*Wise Man from the East
Lit-sen Chang (Zhang Lisheng)*

Studies in Chinese Christianity

G. Wright Doyle and Carol Lee Hamrin, Series Editors

Wise Man from the East: Lit-sen Chang (Zhang Lisheng)

Critique of Indigenous Theology; Critique of Humanism

Lit-sen Chang

Edited by G. Wright Doyle
Translated by G. Wright Doyle
and Samuel Ling

◦PICKWICK *Publications* · Eugene, Oregon

WISE MAN FROM THE EAST: LIT-SEN CHANG
Critique of Indigenous Theology; Critique of Humanism

Copyright © 2013 Global China Center. All rights reserved. Except for brief quotations in critical publications or reviews, no part of this book may be reproduced in any manner without prior written permission from the publisher. Write: Permissions, Wipf and Stock Publishers, 199 W. 8th Ave., Suite 3, Eugene, OR 97401.

Permission to translate *Critique of Indigenous Theology* (*Bentu Shenxue Pipan*) and *Critique of Humanism* (*Renwen Zhuyi Pipan*) granted by Dr. John K. Chang.

Pickwick Publications
An Imprint of Wipf and Stock Publishers
199 W. 8th Ave., Suite 3
Eugene, OR 97401

www.wipfandstock.com

ISBN 13: 978-1-61097-307-6

Cataloguing-in-Publication data:

Chang, Lit-sen (1904–[1996])

    Wise man from the east : Lit-sen Chang : critique of indigenous theology ; critique of humanism / Lit-sen Chang ; edited by G. Wright Doyle ; translated by G. Wright Doyle and Samuel Ling.

    Studies in Chinese Christianity

    xxx + 230 pp. ; 23 cm. Includes bibliographical references.

    ISBN 13: 978-1-61097-307-6

    1. Chang, Lit-sen (1904–). 2. Apologetics—History—20th century. 3. China—Western influences. 4. Christian life I. Doyle, G. Wright (George Wright), 1944–. II. Ling, Samuel. III. Global China Center IV. Title. V. Series.

BR1288 W58 2013

Manufactured in the U.S.A.

Unless otherwise noted, Scripture is taken from the New King James Version®. Copyright © 1982 by Thomas Nelson, Inc. Used by permission. All rights reserved.

Scriptures marked (NASB) come from the NEW AMERICAN STANDARD BIBLE®, Copyright © 1960,1962,1963,1968,1971,1972,1973,1975,1977,1995 by The Lockman Foundation. Used by permission.

Contents

Acknowledgments | *vii*
Editor's Introduction | *ix*

Critique of Indigenous Theology

Translator's Preface | *3*
Author's Preface | *5*

1. Introduction | 13
2. The Source of the Disaster of Indigenous Theology: Historical Review and Reflections | 25
3. Fallacies of Indigenous Theology | 42
4. Indigenous Theology and Philosophy | 70
5. Indigenous Theology and Culture | 78
6. Indigenous Theology and Religion | 92
7. Indigenous Theology and Humanism | 104
8. Indigenous Theology and Indigenous Church | 120
9. Christian Doctrine and the "Substance-Use [Essence-Application] Principle" | 129
10. Conclusion | 160

Critique of Humanism

Translator's Preface | *175*

1. The Tradition of Chinese Humanism: Confucianism, Daoism, and Buddhism | 178
2. The Renaissance of Chinese Humanism in the Twentieth Century | 194
3. Twentieth-Century Chinese Humanists | 203
4. Humanism in Christian Guise: Lin Yutang | 211

Bibliography | *231*

Acknowledgments

THE TRANSLATION OF THE *Critique of Indigenous Theology* could not have been completed without the help of numerous people, including Dr. Yi Hao, Jing Lu, Meng Ma, Xiuxi Zhu, and Yuziao Zhouzheng.

For both works translated in this volume, Dr. Liu Zhaohua spent a great deal of time applying her expert knowledge of Chinese classics to the rendering of Chang's numerous quotations from Chinese religious and philosophical literature into English. She also checked most of the translation against the original Chinese. I am most grateful to her and to all the others who located characters that I could not find in my Chinese dictionaries. Remaining errors are entirely my responsibility, of course.

Laura Mason and Anna Barnes formatted the final text and helped with some of the proofreading.

Global China Center Senior Associate Dr. Carol Lee Hamrin, who is coeditor of the Studies in Chinese Christianity series, read the Editor's Introduction and made helpful suggestions for its improvement, as did Global China Center Associate Dr. Gloria Tseng.

Dr. John Key Chang, son of Lit-sen Chang, graciously supplied both firsthand information about his father and a precious Chinese copy of *Critique of Indigenous Theology*, which is out of print.

Dr. K. C. Hanson, editor in chief of Wipf and Stock Publishers, has been supportive of the entire Studies in Chinese Christianity project since its inception. We are grateful to him and to the others who are making this series possible.

Finally, I (Wright Doyle) thank my wife, Dori, who has enthusiastically encouraged me throughout the arduous months of translation, and to whom I dedicate this book.

Editor's Introduction

Recently a renewed interest in Lit-sen Chang (Zhang Lisheng) has become evident in both Greater China and the West. Among his works in Chinese, the four-volume *Systematic Theology*, previously out of print, can now be found on the Internet,[1] and a two-volume edition on fine Bible paper has been unofficially printed outside China. There is some talk of reissuing the original set. A young Chinese scholar who wants to write his doctoral dissertation on the thought of Lit-sen Chang recently called me for advice. Another scholar said, "China needs this man, because Christianity still has a foreign flavor to most Chinese people, and Chang is so thoroughly and authentically Chinese; he understands us and can speak to our hearts and our minds." In Taiwan, a lectureship in honor of Chang has been established at Holy Light Seminary in Kaohsiung.

Dr. Daniel Chan, whose unpublished dissertation has proved invaluable in the preparation of this Introduction, is currently writing a biography of Lit-sen Chang for Chinese readers, so convinced is he of the continued relevance of Chang for Chinese Christians today.[2] Chang's writings on law and government, composed before he became a Christian, are now also available in China. Dr. Samuel Ling has already provided the English-speaking world with translations of parts of Chang's *Comprehensive Christian Apologetics: What Is Apologetics?* and *Asia's Religions: Christianity's Momentous Encounter with Paganism*. The editors of the Studies in Chinese Christianity series plan to issue, as complements to this volume, reprints of two works composed in English: *Strategy of Missions in the Orient* and *Zen-Existentialism: The Spiritual Decline of the West*.

Reasons abound for this resurgence of attention to Lit-sen Chang. Though Lit-sen Chang has passed from the scene and his writings are

---

1. "Index of/system/system_b5," Bible CCIM. Online: http://bible.ccim.org/system/system_b5/.
2. Chan, "Quest for Certainty."

not as widely read as they were a few decades ago, the relevance of his work only increases with the passage of time, for he clearly discerned trends in the church and in the world that he believed would continue long into the future.

In an unpublished dissertation submitted to Boston University in 2000, Daniel Chan offers several reasons why we should be attentive to Chang's voice even today. To begin with, Chan notes that earlier Chinese Christians either failed to reach intellectuals with a whole gospel, or failed to reach intellectuals with any gospel at all. Chang saw that intellectuals want something that will lead to cultural transformation as well as personal renewal, and that is scientifically sound. Chang attacked humanism, including scientism, and proclaimed a Christianity that could meet the challenges of philosophy, science, Chinese culture, and personal crisis. His published writings addressed the problems of Chinese intellectuals of his time, while privately, in the 1950s and 1960s he corresponded with leading intellectuals such as Qian Mu and Tang Junyi, whose ideas he critiqued.

In the 1920s and the following decades, Chinese Protestants split into modernists and fundamentalists. The former controlled the seminaries and mainline denominations; the latter worked through churches, revival meetings, and Bible studies. The former downplayed the supernatural elements of Christianity and emphasized the social. The latter almost ignored the social implications of Christianity and built trenches around themselves, for they thought that the Social Gospel was heretical. Chang, however, while severely critical of the modernists, also rebuked those who would not apply the gospel to renew society and redeem the culture. He firmly believed that the goal of evangelism is also to remove roadblocks to the Christian message and renew culture, thus transforming society. He urged Christians to engage society and aim for structural transformation of culture through the gospel. To evangelize effectively, he wanted to expose the flaws of scientism, materialism, and pragmatism. It was necessary to go on the attack in order to show the inadequacies of other views.

Since a similar dichotomy exists in the Chinese Protestant churches today, Chang's holistic, biblically based, and rationally argued approach has a great deal to offer Christians who seek to engage their culture in a fresh and relevant manner.

Chan believes that Chang's values and concerns represent those of Chinese intellectuals in several ways: Chang was concerned for the uplifting of China; he shared with other intellectuals a sense of crisis about the state of China, including the moral condition of Chinese intellectuals; he

Editor's Introduction

lived a quest for spirituality, which is consistent with the spiritual component of Confucianism, as a means not only to benefit the nation, but also to "anchor one's soul."[3] His efforts led to the conversion of some prominent intellectuals, including Zhang Guotao[4] and Zhou Yongneng.[5] Significant was his awareness of the need to balance "application" and "substance."[6]

As a writer, Chang issued thirty stand-alone volumes on Christian themes, plus his *Systematic Theology* and *Comprehensive Christian Apologetics*. Chan believes that Chang's achivement is unique. Daniel Chan quotes Huo Shui, who wrote "that the only effective way to persuade the Chinese intellectuals to consider Christianity was the production of more theological literature by Chinese Christian writers."[7] In order to make an impact, however, these authors must have good language and academic credentials. Dr. Samuel Ling, translator of *Critique of Humanism*, says that Chang's Chinese language was "rich, beautiful, elegant, and clear."[8] Daniel Chan quotes Calvin Chao,[9] who said that his books had "very high scholarly value," and they received favorable reviews at the time of publication.[10] Despite the fact that his citations are not always precisely accurate, in an age when footnoting was almost nonexistent in Chinese writings, Chang provided extensive footnotes, and in this regard he was a pioneer. He had an impact on many, including Stephen Tong, the widely

---

3. Chan, "Quest for Certainty," 250–51.

4. "Chang Guotu [Zhang Guotao] was born in 1897. He graduated from Beijing University and was a leader in the May Fourth Movement. He founded the Chinese Communist Party with Chen Duxiu and Li Dachao in 1920. He was the chairman of the first national meeting of the Chinese Communist Party in 1921. During the Communists' war with [the] Guomingdang he was chairman of the Military Committee. He was once the vice-chairman of the Communist Party and Chairman of the Border Provinces." Chan, "Quest for Certainty," 252.

5. Zhou Yongneng had been "mayor of Shanghai, general secretary of the Guomingdang's military committee, and cochairman of the national congress" of the Republic of China. Chan, "Quest for Certainty," 252.

6. The "substance-use" or "essence-application" principle refers to the need to retain essential truth while applying it to particular situations; Chang refers to this principle often.

7. Huo Shui, "Can Chinese Intellectuals Carry their Cross?," quoted in Chan, "Quest for Certainty," 256. Huo Shui is the pen name of a Chinese intellectual writing in the 1990s.

8. Chan, "Quest for Certainty," 272.

9. Zhao Junying, a Chinese evangelist in the 1940s and later a prominent overseas Chinese Christian leader.

10. Chan, "Quest for Certainty," 258.

influential Indonesian Chinese evangelist and theologian.[11] The effect of his writings was to diminish the dominance of the West over the Chinese church in the area of theology, which had always been a principal goal of those who promoted Indigenous Theology.

There is more recent evidence of the pertinence of the themes that Chang so passionately elucidated. The papers from the Sino-Nordic Conference on Chinese Contextual Theology, held in Lapland, Finland, in August 2003, were published as *Christianity and Chinese Culture* in 2010. A glance at the table of contents quickly shows just how much the issues confronted by Chang remain alive today. Out of nineteen chapters in that compendium, at least thirteen discuss the relationship between Christianity and Chinese religion or philosophy, as the contributors wrestle with how to reconcile Christianity with Confucianism, Buddhism, and Daoism. Different positions are taken, some of them quite similar to the stances of the proponents of Indigenous Theology whom Chang criticizes so vehemently; others voice a perspective closer to his. One could not help thinking of how Lit-sen Chang would approach the question; usually, his perspective would be quite helpful and illuminating.

Chang is relevant also to the phenomenon of Sino-Christianity, or Sino-Christian theology, a movement among Chinese intellectuals that has flourished over the past three decades.[12] Some scholars are interacting solely with the Western theological tradition, seeking to translate it into Chinese words and thought forms. These contemporary thinkers could benefit from Chang's perceptive analysis of the weaknesses of all liberal theology and humanistic philosophy. Many others who write on Sino-Christian theology directly address the question of how Christianity, traditional Chinese religions, and philosophy can be related to each other in a way that preserves the essence of biblical faith while acknowledging the value of Chinese thought over the millennia. Clearly, Lit-sen Chang's burden for a Christianity that would be both faithful to the Scriptures and also fully Chinese (as evidenced by both works translated for this volume) presses heavily upon Christians in China today as well.

---

11. Tang Chongrong (born 1940) is a Chinese Indonesian Reformed pastor, evangelist, theologian, philosopher, and musician of Hakka ancestry. He has been called the Billy Graham of the East because of his wide-ranging ministries in East Asia and Southeast Asia.

12. See, for example, Lai and Lam, *Sino-Christian Theology*; and Yang and Yeung, *Sino-Christian Studies in China*.

Editor's Introduction

Life of Lit-sen Chang

Considering his own life to be a dramatic instance of deliverance from darkness into light, the author frequently recounts his story in his works, including the ones contained in this volume. A brief overview will provide necessary background to these autobiographical references.[13]

Childhood and Youth

Lit-sen Chang (Zhang Lisheng) was born in Wuxi, Jiangsu Province, into a traditional religious family: His father had given up his business pursuits in order to concentrate on Confucianism, Daoism, and Buddhism, and became a religious master in their region. His mother was a devout Buddhist. Zhang studied Buddhist literature with her from boyhood and loved hearing stories about visions that she had received from the Buddha. Even as a young boy he cherished great ambitions to go out from there to all parts of China and around the world in order to build a lasting reputation.[14] His fellow villagers laughed at this studious youth who did not join in their games but applied himself to his books.

Education and Early Career

He says that he was a believer in materialism in the years 1922–24. While studying at Shanghai Baptist University, he loathed compulsory chapel and "read the Bible with hatred," so he later left the school. He eventually graduated from Fudan University, Shanghai's most famous. At the time he identified Christianity with Western culture and imperialism, and sympathized with the anti-Christian movement, which swept China's colleges in the early 1920s—so much so that he joined in the general attack on the church by writing articles for newspapers.[15]

---

13. Compiled from the autobiographical sources listed in the bibliography and from conversations with Chang's son, John Key Chang.

14. Chan, "Quest for Certainty," 9.

15. The anti-Christian movement grew out of the New Culture Movement, which was "an integral part of the May Fourth Movement," and was itself antireligious in general and anti-Christian in particular. Bays, *A New History of Christianity in China*, 108. The situation became so tense in 1926 that many missionaries were ordered to evacuate their posts.

While a student in college, he published *The Land Problem of China*,[16] an exposition of the teachings on national reconstruction of Dr. Sun Yat-sen, the founding father of the Republic of China. On the basis of this and other writings, Chang writes that he became Beijing's "youngest professor" at age twenty-one after receiving the bachelor's and master's degrees.[17] He says that "the President of the university sometimes audited his classes."[18]

From 1925 to 1932, he was a "legalist, believing that better laws would create a better Nation, to maintain peace and order, and to safeguard righteousness and justice."[19] Chang thus went to France for advanced studies in law at the University of Paris, and on to further research on political and legal sciences in Belgium, England (London, Oxford, and Cambridge), Germany, and Switzerland from 1927 to 1929. Upon his return to China, he became a professor of the National Central University of Law in Nanjing.

Serving the Nation

After only a year, however, he was sought out by the former Chinese ambassador to Belgium, by then the president of National Labor University in Shanghai, to be dean of the College of Social Sciences. After initial hesitation because of his youth (he was twenty-six), he "had no choice, but to accept his invitation."[20] From 1932 to 1937, he taught at Suzhou University, Fazheng University, and Jinan University,[21] devoting himself to the study of Confucian and Neo-Confucian thought. He lectured widely to promote "'the unity of knowledge and action' of the Neo-Confucian philosopher Wang Yangming, and a spirit of self-determination."[22] Beginning around 1932, he realized that an effective legal system had to be built on a moral foundation. After the nation's humiliation at the hands of Japan's military forces in 1931 and 1932, he saw that "the root cause of our national humiliation was not external but rather internal, i.e., our moral

---

16. Or *Zhongguo Tudi Wenti*.

17. Since his master's degree was from Eastern University, that may have been where he served as "professor." He does not name the institution in his autobiographical writings. Chan, "Quest for Certainty," 12.

18. Chang, *Contending for Truth*, 2.

19. Chang, *Strategy of Missions in the Orient*, 220.

20. Chang, *Asia's Religions*, 288.

21. All these schools are in East China.

22. James H. Taylor III, foreword to Lit-sen Chang, *Asia's Religions*, xxii.

Editor's Introduction

degeneration."²³ He became a Confucianist, seeking moral perfection both for himself and for "national regeneration."²⁴

Shortly afterwards, the Sino-Japanese War (1937–1945) erupted, throwing the whole nation into turmoil. Once a great riot broke out in school, and the president of the college was very concerned, but Zhang spoke to the students with great courage, and "by the grace of God, the students listened to me and were pacified."²⁵ From that time onward, his heart was greatly burdened by China's national crisis, and Chang became a dynamic speaker for national reconstruction and renovation for noted institutes and social groups in Shanghai and Nanking. He claims that political and educational leaders were very much inspired by his speeches, praising them highly as a great blessing to the nation.

During this period Chang wrote nearly twenty books, such as *National Regeneration*, *Constitutional Law*, *Principles and Practices of Constitutional Government*, *Modern Legal Systems*, and *Principles of Modern Legislation*, in addition to political and legal essays. All this amounted to one million words. For this reason, the minister of justice, Wei Daoming, the board chairman of Shanghai College of Law and Politics, sought him out to become the president of that institution when he was about thirty-five years old. Shortly after Chang's installation as college president, however, the mayor of Shanghai was appointed to be the governor of Guangdong province. It was a province of strategic importance, and urgently needed reform. He urged Chang to go with him to plan for reformation, so Chang started a new political career as a "reformer." As the war with Japan spread across the nation (1937–1938), the capital was moved west to Chongqing. The governor of Guangdong was promoted to be the General Secretary of the Nationalist Party, and Chang became his chief secretary as well as a strategist of "the Supreme National Defense Council," charged with formulating a strategy to defeat Japan. In 1937, Chang married Ling Nie, the daughter of a former tutor to the last emperor. She soon bore him two sons: Chang Qi (John Key) and Chang De.

Eventually deciding that Confucianism could not bring real change to the nation, from 1937 to 1941 he turned to Daoism. Then in 1941, he switched his hopes to Zen Buddhism, practicing Zen exercises every day and convinced that he had attained enlightenment.

---

23. Chang, *Strategy of Missions in the Orient*, 221.
24. Ibid.
25. Chang, *Contending for Truth*, 3.

Shaping a New China: A Constitution and a University

After the Second World War (1945), the leaders of Nationalist China planned for a constitutional convention in order to launch the "constitutional stage" according to the principles of Dr. Sun Yat-sen. Chang was elected as a member of the convention; he became a signatory of the final document. After a long period of deep introspection and rethinking, however, he came to the conclusion that the human problem did not lie in politics but in the heart of man, so he gave up politics, resisting repeated requests to join the cabinet. He was "intoxicated" with Confucianism, Buddhism, and Taoism, as were many other Chinese scholars who had not given their sympathies to the Communists. Returning to his childhood village of Taihu, he became the founding president of Jiangnan (Kiang Nan) University, which was to be the center of a resurgence movement of Asian religions and culture. His purpose was "to revive Asian religions and to destroy Christianity."[26] He was forty-five years old.

Conversion to Christianity

In 1949 Chang was invited by a university in India founded by the Indian philosopher Rabindranath Tagore (1861–1941) to give a series of special lectures on "Asia's Destiny." He accepted, aiming to persuade the religious leaders of India to join him in launching his religious renaissance movement. Unable to obtain a visa to India, he found himself stranded in Java, Indonesia, where his family moved into a house just beside a church that was under construction.

Chang and his family often took a walk together after supper. One evening in 1951, they heard beautiful music coming from within the church, so the children suggested that they find out what was going on inside. A deacon of the church came out to talk with them and invited them to attend the building dedication service on the coming Sunday, knowing that Chang was not a Christian and would not want to go to a regular worship service. Out of curiosity, however, Chang decided to attend the special ceremony. To his amazement, during prayers he was "deeply touched by the Holy Spirit; and from that time on, [he] could not stop going to church, and was eager to search the truth and to read the Bible avidly, often with tears of repentance and joy."[27]

---

26. Chang, *Asia's Religions*, 290.
27. Ibid., 291.

Editor's Introduction

He soon became a news item in Christian circles, with a number of Christian leaders wanting to interview him, amazed at his knowledge of the Bible. From that time on, he was often invited to preach in different churches throughout Java. His audiences responded in two ways. Some said that this must be another Lit-sen Chang with the same name. It could not be the same anti-Christian Lit-sen Chang! But other people said that if Lit-sen Chang, the former enemy of the gospel, could believe in the Christ, they had no reason not to believe.

Theological Training

At that time he was also chaplain of a Christian school in Melang, Indonesia, founded by Dr. and Mrs. Leland Wang. From 1954 to 1956, at the invitation of Dr. Andrew Gih,[28] president of the Chinese Evangelization Fellowship, he served as professor of philosophy at the Southeast Asia Bible College. From 1955 to 1956, he taught concurrently as professor of comparative religions at the Baptist Theological Seminary of the American Southern Baptist Mission in Semarong.

In 1956 Chang enrolled in Gordon Divinity School in Wenham, Massachusetts. Almost immediately he was asked to teach, but he insisted on studying full time at the seminary and teaching only a few courses on comparative religions at Gordon College. He was invited to join the faculty as soon as he finished his Master of Divinity degree *magna cum laude* in 1959. For the next two decades he taught courses on missions at the seminary, but mostly dedicated himself to writing theological and apologetical works. When he retired in 1978, he was honored with the designation of Distinguished Lecturer in Missions Emeritus in a special honor chapel, attended by many Christian leaders and American political dignitaries such as the Speaker of the US House of Representatives.

Work Habits

Lack of material reward has discouraged many, but not Chang, for he toiled away at his desk for decades without financial remuneration. In keeping with the Chinese ideal of the sage, who must have virtue as well as wisdom, Chang possessed an "impeccable character." Friends and family say that he was humble and unassuming, and always thought of others first. He led a

---

28. Or *Ji Zhiwen*.

simple life, totally free of covetousness, often turning down honoraria and remuneration for expenses. Constant overwork and lack of rest resulted in a very serious bleeding ulcer in the stomach and also a bleeding hemorrhoid. He vomited a flood of blood, and for many years afterward could not eat solid food; he could only drink some juice and milk. He wrote, "As I had been working hard day and night since my youth, before my conversion I endeavored to save our nation. After my conversion, I dedicated my life to serve the Lord, to preach the gospel and to save souls. Moreover, in order to redeem my time lost in pagan darkness for fifty long years, I took my supper as my 'second breakfast,' so I could work another day after 8:00 p.m. to 4:00 a.m. I only got two hours of sleep a day."[29] Such diligence and self-denial were not without cost, for Chang neglected his health and had little time for his family, leaving almost all care of the children and the home to his wife, who also had to work full-time in order to make up for his meager stipend from the seminary. He explains the reason for such strenuous labor in this way: "Before my conversion, God, in His 'negative preparation' (a term used by theologian Louis Berkhof), had trained me to write nearly five million words, so as 'to give an answer to every man ... a reason of hope that is in [us]' (cf. 1 Pet 3:15), and to 'earnestly contend for the faith which was once delivered unto the saints' (Jude 3)."[30] From around the world, readers, students, and those who heard him preach testified that they had been greatly impacted by Chang's ministry. Many were converted through his evangelistic books in Chinese.

Writings

He published works in English also. He recalled:

> After World War II many people in the West were frustrated and disillusioned with their culture and religion. They began to be intoxicated with Asian religions and cults. Dr. Carl F. H. Henry, the founding editor of *Christianity Today*, came to Gordon, urging me to write a book to awaken the West. In my early 20's I was in France; I never learned to write in English. But upon his earnest petition, I had no choice, but yielded to his request. The result was a book, *Zen Existentialism: The Spiritual Decline of the West*, which Billy Graham called "a valuable contribution to the West."[31]

29. Chang, *Contending for Truth*, 7.
30. Ibid., 8.
31. Ibid., 9.

Editor's Introduction

The Strategy of Missions in the Orient was composed upon request for the Asia–South Pacific Congress on Evangelism in 1968.

In 1999, two books by Chang and edited by Dr. Samuel Ling, translator of part 2 of this volume, were issued. The first was *What Is Apologetics?*, an English translation of the first six chapters of the first volume of *Comprehensive Christian Apologetics*. The second was a book written by Chang "in the early 1980s,"[32] *Asia's Religions: Christianity's Momentous Encounter with Paganism*. Most of the material in this work was contained also in the Chinese *Comprehensive Christian Apologetics*. In these two books, Chang challenged Christians to understand pagan culture well in order to communicate Christianity in a way that would be clear and convincing. He rejected the "eclectic approach" that called for integration of Christianity with other religions, as well as the "expulsive approach" of pietists, fundamentalists, and neo-orthodox, who called for total rejection of, or at least for ignoring, non-Christian religions. Instead, he espoused an "evangelical approach," which clearly distinguished between general revelation, which is given to all men, and special revelation, which was communicated only to God's chosen spokesmen and written down in the Scriptures. The former conveys some general truths about man, God, and the universe, but these cannot lead us to salvation. Only the knowledge communicated through special revelation can bring us to faith in Christ and thus to reconciliation with God.

Indigenous Theology

Though the two terms are often used interchangeably, *indigenous theology* and *contextual theology* are sometimes distinguished from each other. In Chinese Christian history, indigenous theology was a movement to combine Christian ideas with those from other belief systems, especially Confucianism, Buddhism, and Daoism, as well as to deal with the perceived need to address China's pressing social and political problems. In current missiology, contextual theology is now more strictly used for the efforts to apply Christian principles to society and politics, but in the 1920s, when most of the writers whom Chang criticizes were flourishing, "Chinese Christians did not entertain the distinction that we now make."[33] In each case, the starting point was the context, either that of religion and philosophy or that of social and political crisis, so *contextualization* is often employed as the larger

32. Chang, *Asia's Religions*, xiv.
33. Lam, *Chinese Theology in Construction*, 190 n. 1.

category.³⁴ In other words, Christianity was to be adapted to the current situation. Biblical ideas were not to interpret, correct, and redefine either tradition or contemporary conditions. For the sake of consistency, I shall use *indigenize* and *indigenous theology* to refer to both contextual theology and indigenous theology, since Chang's major aim is to refute theologians who claimed to be Christian, but who, in his opinion, were compromising vital biblical truths for the sake of harmonization with other thought systems and worldviews, and who were also, often, advocating sociopolitical change instead of promoting evangelism.

The indigenous theology movement arose in the maelstrom of the incessant crises that wracked China in the first few decades of the twentieth century, beginning in the 1920s with the May Fourth Movement and its antiforeign flavor.³⁵ Chinese intellectuals, especially, began to turn from an attitude of benign neglect of, or even admiration for, Christianity to open hostility. As part of their rejection of old ways, they warmly received Western concepts of science and democracy, and criticized Christianity as out of date. At the same time, they began to question, and even renounce, all dependence upon or reverence for the West, which had just demonstrated its cultural and moral bankruptcy in the First World War. Christianity was perceived as a Western religion and carried a heavy load of baggage associated with imperialism, past and present, as well as the stench of being non-Chinese. Christians sought to declare their own independence from Western missionary control by forming their own autonomous congregations and even a National Christian Council, which led to the formation of the Church of Christ in China (CCC).

In short, as one historian has written, "Theological contextualization in the twenties was the ideological side of the broader indigenous movement of the Chinese Church which was an effort to establish independence from Western churches through self-support, self-government, and self-propagation."³⁶ Further, it must be understood in light of wider cultural movements of the period, in which three views about the relationship between Chinese and Western civilizations were propounded: One group believed in total Westernization, especially through adopting modern science and democracy. A second position was that traditional Chinese culture,

---

34. See Bevans and Wu, "Contextualization," 211–14.

35 The May Fourth Movement was at first a violent reaction to the granting of Shandong to the Japanese by the Treaty of Versailles. For this period and the church's responses to the challenges it posed, see Bays, *A New History of Christianity in China*, 92–157, as well as Lian, *Redeemed by Fire*, 118–29 and often.

36. Lam, "Patterns of Chinese Theology," 328.

especially Confucianism, must be revived in order to save the nation. Finally, some advocated a synthesis of both Chinese culture and Western values. Proponents of indigenous theology fell into the last category.[37]

The Protestant church, meanwhile, was riven by the fundamentalist-modernist controversy, which mirrored what was happening in the West, especially North America, and split both missionaries and Chinese Christians into two camps. Most academics and seminary professors welcomed the new, modern theology, which considered the Bible to be filled with myths and mistakes, and which thus rejected miracles, including the resurrection of Jesus Christ. Gone also was belief in his deity or unique status as sole savior of the world. Many leaders in the Christian Church of China belonged to this group. Other Chinese Christians resisted modernist theology, however. Some of them formed independent congregations or remained in larger networks outside the CCC, as did, for example, the churches connected with the China Inland Mission.

This division into what we now call liberal and conservative (or evangelical) Christians in China persists to the present. Though most people in the state-sponsored Three-Self Patriotic Movement[38] hold to conservative theology, the leaders have historically been liberals, while house-church Christians are overwhelmingly conservative, even fundamentalist. In the 1960s, when Lit-sen Chang was composing his polemical works, both in China and among overseas Chinese, the liberal views of the earlier proponents of indigenous theology still exerted influence.

For those who promoted indigenous theology, "[t]he dominant problem of the Chinese Church in the twenties was not the infallibility of Scripture but the salvation of the nation."[39] The problem they faced was how to balance loyalty to their culture with fidelity to the Christian faith. The emphasis, however, was upon accommodating, harmonizing, even unifying, Christian faith and Chinese culture. In other words, the contemporary political and social needs and cultural heritage of the Chinese were paramount in the process. Wing-Hung Lam writes, "Their conviction was that the Chinese heritage"—especially Confucianism—"was good . . . They saw Christianity not as the ultimate and absolute religion to substitute for the time-honored deposit of cultural excellences but as a

---

37. Ibid., 329.

38. "Three-Self" refers to "self-supporting, self-propagating, and self-governing," a goal originally promoted by missionaries and later taken as a slogan by the state-sponsored organization.

39. Lam, *Chinese Theology in Construction*, 53. See also his discussion in "Patterns of Chinese Theology," 335–38.

collaborator for mutual service. Christianity and Chinese culture would enrich each other. Christianity was interpreted from the standpoint of Chinese culture, seeking elements of the Christian doctrines that would agree to certain classical precepts."[40]

Their chief spokesmen included Wu Leiquan (Wu Lei-chuan) of Yanjing (Yenching) University. Like others in the movement, he believed that "Truth is one and its expressions are many," and that the Confucian Classics held timeless truths similar to those in the Bible.[41] He thought that both traditions could be used to reform the Chinese nation. Others also sought to harmonize the Christian faith with Chinese culture, especially Confucianism. These thinkers sought to find concepts in that tradition that were similar to Christian ideas. Actually, they were hoping to find "Christian support for . . . selected portions of Confucian thought."[42] Still others, including Zhao Zhichen (T. C. Chao) thought that, as Christ came not to abrogate the Law and the Prophets, but to fulfill them, so Christianity would fulfill Chinese culture. In turn, Chinese culture could enrich Christianity by bringing new elements of understanding, new perspectives to use in examining Christian truth.[43] For example, the lack of a sense of sin in Chinese culture needs the Christian understanding of man's fallen condition, and the traditional absence of a clear sense of a personal, transcendent God, needs biblical revelation.

Not all agreed with the primacy of social issues in indigenous theology. Wang Mingdao, the pastor of an independent church in Beijing, preached a message of personal salvation and incorporation into the church by regeneration by faith in Christ, leading to a changed life and thus transformed conduct and more harmonious relationships with others, with an inevitable impact on society.[44] Ni Tuosheng (Watchman Nee) focused on the relationship of the individual Christian to God and to other believers, with little reference to Chinese culture or society.[45] He later called on his followers to "hand over" their lives, including their possessions, to the leaders of the church.[46] Society could not be redeemed, and the Lord's return was imminent; one must consecrate oneself entirely

---

40. Lam, *Chinese Theology in Construction*, 60.
41. Ibid., 61.
42. Ibid., 68.
43. See also Lian, *Redeemed by Fire*, 106, 123, 135, 187, 198, 202–3.
44. See ibid., 109–30; also Harvey, *Acquainted with Grief*.
45. Lian, *Redeemed by Fire*, 155–78.
46. Ibid., 194–97.

to Christ.[47] Song Shangjie (John Sung) urged repentance from sin, faith in Christ for forgiveness, and faithful obedience to Christ, even to the point of death.[48] Wang, Ni, and Song were all what Lit-sen Chang would call "Pietists," that is, those who spoke only about one's individual relationship with God and with the church but did not seek to apply the implications of biblical thought to all aspects of human life, including society and culture.

Cheng Jingyi,[49] though theologically conservative like Wang Mingdao, entered more into dialogue with traditional Chinese culture, which he believed contained some remnants of truth, though vitiated and obscured by pervasive human sin. He used Christianity to criticize and then transform Chinese ways of thinking, including Confucianism. For him, the difference between Confucius and Christ was the difference between man and God, though Confucius possessed some wisdom as a result of being created in the image of God.[50] Cheng considered the world not a place to be shunned, but a "mission field where the reforming power of the Gospel is to be made manifest."[51] Though he respected Confucius, he saw a fundamental difference of epistemology between him (and other Chinese sages) and Christianity. The first began with man and his natural reason; the second derived from God's revelation. The Dao cannot be understood without divine enlightenment from the Scriptures. Likewise, both personal and national reformation can only be found through repentance, faith in Christ, and reliance on divine power to change. In general, it would seem that Lit-sen Chang agreed with the approach of Cheng Jingyi.

Lit-sen Chang and Indigenous Theology

As we shall see, Lit-sen Chang devoted most of his criticism toward the proponents of the more liberal proponents of indigenous theology. Like Cheng Jingyi, he saw a vast gulf between Christianity on the one hand and all other Chinese thought systems on the other. Clear knowledge of the truth comes only from God's self-revelation in Christ, as recorded in the

---

47. Ibid., 215–16.

48. Ibid., 131–54; see also Song, *The Diaries of John Sung*; Lyall, *A Biography of John Sung*.

49. His name is spelled *Chang I-ching* by Lam. See also Ng, "Cheng Jingyi: Prophet of His Time," in *Chinese Christianity*, 133–42; Bays, *A New History of Christianity in China*, 99, 101–4, 108, 110–11, 113, 144–45.

50. Lam, *Chinese Theology in Construction*, 79.

51. Ibid.

Bible. The man-centered approach of Confucianism and of Confucianist indigenous theology must be replaced by a God-centered approach derived from the Scriptures.

Though Chang agreed that there are some similarities between Christianity and Confucianism, Daoism, and Buddhism, he was convinced that the dissimilarities were more numerous and serious.[52] In fact, in his earlier works, he quoted so many passages from the Chinese Classics that some in the church believed that he was a proponent of indigenous theology. As he tells us, that was a major reason for his composition of this *Critique of Indigenous Theology*: he wanted to distinguish his approach from that of others holding to a more liberal theology. He repeatedly emphasized that biblical Christianity is a system fundamentally different from other religions and philosophies. At best, the apparent agreements between it and other worldviews should be seen only as "points of contact" that can serve as avenues for communicating the gospel in ways that are understandable to people of other faiths. There can be no question of compromise or integration.[53]

Like Cheng Jingyi, Lit-sen Chang was firmly convinced that national salvation could only come from thoroughgoing personal acceptance of the gospel of Christ, along with a radical transformation of the mind that in turn would produce fundamental social and political change. He agreed with Cheng that the purpose of faith in Christ is not to save China, but to receive personal salvation, which would, in time, influence all of society and culture, as it had in the past in the West. He thus shared the view that Wang Mingdao's message was not sufficient; as a Reformed theologian, Chang argued for the application of the Scriptures to all of life, including philosophy, education, politics, economics, and individual ethics. At the same time, he did not put much faith in political action to effect lasting beneficial change in society; such change would come only from a careful, comprehensive reworking of thought systems in the light of biblical revelation by all members of the church.

This volume contains translations of two works of Lit-sen Chang. The first is his *Critique of Indigenous Theology*. In the second part of the book, we offer a translation of most of his *Critique of Humanism*, taken from the four-volume *Comprehensive Christian Apologetics*. Major sections of the *Critique of Humanism* are also found in the earlier book, *Criticism of Humanism*, published in his *Zongti Biandaoxue* (*Comprehensive Christian*

---

52. His position resembles that of Dr. Chow Lien-Hwa as expressed in "Towards Evangelical Theology in Buddhist Cultures."

53. The same viewpoint is found in Weerasinga, "A Critique of Theology from Buddhist Cultures," 290–341.

Editor's Introduction

Apologetics). The two are integrally related, for Chang was convinced that indigenous theology, like all of Chinese religion and philosophy, was essentially humanistic. He resolutely opposed humanism of all varieties, whether outside the Christian church or within it.

Apologetics and Polemics

In many theology books today, *apologetics* includes debate within the community of those who profess to be Christians, which is what Chang's *Critique of Indigenous Theology* is about.[54] This book can also be more strictly categorized as a work of *polemics*. His arguments are directed at professing "Christians," that is, those who call themselves followers of Christ. The word "Christians" is put in quotation marks because Chang believed that proponents of indigenous theology were, for the most part, not true Christians. Rather, he considered them "wolves in sheep's clothing," "false prophets," deceivers, and charlatans, because they denied fundamental tenets of the Christian faith. Though professing to be Christians, they were (he thought) in fact traitors to the basic beliefs of Christianity, such as the inspiration and full authority of the Bible, the deity of Jesus Christ, miracles (including the resurrection of Jesus from the dead), the necessity for faith in Jesus in order to receive forgiveness of sins and eternal life, the need to be "born again" and receive the Holy Spirit in order to have the power for Christ-like living, the return of Christ, the Last Judgment, and heaven and hell. How, he asks, can those who reject such core elements of Christianity be called true Christians?

Thus, in this *Critique of Indigenous Theology*, Chang uses very sharp language to characterize these men and to describe their opinions. Contemporary readers, especially those reared in a multicultural, postmodern society, will find his tone quite harsh, and will probably be offended by it, so much so that I have been tempted to excise his scathing denunciations from the text. To do so would be unfair to the author, however, and would violate the most basic rule of translation, which is to reflect the original text faithfully.

---

54. See, for example, the "Apologetic Interaction" sections in each chapter of Lewis and Demarest, *Integrative Theology*, in which the authors seek to defend their position from rival points of view held both by Christians and by non-Christians. Calvin's *Institutes of the Christian Religion* long ago displayed a similar method, with refutation of Jews, Muslims, and Roman Catholics all within the same text. Carl F. H. Henry follows the same method in his six-volume *God, Revelation, and Authority*.

Before we dismiss Chang as a curmudgeon, however, we should pause to consider several things: First, Chinese intellectuals have often used this sort of ridicule to criticize those with whom they disagree. In fact, some of the authors he quotes did the same thing, even calling fundamentalist preachers "world-class criminals"! Thus, his writing often seems to be black and white, with no room for compromise. He writes with passion, convinced that both the advocates of indigenous theology and those who adhere to pagan religions and philosophies are in danger of eternal loss. The imminent danger to the Christian church posed by false teaching weighs no less heavily on his heart. Chang paints with a broad brush, making generalizations about theologians in church history that reflect wide reading and research, and which are usually documented by reference to reliable sources, but which might seem unduly harsh and unwarranted to readers accustomed to more nuanced critiques of those with whom one disagrees. Chang frequently employs the vocabulary of warfare: words such as "strategy," "offensive," "total mobilization," and the like—mostly, it would seem, because of his controlling passage of Scripture, 2 Corinthians 10:3–5, where Paul speaks of a spiritual warfare and weapons that are "mighty in God for pulling down strongholds." His experience as a member of the Republic of China's strategy commission in the war against Japan may also have influenced him.

Second, Chang's polemical style stands firmly (though perhaps not consciously) in a long tradition of Christian polemics against those who were considered dangerous heretics. We can see it in Irenaeus, who ridiculed the Gnostics in the second century AD; in the Reformers, particularly in Luther but also in Calvin; and in many other writers. More important, however, when we read the Old Testament prophets or the letters of Paul, we are confronted with powerful denunciations of hypocrites and false teachers. Jesus himself spared no words in describing and castigating the religious leaders of his day, whom he considered to be "blind leaders of the blind," "whitewashed tombs," "false prophets," and hopeless hypocrites.[55] We have to remember that, for all these men, issues of eternal life and death were at stake. They could be gentle with outright unbelievers and notorious sinners, but would not tolerate those who pretended to be reliable guides for sincere seekers of the truth but who were to them in fact dangerous deceivers, whose doctrines would lead others to eternal ruin.

---

55. See especially Matthew 23.

Critique of Humanism: Apologetics (With Some Polemics)

Lit-sen Chang believed that Chinese religion and philosophy were fundamentally humanistic, like the Western Renaissance, Enlightenment, and modern non-Christian systems of thought. In fact, his *Critique of Indigenous Theology* also refers often to the humanistic assumptions of the theologians whose writings he criticizes. Chang's *Critique of Humanism* appeared in his four-volume *Comprehensive Christian Apologetics*, in which Chinese religions, culture, and philosophy were also discussed in detail, as was as his approach to apologetics as a Christian endeavor. For Chang, apologetics must not only demonstrate the reasonableness of Christianity but clear away obstacles to the proclamation of the gospel. Humanism was for him a major obstacle, especially among Chinese, so he tried to unveil the humanistic core of traditional Chinese religion and philosophy as well as the humanistic positions of leading twentieth-century intellectuals.

Apologetics and polemics merge in his chapter on Lin Yutang, an international literary figure who moved away from his childhood Christianity and then, he claims, back to Christianity in his later years. Chang, however, doubts whether Lin is a true Christian, and tries to demonstrate this through an analysis of Lin's words spoken after his "return" to the Christian fold. Interesting is that one recent article on Lin Yutang comes to a similar conclusion, though the author highlights Lin's commitment to Daoism more than to humanism.[56]

Theology

Lit-sen Chang belongs to the school of Reformed theologians.[57] That is, he is a Protestant in the Calvinist tradition, as one can see from the theologians whom he quotes with most approval. Calvin emphasized the priority and sufficiency of the Bible as the sole source of Christian revelation, the sovereignty of God over all creation and in the salvation of sinners, the comprehensive scope of biblical revelation, and its relevance for all of life and thought. More than Lutherans and certainly much more than Anabaptists and Pietists, Reformed thinkers seek to apply the general principles of

---

56. See He, "Dialogue between Christianity and Taoism," 124–44. For a dissenting view, see Yang, "Lin Yutang," 171–75.

57. For a more extensive description of Reformed theology, see Doyle, *Carl Henry*, 38–50.

Scripture to both personal and public life, including politics, philosophy, education, the arts, and other major spheres of human thought and activity.

Apologetic Method

Negative

As is evident in the two books translated in this volume and in his English-language works, Lit-sen Chang believed that non-Christian points of view can be shown to fail even on their own terms. They are internally inconsistent, incomplete, and unable to solve the problems they pose. Confucianism cannot produce the superior man; Daoism cannot describe the Dao or show us the way to the Way; Buddhism cannot solve the problem of suffering; humanism cannot bring happiness or even mental clarity to human beings. Thus, the negative role of apologetics consists in pointing out the defects and deficiencies in other religions and philosophical systems.

Positive

Lit-sen Chang rejected what he considered to be the compromising and even syncretistic approach of liberalism, such as was found among the proponents of indigenous theology. Chang also disagreed with those who saw no point of contact whatever between Christian truth and pagan religions and philosophy. The former derives from special revelation, and is contained in the Bible. The latter mixes both truth and error, which must be differentiated by those who are knowledgeable about the Scriptures. Because of what theologians call general revelation, non-Christian religions and philosophies do include some truths in their worldviews. These can form points of contact between Christianity and other belief systems. Thus, Chang advocated taking advantage of these points of contact when presenting the Christian message to nonbelievers, rather than merely stating that all they held true was totally false. He took his cue from the method used by Paul in the New Testament. The apostle acknowledged that the Gentiles had some awareness of a God but that their understanding was incomplete and even inaccurate, so he had come to tell them the whole story.[58]

---

58. See, for example, Acts 22–29; Romans 1:18–21.

Presuppositional Apologetics

Lit-sen Chang practiced what has been called presuppositional apologetics.[59] That is, he started with certain assumptions, which he did not try to prove. God exists. He has created the world, including humankind. We are made to know him, but cannot find him on our own. He has revealed himself and all necessary truth about himself in the Bible.

At the same time, Chang firmly believed that faith in the Bible as the Word of God was a reasonable assumption to hold. He did not think that either science or philosophy, and much less history, had disproven the narratives or the principle doctrines of the Scriptures. In other words, he was convinced that the evidence fully supported the truth claims of Christianity as derived from the Bible. He used reason to counter arguments in other belief systems, and pointed out the unreliability of the so-called findings of modern science that seemed to disprove the Scriptures. In that sense, he agreed with the so-called evidential school and method of apologetics.[60]

Style

Born in 1904 and educated in the classical literature of China, Lit-sen Chang wrote in a semiliterary style. That is, coming after the vernacular literary revolution of the May Fourth Movement, he did not use the highly stylized, even stilted mannerisms previously required of educated writers; his composition is clearly modern and not classical. On the other hand, neither are his writings contemporary, for he filled the pages with traditional four-character phrases and even some vocabulary that seems archaic today, at least to younger people. Like classical Chinese authors, Chang enriched his prose with numerous quotations. Because he had given his allegiance to the Bible as the source of ultimate authority, and had evidently committed much of it to memory, most of the quotations come from the Bible. In addition, when discussing Chinese religion or philosophy, he quoted extensively, and apparently from memory, famous passages from Chinese classics.

In addition, in his arguments against those with whom he disagrees, he reproduced the very words of his interlocutors. This abundance of

---

59. For a general survey of Protestant apologetic methods, see Evans, "Approaches to Christian Apologetics," 15–21.

60. Carl F. H. Henry, who encouraged Lit-sen Chang in his work, employed a similar apologetic strategy. See Doyle, *Carl Henry*, 65–77.

quotation makes his case more credible, for clearly he had read what others had written and was not just responding to a vague impression he had gained. As caustic and scathing as he often is, we nevertheless know that he was responding to the actual positions of those whom he was trying to refute. At the same time, however, Chang did not usually provide publication information about the works he cited, and frequently even the page numbers he gives are not accurate. Thus, the bibliography at the end of this volume does not contain the usual citation of place, publisher, and date of publication for some of the Chinese works that he quotes or references, and we have given information on later English language editions from the ones he may have used. Many footnotes also lack page numbers and cite only the book title and author.

We should take particular note of Chang's utter conviction that the Bible was the Word of God and his habit of quoting from the Scriptures at length. His own mind seems to have been soaked in the words of the Bible, as these appear to flow freely from his pen. Frequently, he will quote one passage after another, from various parts of the canon, both to reinforce points and to advance a well-developed argument.

We hope that this volume will open up the wisdom of Lit-sen Chang to Western readers and perhaps also receive attention from Chinese scholars around the world.

G. Wright Doyle
Director, Global China Center
Coeditor (with Carol Lee Hamrin),
Studies in Chinese Christianity series

Critique of Indigenous Theology

Translated by G. Wright Doyle

Translator's Preface

READERS WILL QUICKLY NOTE that Chang often repeats himself. He does this not only within this one book, but also across several works. It seems that he had some important concepts, as well as stock phrases, including favorite biblical passages and Chinese proverbs (usually "four character sayings") that he had either memorized or, less likely, had written down, and he returned to these again and again. Usually I have retained this repetition, but sometimes other possible translations of the same Chinese phrase have been employed for the sake of variety. With proverbial sayings, I have usually attempted to render these literally as well, though sometimes I have given the general meaning without reproducing the original figures of speech.

Chang typically constructs very long sentences with many subordinate phrases and clauses, especially participial phrases. He delights in piling up parallel descriptive phrases and clauses. I have retained most of his grammatical structure, but have also sometimes split up sentences in order to conform a bit more to modern English usage.

Consistent with Chang's own English usage, both translators have used the general term *man* or *mankind* to include men and women. This also prevents awkwardness of style.

In the notes, when the author cites his own works, the following method has been used: The author will be listed as Lit-sen Chang, the name by which he is known to English readers. Works in Chinese will be given their title in Pinyin (Chinese Romanized spelling), followed by an English translation of the title in parenthesis. Works in English will be listed simply by their English-language titles.

As much as possible, Chinese names and technical terms have been transliterated into Pinyin, but when they are found in quotations, or when common usage (such as Lit-sen Chang's own name) requires it, the Wade-Giles or other original form of spelling is retained. Frequently, alternative

3

English spellings are contained within quotations marks in the text; almost as frequently they are found in footnotes. When *Tian* (heaven) refers to a supreme being, it is capitalized; at other times, the lower case is employed, except that the form in quotations from printed English translations is always retained. Since the distinction between references to a supreme being and to the realm above (as distinct from the earth) is often difficult to determine, readers may disagree with the choices that we have made; we fully respect such difference of opinion, along with any other criticism of the translation decisions Samuel Ling and I have made.

Unless otherwise indicated, biblical quotations throughout this volume are from the New King James Version.

Lit-sen Chang does not always cite his sources with precision.[1] For that reason, it is frequently almost impossible to trace the original quotation. We both have followed the practice, therefore, of citing only the authors and the titles of the works from which quotations are taken, to give an idea of the range of Dr. Chang's scholarship and the types of resources upon which he drew. Much of the time, in the *Critique of Indigenous Theology*, I have had to translate Professor Chang's Chinese rendering of English quotations back into English, without always being able to find the original statement. I apologize for any resulting inaccuracy or infelicity of rendering.

—G. Wright Doyle

---

1. Chang, *Asia's Religions*, iv.

Author's Preface

IN THE TIME OF missionary Hudson Taylor, a conference of missionaries was held in Shanghai, during which Dr. Joseph Edkins spoke words to this effect: "The three great religions of China—Buddhism, Confucianism, and Daoism—are strong fortresses erected by Satan among the Chinese. Their intent is one of opposition to the spread of Christian truth, and we must exert every effort to destroy them. After their demolition, China will become a nation ruled by the Prince of Peace, the Messiah, and this will be one of the greatest triumphs since the overthrow of Roman political and religious power and Greek philosophy."[1] Sadly, these strongholds have to this day not yet been destroyed. On the contrary, those scholars who advocate "indigenous theology" want to come to their aid, even surrender to them, and promote a pagan religion—which would bring pain to the friends of our faith, joy to its enemies, and hidden disaster to the Chinese church!

Early in life, the author was immersed in the three religions of Buddhism, Confucianism, and Daoism, and was cruelly deceived by them; with the endorsement of Dr. Ouyang Xiu, Dr. Luo Han, and other outstanding scholars, he founded Jiangnan (Kiang Nan) University, which became a center for the revival of Eastern culture and religion. In 1950, on a trip to the university founded by Tagore in India to lecture on "Asia's Destiny: The Hope of Mankind," I planned to confer with leaders there and initiate a movement for the revival of Eastern religion and culture. I thought that this was the way to save the world, in fact the only way. During this trip, however, I was obstructed by God, who closed the door to India. At this critical point in my life, when everything hung in the balance, God brought me from death to life, from disaster to blessing, the mystery of which cannot be fathomed by human understanding. Thenceforth, I forsook everything,

---

1. *Records of the Shanghai Missionary Conference,* 1877. James Hudson Taylor (1832–1905) was a British missionary to China, the founder of the China Inland Mission. Joseph Edkins (1823–1905), also British, served with the London Missionary Society.

Critique of Indigenous Theology

considering all I had previously learned as worthless, and studied theology, dedicating myself to the proclamation of God's Word.

I must briefly summarize my past experiences[2] so that those who advocate indigenous theology can know that before I turned to the Lord, I was like them. You could even say I was a fellow traveler, and went even further than they did. As a result, my earnest prayer and hope is that indigenous theologians may see that their fellow traveler could suddenly see the light, pass from death to life, and say, like the Apostle Paul, that "what things were gain to me" "(i.e., indigenous theology), "these I have counted loss . . . for the excellence of the knowledge of Christ Jesus my Lord . . . forgetting those things which are behind and reaching forward . . . toward the goal for the prize of the upward call of God in Christ Jesus" (Phil 3:7–14), that I may gain "an inheritance incorruptible and undefiled and that does not fade away, reserved in heaven for you" (1 Pet 1:4).

After my conversion, my earliest writings, *Yuan Dao* (*The Way*), and *Sheng Dao Tong Quan* (*A General Interpretation of Christian Truth*), drew upon the ingrained Chinese concept of the Heavenly Way, quoting many passages and proverbial sayings from various Chinese classics and authors (such as the *Book of History*, *Book of Songs (Odes)*, *Book of Changes (I Jing)*, *Analects* of Confucius, *Doctrine of the Mean*, *Dao De Jing*, *Zuo Juan (Tso Chuan) Commentary on the Spring and Autumn Annals*, *Historical Records*, and Confucian writers like Dong Zhongshu, Zhou Dunyi, Chen Mingdao, Chen Yichuan, Lu Xiangshan, Zhu Xi, Shao Kangjie, Wang Yangming, etc. This caused misunderstanding in the church, because people thought I was promoting indigenous theology and many were prepared to come and to rebuke me. Their motives were totally good, for they wanted to guard against heresy and prevent me from confusing the truth of God. But they completely misunderstood, and did not realize that I meant to oppose indigenous theology. In particular, they did not see what I was striving mightily to accomplish, or perceive my strategy for proclaiming the truth. My goal was to "pull down strongholds" (2 Cor 10:4), to utterly shatter my countrymen's traditional view of Confucianism, Buddhism, and Daoism, to pull the rug completely out from under their teaching, to eradicate indigenous theology's poisonous root, and clear away obstacles to the Christian gospel.

My strategy was to lead them along naturally, bringing them to hearty assent to the truth and causing them to turn from their previous futile conception of the Heavenly Way. I hoped that they would seek the

---

2. See also Chang, *Jiushi zhi Dao* (*The Way of Salvation*).

Author's Preface

truth with a sense of their spiritual poverty; accept the Truth of God with a sincere heart; and not consider Christianity a Western religion, or heed the voice of indigenous theology's claim that it had a "foreign stench" (actually, it is closer to our nation's ancient concept of the "Heavenly Way") and not accept the slander that Christians were "forgetting their roots." In this strenuous effort, I was not attempting to prove a point with specious arguments. On the contrary, I meant to oppose the specious reasoning of indigenous theology. In this manner of communicating the gospel to my compatriots, I am following the Apostle Paul's strategy: "To the Jews I became as a Jew, that I might win Jews . . . To the weak I became as weak, that I might win the weak" (1 Cor 9:20, 22). Thus, to the Chinese, I have become a Chinese, that I might win Chinese; to the weak, like the indigenous theologians, who are "weak in faith," I have become "weak," even to the point of being misunderstood, causing others to think that I am promoting indigenous theology. Actually, I aim to use what my fellow Chinese, especially the Indigenous Theologians, treasure, namely, our "ancient traditions" and "our people's cultural heritage," to redirect these people away from their weak way of thinking, so that they might perceive clearly the reality of Christian doctrine, not rejecting it out of hand, but receiving it with faith. In fact, this method is very effective. The "maiden works" of my early years as a Christian were immature, but some eminent scholars, as a result of reading these books, did "see the light" and turn to the Lord as Savior. Since then my efforts to expound the Christian faith, written with the same spirit, have often received a warm welcome from both Chinese and foreign readers. One reader, who had attended church for decades, was marvelously converted—may God be praised.

When a people is about to depart from its traditional religion and accept a new faith, there will inevitably be cultural and philosophical questions that must be thoroughly resolved. For this, a comprehensive strategy must be adopted in order to tear down Satan's strongholds, transform its rebellious cultural system, and clear away obstacles to the gospel. Only thus can the "seed of the Word" "take root downward, and bear fruit upward" (Isa 37:31). China is an ancient nation with a five-thousand-year culture, so the difficulty is even greater. We cannot rely on the flesh or our impulsive feelings to resolve the issues. Nor can we gain the acceptance of men's hearts with warmed-over platitudes written in formulaic "Gospel" style.[3]

---

3. Schaeffer, "The Evangelical Outlook." See also Chang, *Strategy for Missions in the Orient*; Chang, *Zongti Bian Dao Xue* (*Comprehensive Christian Apologetics*); and other works.

Critique of Indigenous Theology

Theologian John Calvin wrote, "That pagans possess religion is a testimony to God's infinite mercy; that is, because he has planted in their hearts a 'seed of religion.' It is a pity that because of man's sin and corruption, he does not cherish or hold onto God's gracious gift, but damages and perverts the 'mind of God' or 'seed of religion' which has been implanted in his mind; this is precisely the tragedy of human history."[4]

From Chinese history, we can see the unfolding of this tragedy. When we peruse the ancient classics, our people's "concept of the Heavenly Way," which Calvin called "God's mind," constantly established upon the foundation of such vain and empty notions as "the Supreme Unity" (*Tai Yi*); "the Supreme Ultimate" (*Tai Ji*); "the Supreme Ultimate" (*Wu Ji*);[5] and similar empty notions by the scholars who have cumulatively developed Chinese thought. It is no surprise, therefore, that "the seed of religion" cannot take root and flourish or prosper in Chinese soil. If we want to see a revival of true religion, therefore, starting with foundational issues, we must first reestablish for our nation a religious faith of the fear of God, from concepts that are "empty fantasies"—"sand"—to the foundation of an incorruptible, eternal Rock. From a spiritual standpoint, the people of China are facing a crisis of the spirit, which is the very tragedy of human history of which Calvin spoke.[6]

Sadly, indigenous theology not only does not rescue us from this fate, but has replayed the tragedy of the ancients. They have not only imbibed the poison of the modernistic theology of the West, but have taken it further, and greatly worsened the tragedy! They have completely misunderstood the essence of Christian truth; reversed cause and effect; confused essence and function; mixed the false with the genuine; and made philosophy the foundation for theology, rather than taking the Bible as the standard for faith. They totally miss the supernatural, space-and-time-transcending absolute truth of Christian doctrine and the truth of "one Lord, one faith," which is a universally valid standard that is true for all ages, and forgotten that "Forever, O LORD, Your word is settled in heaven" (Ps 119:89). Indigenous Theologians do not distinguish between true and false in their search for an indigenized (contextualized) theology, a Chinese theology. They put the cart before the horse; elevate the sages; promote human wisdom; replace the

---

4. Calvin, *Institutes of the Christian Religion*, bk. 1.

5. Or *wu chi*. Chan, *Source Book*, 639.

6. See Chang, *Minzu Xinling zhi Weiji* (*The Spiritual Crisis of a Nation*); *Jizu Yundong Boyi* (*A Rebuttal of Ancestor Worship*); *Liguo zhi Dao* (*The Foundation of a Nation*); *Sunwen Zhuyi zhi Shenxue Jichu* (*The Theological Basis of the Teachings of Dr. Sun Yat-sen*); and *Shengdao Tong Quan* (*A General Interpretation of Christian Truth*).

Author's Preface

Bible with philosophy; put man in God's place; and replace God's revelation with human speculation. Consequently, in their conviction that "theology can change according to race[7] and time," they want to have a "Chinese" Bible; create a "Chinese" Christianity; possess a "Chinese Old Testament"; establish with God a "Chinese New Covenant."[8] They also say, "Each person and each age can have its own view of God." "Man is the epitome of God, and God is the completion of man."[9] That is like saying, God is created by man, and children give birth to their parents, which amounts to a massive rebellion against standards of virtue.

Because they reverse cause and effect, they also make no distinction between essence and function. Though I have often emphasized that we must know the essence of things in order to put what we know into action,[10] that does not mean that we may confuse "essence" (substance) and "function" (use) in order to do that. I recall that in 1968, when I was on an evangelistic lecture tour in Asia, speaking at seminaries in the Philippines, Hong Kong, Taiwan, Singapore, and Indonesia, I stressed that we must know the essence of things in order to put what we know into action[11] but may not "cherish the outmoded and preserve the outworn"; block one's own progress; adhere to traditional ideas without really comprehending them; or act blindly by divorcing oneself from reality. On the contrary, we must adapt according to place and time; stop hitting our head against the wall; leave the ivory tower; and ascend Mars Hill (Acts 17:22) to contend earnestly for the truth.[12] But we must make one point completely clear: Function is only strategy, and must vary according to the environment and situation, but essence constitutes true doctrine, which is "forever . . . settled in heaven" (Ps 119:89). A thousand changes may be made in the former, but we must never depart from the fundamentals. Sadly, indigenous theology makes no distinction between essence and function, and

---

7. Or, culture, people.—Ed.

8. See Xie, "Zhongguo Wenti yu Jidujiao" ("China's Problems and Christianity"); and Hu, "Jiuyue yu Xinyue" ("Old Testament and New Testament").

9. Xie, *Zongjiao Zhexue* (*Philosophy of Religion*), 154–220.

10. The Chinese phrase is *mingti dayong*, which the author repeats at the end of the sentence and often throughout the book; it means "to understand the essence (substance) and apply it to particular circumstances and situations."

11. Or *Mingti dayong*

12. See Chang, *Dongzheng Ganhuai Lu* (*Remembering My Eastern Journey*); Chang, *Strategy for Missions in the Orient*; Chang, *Christian Impact on the Pagan World*; Chang, *Asia's Religions*; Chang, *A Critique of Humanism* [in this volume]; and Chang, *Zongti Biandaoxue* (*Comprehensive Christian Apologetics*).

therefore retreats, compromises, "cuts off the foot to make the shoe fit," mixes Christianity with paganism, keeps Chinese Christians unable to distinguish between truth and error, and retains the name of true doctrine while losing its reality.

Authentic Christian doctrine respects God's special revelation as the only truth, which cannot be mentioned in the same breath with worldly religions, and especially cannot be put on a par with culture, philosophy, etc. Indigenous theology does not see the fundamental difference between special revelation and general revelation, with the result that it not only confuses the truth but replaces truth with falsehood and elevates heresy. For example, Xie Fuya considers Christianity inferior to the Three Teachings,[13] and has even said, "Of the world's religions, there is none which can enable one to know himself clearly more than Buddhism."[14] Thus, he does not believe the gospel, rejects the Lord as Savior, and believes that "regeneration is nothing other than paying close attention to the work of self-cultivation." He holds to a superstitious faith in the way of the Confucian method of self-cultivation, stating that "by coming to sudden understanding and practicing bringing out the best in oneself, . . . one can make himself into a virtuous man, . . . that is to say, into what Paul called the born-again new man."[15] This is the heresy of autosoterism![16] Xie has definitely departed from the truth, and thus has become arrogant. He states: "This age is one of political greatness." "The 'gospel of peace' is nothing other than a 'gospel of struggle.'" Consequently, he advocates Marxism, saying that it has "biblical support." He continues, "We must rise up as an independent, autonomous electorate; resist God; establish the kingdom of heaven ourselves; and escape from being monopolized by God"![17]

Yanjing (Yenching) University president Wu Leichuan, another advocate of indigenous theology, says, "Most of the teaching of Jesus can be corroborated by statements from China's ancient sages." He also equates the Holy Spirit with Confucianism's *ren*.[18] Because he did not know true Christian doctrine, he became a left-wing proponent of the Social Gospel and a believer in Marxism, approving of revolutionary dictatorship and of

---

13. I.e., Confucianism, Buddhism, and Daoism.—Ed.

14. Xie, *Zongjiao Zhexue* (*Philosophy of Religion*), 200–268.

15. Ibid., 225–49. "Virtuous man" is my translation for *youde junzi*—"a gentleman with virtue [moral excellence]."—Ed.

16. Self-salvation.—Ed.

17. Xie, "Zhongguo Wenti Zu Jidujiao" ("China's Problems and Christianity").

18. Variously translated as "benevolence," "love," "humanity," "humaneness."—Ed.

Author's Preface

overturning political authority by military violence. He thought that "the Kingdom of Heaven proclaimed by the Lord Jesus is a sort of ideal new society. When people interpreted it as another world, a Heaven attainable only after death, they created a superstition that inflicts harm upon people." He therefore sympathized with the traitor Judas, calling him a person whom we can easily excuse, "because Jesus' earliest plan was to carry out a policy of the transformation of society after he had gained political power."[19]

Merely to quote these statements without comment is to expose the danger of indigenous theology's confusion of the truth.[20] I hope that the Chinese seminaries that still hold to pure doctrine, if they offer a course on indigenous theology, will stand up and offer a critique and refutation, thereby enabling the people of our nation to understand the true nature of this teaching and "earnestly contend for the faith."

When I was younger, I was addicted to the Three Teachings,[21] opposed the truth, and was even worse than the proponents of indigenous theology. Little did I know that in my later years I would receive God's mercy, be turned from error to an understanding of the Truth, and pass from [spiritual] death to life. Beginning at the age of fifty-three, I decisively gave up my position as president of a university, high offices in the government, and other posts, and became a student once again, devoting all my energies to the study of the truth. Though I am more than eighty now, working around the clock, I continue to write books and preach the gospel; putting myself in the place of those who are still lost, I cannot stop this work. All my books are not just the products of book knowledge and my own mind, but are the distillation of a life of unremitting toil.

So, relying on God's grace and by the power of the Holy Spirit, [I have composed works that have resulted in] the conversion of readers both within China and beyond. For a former stubborn opponent of Christianity, who was deeply addicted to the evil teachings of paganism, to realize his errors and mend his ways, and to see the distinction between truth and falsehood, shows that our God "is not willing that any should perish" (2 Pet 3:9). I believe that others who have been led astray by indigenous theology will likewise come to an understanding of the truth and be saved. As the Scripture says, "There is a way *that seems* right to a man, but its end *is* the way of death" (Prov 14:12; 16:25). Beware lest, by a small slip of the

---

19. Wu, *Jidujiao yu Zhongguo Wenhua* (*Christianity and Chinese Culture*), 82.
20. Ibid., see chapter 3.
21. Confucianism, Buddhism, and Daoism—Ed.

mind, you fall into an error that will lead to ruin. I repeat myself so that you might be vigilant and repent. For this I pray fervently to God.

Lit-sen Chang (Zhang Lisheng)
1984
United States of America

1

Introduction

The Lessons of Old Testament History

IN HIS LETTER TO the Romans, Paul writes, "For whatever things were written before were written for our learning" (Rom 15:4). To the Christians at Corinth, he says, "our fathers . . . all ate the same spiritual food, and all drank the same spiritual drink" (like scholars promoting Chinese Indigenous theology, who read the same Bible, of whom are even presidents of Christian colleges and seminaries). "But with most of them God was not well pleased, for *their bodies* were scattered in the wilderness. Now these things became our examples, to the intent that we should not lust after evil things as they also lusted . . . Now all these things happened to them as examples, and they were written for our admonition" (1 Cor 10:1–11). In Peter's second epistle we also read, "But there were also false prophets among the people, even as there will be false teachers among you, who will secretly bring in destructive heresies, even denying the Lord who bought them" (note that a number of indigenous theologians do not acknowledge the deity of the Lord Jesus, considering him an ordinary man like Confucius and Mencius), "bringing on themselves swift destruction . . . because of whom the way of truth will be blasphemed . . . for a long time their judgment has not been idle . . . For God . . . did not spare the ancient world . . . bringing in the flood on the world of the ungodly; and turning the cities of Sodom and Gomorrah into ashes he condemned *them* to destruction, making *them* an example to those who afterward would live ungodly" (2 Pet 2:1–6).

Critique of Indigenous Theology

In the Old Testament it is recorded twice that "Nadab and Abihu, the sons of Aaron, each took his censer and put fire in it, put incense on it, and offered profane fire before the LORD, which he had not commanded them. So fire went out from the LORD and devoured them, and they died before the LORD. Then Moses said to Aaron, 'This is what the LORD spoke, saying: "By those who come near Me I must be regarded as holy; and before all the people I must be glorified."' So Aaron held his peace" (Lev 10:1–6). In Numbers we read, "These are the names of the sons of Aaron . . . the anointed priests, whom he [Moses] consecrated to minister as priests. Nadab and Abihu had died before the LORD when they offered profane fire before the LORD in the wilderness of Sinai" (Num 3:2–4). Our Chinese indigenous theologians make idols out of secular Western and Chinese scholars, and take their theories as the bases of their own thought, while despising the Scriptures (God's Word), even to the point of defaming the truth. The opinions of the scholars that they follow are all far from the Bible and opposed to the truth. In the eyes of our most holy God, "every high thing that exalts itself against the knowledge of God" (2 Cor 10:5) is just like "unauthorized fire," and is an abomination that will incur God's wrath.

Looking again at the Scriptures, we read that in the period of the judges, the Israelites forsook the LORD, not wholeheartedly worshiping the one true God, but disobeying his commandments. They sought to "Canaanize" theology ("indigenization") and make an idol out of God[1] by fashioning images. As a result, idolatry was very rampant, leading to various sorts of harm: in the realm of morals, life became corrupt, immoral and debauched, full of violence and wickedness. Politically, anarchy reigned, laws and moral standards ceased to be binding, and "everyone did *what was* right in his own eyes" (Judg 21:25). Throughout the time of the judges, the whole nation was rebellious; they were repeatedly given over by God into the hands of the peoples around them as punishment. In his mercy God forgave them many times, raising up judges to deliver them. Human nature is hard to change, so that the people continued to do what was abominable in the eyes of the LORD in their rejection of him, provoking his anger, which led to their being turned over yet again to the power of their enemies, who despoiled them. After the era of the judges, the people still did not learn from repeated painful experiences how to repent sincerely, but continued in stubborn rebellion. As the LORD said

---

1. Chang uses two words for "God": *Shen* and *Shang Di*. For reasons that I have explained elsewhere, I have rendered both *Shen* and *Shang Di* as "God," since it is clear that Chang sees these two Chinese terms as synonymous.—Ed.

Introduction

to Samuel, "According to all the works which they have done since the day that I brought them up out of Egypt, even to this day—with which they have forsaken Me and served other gods" (1 Sam 8:8). During the centuries of the kings, most of the monarchs "did what was evil in the LORD's sight," and "caused the people to sin" (1 Kgs 22:52). God repeatedly sent courageous prophets who spoke from the heart to warn the people, especially the prophet Jeremiah, who wept day and night, wishing that his "head were waters, and [his] eyes a fountain of tears" (Jer 9:1). Still, though the speakers were earnest, the hearers were obdurate and contemptuous, and even wanted to kill the messengers of the Lord. Finally, when God's patience was exhausted, his anger shattered the nation and sent them into exile among the Gentiles. They wandered through many lands and suffered great humiliation and persecution. The source of their troubles was that they had violated God's commands and failed to worship the only true God with all their heart, thus "Canaanizing" him ("indigenizing") and making him into an idol. The sacred history of the entire Old Testament "was written for our instruction," to warn those who live in these last days, and serve as a warning to us.[2]

Repeating the Same Old Mistakes

Dr. B. B. Warfield, a theologian with orthodox convictions, said, "When describing the science of the relationship between God and the world, theology must be based entirely upon the Bible, using the Bible as its only source."[3] Clearly, the Scriptures are the only foundation upon which to build theology. Proponents of indigenous theology, however, lack an accurate understanding of the Scriptures. One Chinese scholar has posited the Bible as an "assumption,"[4] asserting that "Chinese Christianity should have a third kind of great assumption. Before the arrival of Christianity in China, what we had was a Chinese 'Old Testament' . . . After the entrance of Christianity, we must also establish a Chinese 'New Covenant' with God."[5] There is another scholar, who wants to write a "Chinese Bible" and

---

2. See Chang, *Sheng Dao Tong Quan* (*A General Interpretation of Christian Truth*) and *Jidu Jiao de Lishi Guan* (*A Christian View of History*).

3. Warfield, "The Idea of Systematic Theology," 56; [Warfield] "An Introduction to Beatie's *Apologetics*," 23ff.

4. Or *supposition*.—Ed.

5. Hu, "Jiuyue yu Xinyue" ("Old Testament [Covenant] and New Testament [Covenant]"), *Jing Feng*, vol. 3.

Critique of Indigenous Theology

create a "Chinese Christianity,"[6] thus "indigenizing" a Christianity that is universally valid as a standard. By not building doctrine upon correct presuppositions, with such an erroneous view of Scripture they establish their theology on an erroneous foundation, one that is not a solid rock, but shifting sand (see Matt 7:26–27). It is not surprising, then, that their theology contains so many absurd heresies and must collapse.

Their View of God

They say, "God is known[7] through men; men can make God known and thus can be worthy of heaven; the sage is worthy of heaven. This is China's original teaching."[8] Another writes, "If we say that God is omniscient, omnipotent, completely loving, omnipresent, infinite, and eternal, this is irrational." "The principle (*li*) of Heaven is China's unique view of God." "In the Chinese mind, the complete human personality is equivalent to God."[9] Again: "Each age and each person can have its own view of God."[10] "The Dao is the God of Laozi; the self is the God of Yang and Zhu.[11] The conscientious person is the God of Wang Yangming;[12] the person in the dark is the God of Wu Zhihui;[13] man is the epitome of God and God is the completion of man."[14] Is this not the same as saying that God is made by man and parents are born from their children, thus violating all the heavenly laws of morality?

---

6. Xie, "Zhongguo wenti yu Jidujiao" ("China's Problems and Christianity"), *Ming Bao Monthly*, vol. 107.

7. Or *expressed*.—Ed.

8. Zhao, "A Few Suggestions for Creating a Chinese Church." Professor Zhao was the dean of the Institute for the Study of Religion at Yanjing University.

9. Xie, *Zongjiao Zhexue* (*Philosophy of Religion*); and Xie, *Nanhua Xiao Shan Pang Wen*, 8:294–316; 4 sec. 5.

10. Xie, *Zonghua Jidujiao Chulun* (*Introduction to Chinese Christianity*).

11. Zhu Xi (1130–1200) was a Confucian scholar who became the leading figure of the School of Principle and the most influential rationalist Neo-Confucianist.—Ed.

12. Wang Yangming (1472–1529) was an idealist Neo-Confucian philosopher, official, educationist, calligraphist, and general.—Ed.

13. Wu Zhihui (1865–1953) was a satirist, anarchist, philologist, and educator.—Ed.

14. See Xie, *Zongjiao Zhexue* (*Philosophy of Religion*), 154–220.

Introduction

Their View of Heaven

Wu Leichuan, former president of Yanjing (Yenching) University, says, "The kingdom of heaven[15] which Jesus preached is a kind of ideal new society. When people interpret it as another world, a heaven to be reached after death, that is an 'extremely harmful superstition!'" In order to bring about the realization of his "view of heaven," he believes in the atheistic materialism of Marxism and supports the use of revolutionary violence to seize political authority.[16] Xie Fuya advocates for "an independent, autonomous, electorate" to arise and oppose God and establish the kingdom of heaven themselves, in order to escape from "the dictatorship[17] of God," thus expelling God from the kingdom of heaven.[18] They are all unwittingly serving as the mouthpiece of the Chinese Communist Party, turning theology into communist doctrine!

Their Christology

They turn Jesus into an ordinary man. John the Baptist was, clearly, one who came to "prepare the way of the Lord" (Matt 3:3; Isa 40:3). John plainly said that he came as a forerunner of the Lord, declaring, "I indeed baptize you with water unto repentance, but He who is coming after me is mightier than I, whose sandal I am not worthy to carry." When he saw Jesus, he declared, "Behold! The Lamb of God who takes away the sin of the world!" He also "bore witness, 'I saw the [Holy] Spirit descend ... and it remained on him ... [T]his is the Son of God" (Matt 3:11–17; John 1:26–34). When Jesus came to John to be baptized, John "*tried to* prevent Him, saying, 'I need to be baptized by you'" (Matt 3:14), but Xie denies the truth when he says, "When Jesus heard John the Baptist say, 'The kingdom of God has drawn near; repent and be baptized,' he suddenly became aware of his divine nature and rushed to John to be baptized." He is thus making a degrading remark about the Lord's position. He imposes his own interpretation on Scripture (2 Pet 1:20). He makes a far-fetched comparison between Jesus' important revelation in John 14:6, misconstruing him to say, "The Way is the realization

---

15. Though for Jesus "kingdom of heaven" meant "kingdom of God," for Wu heaven means only a realm, or state, so that it is not here capitalized.—Ed.

16. See Wu, *Jidujiao yu Zhongguo Wenhua* (*Christianity and Chinese Culture*), 82–98.

17. Or *monopoly*.—Ed.

18. See Xie, *Zongjiao Zhexue* (*Philosophy of Religion*), chap. 2, pp. 92, 95, 96, 100, 101.

of democracy; the Truth is the goal of science; and the Life is the turning point of the combination of the highest truth and the deepest knowledge."[19] In this he is succumbing to the influence of the error of the May Fourth Movement's "Democracy and Science" slogan.[20] He therefore nonsensically degrades the Lord Jesus Christ—the Word made flesh, the God-man, the Savior of mankind, the King of kings—to a mere ordinary man who advocated science and democracy. In this way, he empties Christian truth of all substantial reality, retaining the name but losing the essence. Another advocate of indigenous theology even more absurdly writes, "To rely only on a Jewish Jesus of history is not enough.... Each one of us should also use our own blood to write our own signature."[21] He thus not only reduces Jesus to just an ordinary man like us, but erases the saving work wrought by the blood that he shed for us on the Cross. As Wu Leichuan, president of Yanjing University said, "Jesus' original plan was to gain political power..., restore the nation of Israel..., and carry out a program to reform society," thus making him into a mere politician.

Their View of the Holy Spirit

They do not have an accurate understanding of the Trinity, or a reverent attitude, but arrogantly imagine that "'the sage is worthy of heaven' is China's original teaching." They totally misunderstand the personality of the Holy Spirit and completely deny his supernatural activity, absurdly declaring, "For Chinese, the Holy spirit is no stranger to us. As the traditional Chinese saying goes, '[We] do not start from the Holy spirit to talk about the Holy Spirit,' but from the saying, 'What Heaven has conferred is called the Nature' to explain the Holy Spirit."[22] "The Holy Spirit is nothing other than the personification of love and goodness, as Mencius said, 'All humans have by nature a compassion for others and will not want to see

---

19. Xie, *Zhongguo Jidujiao Chulun* (*Introduction to Chinese Christianity*).

20. The May Fourth Movement arose in 1919 as a response to the provision of the Treaty of Versailles to hand over the former German-occupied territory of Shandong to Japan, but it blossomed into a wide-ranging cultural movement that included promotion of science and democracy as the answers to China's chronic weakness and backwardness.—Ed.

21. Hu, "Jiuyue yu Xinyue" ("Old Testament and New Testament"), in *Jing Feng*, vol. 3.

22. Legge, "The Doctrine of the Mean," 1.1.

Introduction

them suffer; [they all possess] an ability to distinguish right from wrong; a quality of propriety; a sense of honor."[23]

Their View of Religion

Xie Fuya quotes the words of the atheist, antireligionist Luosu: "Religion holds on to what is old, and hinders progress, and so can be compared to unsanitary water." He repeatedly proclaims that the "'believe and be saved' segment of Christianity seems, on the surface, to be vigorous, but in reality is like a man who 'drinks poisoned wine to quench his thirst, thus killing himself.' Those who thus mislead others are world-class criminals!" He therefore values the traditional religions of China, but he is actually destroying the authority of his own position and the theology that he believes. He therefore promotes Confucianism, Buddhism, and Daoism, thus destroying the foundation of the faith, and the authority of his own theology![24]

Their Soteriology (Doctrine of Salvation)

Xie criticizes "the Lord Jesus' teaching 'unless you are born again, you cannot be saved,'" holding that Jesus "is simply emphasizing the importance of the effort to cultivate oneself." He superstitiously believes in the "cultivate one's moral character and nourish one's nature" doctrine of the Confucianists, and denies the saving work accomplished by the shed blood of the Lord, believing that to "realize the truth suddenly and self-consciously and practice self-cultivation" is the way to become a moral gentleman, or what the Israelites called a chosen people. "This is also what Paul emphasized, namely the reborn new person." He superstitiously places his faith in the pernicious doctrine of "autosoterism,"[25] holding that the marvelous experience of regeneration and salvation of Paul on the road to Damascus was really a form a mental illness. He also trusts in modern psychology, thinking that the concept of a soul has already been eliminated by that discipline. Hence, he absolutely does not believe in eternal life, which is the same as making God a liar![26]

---

23. Xie, *Nanhua Xiaozhu Shan Pang Wen*, 4, sec. 5.
24. Xie, *Zongjiao Zhexue (Philosophy of Religion)*, 250–68.
25. Self-salvation.—Ed.
26. Xie, *Zongjiao Zhexue (Philosophy of Religion)*, 225–49.

Critique of Indigenous Theology

Based on what we have said, the advocates of indigenous theology mentioned above do not know how to benefit from the lessons of sacred history, so that they are not only "following the track of an overturned cart,"[27] but also doing even worse, "cutting off the foot to fit the shoe,"[28] misinterpreting the Bible to fit their theory of indigenous theology, thus retaining the name of Christian but losing its reality.

A Testimony Tried by Time and Fire

In my younger days, my thought was leftist; I was addicted to the idea of revolution and advocated a materialistic view of history. When I was twenty-three I went to Europe to conduct advanced studies in politics and law, and investigated the governments of various nations. Upon my return to China, I advocated a "legal" view of history. I lectured and wrote books. I supported the constitutional movement to establish the nation. I had an aspiration to "govern the state well, and pacify the world." When the national calamity erupted,[29] I was summoned to participate in politics. After the war with Japan, I was keenly aware of the current social maladies, and became addicted to the Three Teachings,[30] so that I was called a "reincarnation" of *Ouyang Xiu*[31] and of Luo Han. Commended by the eminent scholars of the time, I founded Jiangnan University as a base for the revival of Eastern religion.

In 1950, I was invited to India to lecture at the university founded by Tagore, the topic being, "Asia's destiny: the hope of mankind." I planned to make contact with the leaders of that nation and launch a movement to revive Eastern religion and culture. Who would have thought that mid-way on my journey, I would be hindered by God, and the door to India would be closed. Indeed, it was a very close call. As the Chinese proverb says, "a thousand pounds hang on a single hair." The turning point between disaster and blessing is a great mystery, something we cannot penetrate.

---

27. i.e., repeating the mistakes of others who had brought disaster upon themselves.—Ed.

28. i.e., sacrificing something essential in order to gain something nonessential.—Ed.

29. Japan's invasion of China.—Ed.

30. i.e., Confucianism, Buddhism, and Daoism.—Ed.

31. Ouyang Xiu (1007–1072) was a statesman, historian, essayist, calligrapher, and poet of the Song Dynasty.—Ed.

Introduction

Not long before this, I had been vice-chairman of the Central Government's Overseas Affairs Commission. The government had seven times ordered me to become chairman, but because my ideal and ambition was to "save the world," I consistently refused. The central government sent me to India and also to other Southeast Asian countries, after which I went to Java. This was God's foreordained, amazing plan. From others' standpoint, my background and my studies would not have equipped me for foreign affairs. Most overseas Chinese are from Shangdong, Fujian and Guangzhou, so most of their leaders are from that area only and not other parts of China. My studies had been in law and politics, and I had been an educator, with a specialty in constitutional law. But at the time of the war against Japan, I was a member of the Supreme Committee of the Ministry of Defense, and was very good at and interested in foreign policy. I predicted the "maritime strategy party" of Japan would follow the "continental strategy party" and launch the Southern Campaign. I recommended to the government that it seize the initiative by striking first to oppose the Southern Campaign and carry out a comprehensive strategy for the sake of the life and property of millions of our citizens. Then I was assigned to visit the people of that region to promote friendly relations with those countries and encourage overseas Chinese. Not long after, the Pacific War broke out, as I had prophesied. Departing from my previous practice, I allowed myself to be placed in charge of overseas affairs, which was God's plan also, to make me a "brand plucked from the fire" (Zech 3:2). Otherwise, had I remained in China, trapped in the errors of the "Three Teachings," I would eventually have been "cast into the lake fire" (Rev 20:15), eternally lost. That I could pass from death to life and be saved in Java is truly God's amazing grace.

After I turned to the Lord, but before I had begun studying theology, I was treated as important by leaders of the church in China. I was already preaching in various places, and served as chaplain at a Christian school, professor at Southeast Asian Bible College and the seminary of the Southern Baptist Church. In light of my background, I would most likely have promoted indigenous theology, but God protected me. In 1950, he led me to America to study theology full time. At the time, the school (Gordon College and Seminary), considering my professional experience, invited me to become an instructor both in the college and in the seminary. But I insisted that I only wanted to become a student again, so I only taught one course in the college, and devoted myself fully to my studies. The school afforded me special treatment, giving me a key to the library, so that I could do research both day and night as I immersed myself in the coursework. By God's special grace, I was able to overcome the language difficulty. I had lived in France in my youth, and had fallen in love with German culture, but my English was quite rusty. After only a month, however, I was able to write a theological paper. The American students wrote only ten pages or so, but, to my professor's amazement, my paper was over one hundred pages long, and was called a "graduation thesis." Henceforth, I wrote more and more, from two hundred to six hundred pages, while at the same time I had to complete other important and very heavy homework. Others thought that for me to do so much in such a limited time and with such limited knowledge was impossible. As a result of my work, all my professors were astounded, and I was kept on as an instructor after graduation, even up to the present. I was well liked by the students and faculty, who designated me as Distinguished Professor Emeritus in a special ceremony that was unprecedented in the history of the school. I felt totally ordinary and ignorant, and give all the glory to God.

By retelling this story, though I feel I have gone on a bit long, I still fear that I have omitted many important things. The purpose is, first, to let advocates of indigenous theology know that before I turned to Christ, like them, I idolized "the wisdom of this world"; was fully addicted to and obsessed with the Three Teachings;[32] and was thus a fellow traveler with them, even going further than they. Second, I wish to glorify God, who has allowed me, over the past fifty years of testing, to be "plucked from the fire," and thus to know clearly the severity of the "sickness" of indigenous theology; to come to know both myself and those with whom I disagree; be equipped by the Lord for service; enter the army of the Lord of hosts; engage in spiritual warfare; and contend for the truth.[33]

Third, and even more important, I cherish the hope that advocates of indigenous theology, as they look at their "fellow traveler," will come to their senses; pass from death to life; renounce what they have learned before; count everything as rubbish; and become like Paul the Apostle, who said, "what things were gain to me, these I have counted loss . . . for the excellence of the knowledge of Christ Jesus my Lord . . . forgetting those things which are behind and reaching forward to those things which are ahead, I press on toward the goal for the prize of the upward call of God in Christ Jesus" (Phil

---

32. i.e., Confucianism, Buddhism, and Daoism.—Ed.
33. See Chang, *Zongti Biandaoxue* (*Comprehensive Christian Apologetics*).

3:7–14), so that I may gain "an inheritance incorruptible and undefiled and that does not fade away, reserved in heaven" (1 Pet 1:4).

In the past few years of unremitting effort at writing and teaching, relying on God's grace, I have written eighty shorter and longer works in Chinese and in English. Most readers in China have viewed my works as too abstruse. Christians, being more advanced, have encouraged me. Though my English is not strong, I have received praise from highly-regarded Western scholars and from well-known theologians and church leaders. Readers within and without China have warmly responded to my writings, causing me to praise the amazing work of the Holy Spirit. For example, one young university student, who strongly opposed religion and absolutely would not listen to Christian preaching, because of his parents' command did go to church. He felt as if he were sitting on pins and needles, but as he casually opened one of my books, some amazing power threw him to the ground, where he cried bitterly, confessing his sins. According to a letter he wrote me, he now reads my works and has offered himself for the ministry of the Word.

Another American young person, who had been addicted to Eastern religion, while meditating in the Zen fashion, was actually possessed by an evil spirit and felt as if he had been plunged into a deep ocean, and then thrust up into the sky by a dark wave. Panic-stricken, he cried out in desperation to Heaven, though unable to speak. Suddenly, he thought of my book, *The Spiritual Decline of the West*. He picked it up and began to read. Who would have known that he would suddenly see a white light, escape from darkness, and enter into marvelous light? He rejected Eastern paganism and entered seminary.

Even more remarkably, ordinary readers think my books are too profound to be of any use, to the degree that they have told me to my face that my writings are not easy to understand, but a reader in Burma[34] who described himself as a member of the Miao people from the border area (a people have do not have a written language), and who only studied two years in an elementary school in China, not only was able to read my books (published, for example, in Singapore in the Guan Shi Bao edited by Yu Zhongmin), but was used to spark a revival in the church. He later risked his life to go to preach in mainland China. When he was seized by the Communists, he prayed, and was miraculously released to return to Burma. In addition, there was a reader who happened to see the *Critique of Chinese Humanism* in a friend's house, and as soon as he began reading

---

34. Now Myanmar.—Ed.

it began to understand the truth. Though he had studied theology and had preached in a church for fifteen years, he had sadly not known the truth or been truly converted. After reading my book, however, he was filled with the joy of regeneration, knelt down and prayed to God all night, thanking him for his grace and praising the name of the Lord.

In my writing, I steadfastly endeavor to render my style easy to read and amiable, and empathize with others' suffering, for which I often shed tears. But when it comes to the truth, I cannot compromise or accommodate, so I often condemn others in my speech and writing. It is said, "Good medicine tastes bitter, but only then can it bring healing." When God disciplines us, it is "for *our* profit . . . no chastening seems to be joyful for the present, but painful; nevertheless, afterward it yields the peaceable fruit of righteousness" (Heb 12:10–11).

Like that reader, the proponents of indigenous theology have all studied theology and have become pastors or teachers, and among them there are college presidents. But because they have possibly not yet been truly born again I deeply hope that when they read they will not think of my book as bitter medicine, but like the person described above see my book as something they wish they had seen sooner and receive the joy of true conversion. My earnest prayer is that God Almighty, the holy and good Spirit, will act upon them by his gracious power.

2

The Source of the Disaster of Indigenous Theology
Historical Review and Reflections

Heresies of the Early Church

CHRISTIAN TRUTH IS THE heavenly revelation from God as well as his great salvation. This "salvation . . . at the first began to be spoken by the Lord, and was confirmed to us by those who heard *Him*, God also bearing witness both with signs and wonders, with various miracles, and gifts of the Holy Spirit, according to His own will" (Heb 2:3–4). Ever since mankind fell into sin, however, human nature has been in rebellion against God, opposing the truth, following the course of this world, and submitting to the prince of the power of the air, the spirit who now works in the sons of disobedience. Men have used their science and empty nonsense, not according to Christ, but according to human tradition and the elementary principles of this world, to lead countless people astray (see Rom 1:18–20; Eph 2:1; Col 2:8). So-called indigenous theology belongs to this sort of heresy that is not according to Christ, but according to the elementary principles of this world and empty nonsense derived from tradition. Advocates of this position are "false prophets . . . false teachers . . . who will secretly bring in deceptive heresies" (2 Pet 2:1). From the beginning of history until now it has been like this, and recently has become even worse, proving that human nature is rebellious.

The earliest effort to use human wisdom to confuse the truth; to degrade the exalted, holy, and heavenly revelation into the status of tradition

Critique of Indigenous Theology

and elementary principles of this world; to turn the truth into something secular, humanist, and indigenized (contextualized), was Gnosticism. An early indication of this heresy can be found in the writings of Paul, Peter, and John. Exegetes believe that Paul was speaking to such an incipient form of gnosticism in the second chapter of Colossians. With his great learning, Paul was especially chosen by God to combat Greek philosophy and actively to attack the fortresses of the philosophical culture of Greece and Rome and to prevent Christian doctrine from becoming Hellenized, that is, indigenized. In Athens, he debated daily with those whom he met in the Agora; he also disputed with the Epicureans and Stoics (see Acts 17:16–18). Later, upon arriving in Ephesus, Paul entered the synagogue and boldly preached the gospel, continually for three months speaking of the kingdom of God and exhorting everyone. After he had met resistance from those who were hardhearted and would not believe, he debated in the lecture hall of Tyrannus for two years, so that everyone in Asia Minor, both Jews and Greeks, heard the truth of the gospel. His fellow apostle John, meeting the gnostic Cerinthus in a public bath, immediately fled the place, shouting, "The enemy of the truth is here; leave, everybody, lest you perish with him when the building collapses!" You can see from this that they shared the same resolute opposition to heresy.

By the middle of the second century, Gnosticism resembled a hurricane, and ran rampant. The wildness[1] of this sect consisted in its masquerading as something precious; employing Christian modes of thought and terminology, even claiming to be the revelation given to elite *illuminati* by God and calling itself an additional revelation secretly passed down from Christ and his apostles; and averring that what they preached was "true Christianity." Even the German theologian Adolph Harnack surprisingly (and wrongly) called them the earliest theologians. From this my fellow countrymen should take note. Our Chinese Christian scholars who advocate indigenous theology are also learned men who cite many classic works. They are familiar with both Chinese and Western literature, are prolific writers, and are respected as on the cutting edge of the church, to the point that even Christians with a pure faith are led astray (Matt 24:24). They don't realize that these indigenous theologians are wolves in sheep's clothing promoting a fearful heresy, and are really a hidden looming disaster for the Chinese church. Although the gnostics bragged that they were true Christians, and were God's specially-chosen *illuminati* and

---

1. The author uses the same word several times in this passage, which I sometimes translate "rampant," sometimes "wild."—Ed.

The Source of the Disaster of Indigenous Theology

recipients of an esoteric revelation that had been secretly transmitted to them, in reality they turned Christian doctrine into something "with the name and not the reality," because they did not believe in God as Creator. They denied that the Lord Jesus died on the Cross (Chinese indigenous theologians also deny the saving work of Christ), so they supplanted faith with knowledge, holding that the meaning of salvation was to put off foolishness and ignorance rather than to receive forgiveness of sins. As the Scripture says, "they . . . became futile in their thoughts, and their foolish hearts were darkened. Professing to be wise, they became fools" (Rom 1:21–22). Sadly, however, this sort of philosophy surprisingly flourished for quite a short time, and because of the baneful effects of the Hellenization/indigenization of Christian doctrine as well as its compromise with Greek philosophy, it is good for the proponents of Indigenous Theology to heed this warning from the pages of history.

The Errors of the Period of the Early Church Fathers

The early church fathers looked with anxiety at the world's troubles and boldly proclaimed Christian truth. They believed firmly in Christian teaching, holding it to be the revelation of God, incomparably lofty, complete, and sufficient, not needing Greek philosophy to make up for any deficiency. They also warned people that if they blindly followed Greek philosophy, it would lead to their destruction. So with all their might they attacked the destructive heresies of the time and would not tolerate any confusing of them with the truth. Thus, although they encountered persecution, they continued to contend earnestly for the truth, never surrendering, steady in their faithfulness no matter how desperate the situation, preparing even to die if necessary.[2] "The blood of the martyrs is the seed of the church."[3]

On the other hand, however, it was unavoidable that among the early fathers there appeared major errors. Some made far-fetched interpretations of Christianity and compromised with Greek philosophy, so that even Justin Martyr did not avoid this step, in an error that advocates of indigenous theology should note carefully, to know where they should be cautious and take it as a warning. Justin said, "The Logos is the Universal Reason that works throughout the world, through philosophical thought, enlightening countless Egyptians, Romans, Greeks, all reasonable men, all Christians. All who are Christians are reasonable, so Socrates and the others can all

2. See Chang, *Zongti Biandaoxue (Comprehensive Apologetics)*, vol. 2, chap. 12.
3. Tertullian, *Apology*, 37.

be considered Christians." Clement of Alexandria held that before Christ came, the Greeks had to obtain righteousness through philosophy, which was a tutor to lead them to Christ.[4] For that reason, he employed Greek philosophy to organize his systematic theology. Later, Origen and Cyprian sought to harmonize Christianity with Neoplatonism—the method of the advocates of today's indigenous theology.

The Dark Period of the Middle Ages

This trend of compromise intensified during the Middle Ages. Roman Catholic Scholastic thinkers like Thomas Aquinas repeatedly tried to harmonize divine revelation and human wisdom, in order to make theology "humanistic and Hellenized." Aquinas believed that the Bible is the Word of God, but he opposed Augustine's approach (see below) in order to return to the old way of Aristotle, using reason to prove what was believed, such as the existence of God and the accuracy of the Bible. He even said that exegesis of the Bible should be based upon the foundation of church tradition, forcing God's revelation to accommodate the opinions of the pope and the church fathers, thus making theology "humanistic" and installing the pope on the throne of God.[5]

We must, therefore, fill out our previous reference to Augustine's theology. Born and brought up in a culture that rebelled against the truth, he came under the influence of the errors of Plotinus, the founder of Neoplatonism. Not only was his thinking poisoned, but his life became dissolute. The change after in his thought and faith was a remarkable work of God. At a time of discouragement and total loss of purpose in life, while sitting under a fig tree in a garden in great sorrow and sobbing, he suddenly heard a voice saying, "Take up and read! Take up and read!" He picked up the Bible, and as he read Romans 13:12–14, "The night is far spent, the day is at hand," an amazing beam of light pierced his heart as God called him out of darkness into light. Thereupon, he became a different person, immediately receiving new life. Doubts completely dissolved, his faith was firm; he was chosen by God to become a path-breaking theologian.[6] Actually, most scholars only look at the similarities between Greek philosophy and Christian truth and do not examine their fundamental characteristics,

---

4. See Chang, *Zongti Biandaoxue* (*Comprehensive Apologetics*), vol. 1, chap. 2. The biblical allusion is to Gal 4:1–2.

5. See Chang, *Renwen Zhuyi Pipan* (*Critique of Humanism*), vol. 1, sec. 2, chap. 12.

6. See Bentley-Taylor, *Augustine, Wayward Genius,* chap. 5.

including their absolute differences. There are many, therefore, both eclectics and compromisers, who try to keep their feet on both sides, seeking the Hellenization of Christianity, combining it with Neoplatonism, which was exactly Augustine's experience. He also fell into this type of thinking, but later he received God's revelation. Realizing his earlier errors, he refuted the current popular thinking and summoned his fellow believers to contend for the truth and oppose the trends of Greek thought without any compromise at all or making far-fetched comparisons. This experience of the transformation of his thought should be an occasion for those who think that Chinese thought, the Three Teachings,[7] and Christianity can be combined in a coherent system, an Indigenous Theology, to learn from the experience of others and engage in critical reflection. In the history of the church, Augustine inherited the past and laid the foundation for the future; he stands at the critical watershed and pivot-point between two ages, two worlds even. For Christian theology, he brought order out of chaos—a contribution that can never be forgotten.

Unfortunately, however, the Roman Catholic theologian Thomas Aquinas rejected Augustine and, surrendering to Aristotle, changed the nature of theology to Hellenize it and make it humanistic.[8] The Vatican in Rome was rotten at the core, mixing the truth with Roman paganism, and therefore losing the light of the gospel and plunging Europe into the Dark Ages. Later, God raised up Martin Luther during the reign of a tyrannical pope. Luther risked death many times in order to promote the Reformation movement. Calvin then took up the revolutionary banner, opposing the traditional Greek system of thought and causing the light of the gospel to shine afresh upon Europe. Sadly, church scholars have not allowed Calvin's theology to flourish; his thought was opposed by evil influences, which gained even more strength, giving the devil more ground.

Intellectual Trends after the Reformation

Following the Enlightenment Movement of the eighteenth century, rationalism, empiricism, and naturalism increasingly gained strength, emphasizing the so-called liberation of the individual to oppose the restrictions of dogma, while advocating reasonable theology and rational religion. All departments of learning became subordinate to sensationalism,

---

7. i.e., Confucianism, Daoism, and Buddhism.—Ed.
8. Or *ren wen hua*: humanize; that is, in this case, to make it more man-centered.—Ed.

empiricism, materialism, and atheism, placing undue faith in the so-called scientific, empirical view of the universe and of life. This sort of thinking, influenced by writers like David Hume, Immanuel Kant, Francois Voltaire, J. Rousseau, Auguste Comte, Charles R. Darwin, William James, John Dewey, and Bertrand Russell, gradually strengthened and spread furiously like a contagious disease, rushing in like a hurricane and overwhelming everything in its path, with disastrous consequences for heavenly doctrine and supernatural theology. The position of theology was turned upside down, for it came under the control of philosophy and became mingled with human wisdom. The modernist theologians of the West took their own nations' scholars' opinions as their standard, not knowing how to rely on the omniscient, omnipotent, true God but following the lead of philosophy. From one standpoint, one could say that their theology was indigenized (contextualized), that is, stained by the colors of the secularized contextual theology of the West, and therefore turning Christian doctrine into something inferior.[9] They confused the real with a fake, neglecting the essential to pursue the trivial, so that "the name was retained but the reality was lost." Chinese scholars who promote indigenous theology, even though they depend on the development of Chinese civilization to wash out the stench of the bad name of Western, are in this way deceiving their countrymen (to the degree that even the elect were led astray, for I have heard that several seminaries that had pure theology have recently been offering courses on indigenous theology, though they added the words *Critique of* to avoid misunderstanding). They really don't know that they themselves have been "spending so much time in a fish market that they can't smell its stench." They have not only themselves been tainted with the odor of the West, but also, because they have been for so long under the influence of the brainwashing of modernist theologians (which have been rightly accused of being "the party of unbelief") that their own thinking has been deeply poisoned, completely dominated by the rationalism, empiricism, and naturalism described above! (See below). They not only don't reflect and come to a clear understanding, but they still want to teach their fellow Chinese. How pathetic!

The fundamental nature of Western contextual [i.e., indigenous] theology is humanism and naturalism, and is thus completely opposed to Christian truth, like fire and water, because Christianity is a revelation from heaven and its essence is supernatural.[10] Modernist theologians,

---

9. Or *"passing off a fish's eye as a pearl."* —Ed.

10. Chinese writers tend to mistake *chao ziran* as a synonym for *chaoran*, but the two

The Source of the Disaster of Indigenous Theology

by rejecting the supernatural nature of Christian truth when they are ashamed to talk about theology, are destroying its lifeline, leaving the name of truth without its reality. They entirely reject its supernatural elements, blindly relying on rigid and unchanging natural law and natural forces to explain the phenomena of the universe and the human questions of religion and morals. They deny miracles, charging that belief in them is superstitious, with tunnel vision,[11] extremely self-important, considering themselves intelligent, but becoming foolish. They vainly presume to be counselors to God, not knowing the one from whom, through whom, and for whom are all things, the omniscient, almighty God; and they are ignorant of his abundant wisdom, knowledge, judgment, and amazing incomprehensibility (Rom 11:33–36). They do not understand science, but absurdly regard it as a talisman, not knowing what the eminent scientist and honorary chairman of the board of M.I.T., Dr. Vannevar Bush, said, "This sort of worship of science is a toxic vestige of the eighteenth century's superstitious faith in the 'Law of Nature.'" According to this "Law of Nature," people thought that by simply relying on superficial observation and deduction they could penetrate the mysteries of the universe as well as predict inevitable trends. If this sort of reasoning were true, then man is a passive puppet, and the universe is nothing but a rigid, robotic structure. Actually, so-called scientific proof cannot guarantee total accuracy. Scientists must construct a hypothesis upon the conclusions of reasoning based on observation, but this sort of hypothesis can always be overturned by new arguments. So many scientific ideas that were accepted as "gold standard" at the time are already considered "here today, gone tomorrow" and are conclusive evidence of the inability of science to attain to irrefutable proof.

Not only is science not absolute truth, but it tends gradually to become more fallacious, separating itself from the fundamental essence of the universe. It sinks into a kind of mechanistic view from which it cannot extricate itself. It cannot provide any answer to mankind's greatest questions, which are, "Where do we come from and where are we going?"[12]

These theologians, therefore, neglect the essentials and concentrate upon trifles, and have become prisoners of eighteenth-century natural

---

differ completely in meaning. *Chao ziran* means "supernatural," like *chaofan*; but *chaoran*, "transcending the worldly," has a neutral connotation, and does not represent the views of any particular school of thought. The two must be strictly distinguished.—Ed.

11. Or "looking at heaven from the bottom of a well."—Ed.

12. See *Fortune* magazine, May, 1965; and Chang, *Shengdao Zhengyan*, chap. 2: "Jidujiaode Kexueguan" ("The Christian View of Science").

law. They have fallen into its residual poison, yet they have become "blind guides," leading people astray and creating a great crisis for our time! These scholars, calling themselves scientific and yet so conceited, not only presume to penetrate the mysteries of the universe but also to solve mankind's religious and ethical problems, so they mount an offensive against Christian ethics, despising the holiness and righteousness of God in the process. The German philosopher Friedrich W. Nietzsche, for example, was originally studying theology in universities in Bonn and Leipzig in preparation for Christian ministry. After coming under the influence of Kant's positivism, Darwin's evolutionism, and Marx's materialism, however, he "departed from the Classics and rebelled against [Christian] orthodoxy," promoting instead the so-called philosophy of the "Superman," positing the "will to power" as the supreme operative principle among men, and thereby constructing his "unique world-and-life view." He thought that the goal of life was struggle, thus turning "right" and "wrong" upside down by advocating the view that "strength is good, and weakness is bad." Smug and complacent, and shamelessly boasting, he said, "I can surpass the rest of mankind because I am able to expose the defects of Christian ethics." "Christian ethical views are the worst expression of every sort of hypocrisy"; they are the "Circe among men, and the cause of the fall of man." This is really a supreme effort at blasphemy, which enrages God on high, an extreme form of mental illness, and a deadly disease. The reason a full-time theologian, trained for Christian ministry, fell into this sort of tragic finale, is that he "depart[ed] from the faith, giving heed to deceiving spirits and doctrines of demons" (1 Tim 4:1). Scholars in the church should be vigilant and careful.

The Deterioration of Liberal Theology

Sadly, now this sort of teaching has appeared in "theological" seminaries, which is not surprising. First it was the "New Morality," based on the theories of Nietzsche and Dewey, denying any sort of eternal truth or fundamental law and emphasizing the needs of the situation, going even to the extent of opposing God's Ten Commandments and the Sermon on the Mount of Jesus. As long as an action springs from love, one can do as he pleases.[13] Then came the death-of-God theology and godless Christianity, both of which worshiped Nietzsche, calling him the greatest prophet, considering that "only Nietszche had the courage and the vision to understand that to

---

13. Henry, *Dictionary of Christian Ethics*, 623–24; Clark, *Situational Ethics*; and Fletcher, *Situation Ethics: The New Morality*.

The Source of the Disaster of Indigenous Theology

have a real man, we must seek the death of God. Only with the death of God can the 'great divine[14] humanity' emerge." "Only as God appears as the devil can he really die; and only then can we be really saved."[15] This is very similar to the extreme wing of Chinese Zen Buddhism, which holds that we must smash Buddha and all Bodhisattvas before we can attain to sudden enlightenment and achieve buddhahood here and now.[16]

Third, liberation theology arose, along with the theology of hope, advocating social revolution. The World Council of Churches (WCC) often used huge resources to assist armed revolts instigated by left-leaning organizations all over the world. German "theological" seminaries became the base for fomenting social revolution, and honored Marx as a prophet. At the WCC meeting in 1972 in Bangkok, one delegate stood up to praise Mao Zedong as a savior.[17] One extremely vigorous advocate of indigenous theology, Xie Fuya, in an article in the *Mingbao*, in the most wildly irrational words not only asked Chinese Christians to "re-cast Chinese Christianity," and "re-edit a [new] Chinese Bible," but also, in an apparent attempt to cast God out of heaven, declared his intention to stir up every sort of "independent, autonomous electorate" to oppose God, create the kingdom of God, and escape from "God's dictatorship."[18] He also beat the drum of the hate-filled, class-struggle materialism of Marxism, claiming that it had biblical support. (I shall speak more of Xie's theories in another chapter.)

In the above remarks, I have written in a simplistic fashion, mentioning only a tiny sampling of their doctrines; to know more, the reader will have to wait for me to complete other volumes devoted to this specific topic.[19] Even from the little that I have said, however, we can observe the errors of Western theology, which derive in part from its use of Greek philosophy as the source of their disaster, and on the other hand has imbibed the poison of recent trends of thought. Those who promote Chinese indigenous theology, though putting the fair name of Chinese theology on it and claiming to

---

14. Or, perhaps, *holy*.—Ed.

15. See Altizer, *The Gospel of Christian Atheism*; Altizer, *Radical Theology and the Death of God*; Hamilton, *God Is Dead*; Montgomery, *The "Is God Dead" Controversy*; and Van Til, *Is God Dead?*

16. See Chang, *Zen-Existentialism*; and Chang, *Transcendental Meditation*.

17. See Moltmann, *A Theology of Hope*; Henry, "Revolution in Theology"; Lindsell, "Dateline Bangkok"; and Chang, "Old Serpent, New Strategy"; and Chang, "The True Gospel vs. Social Activism."

18. Xie, "Zhongguo Wenti yu Jidujiao" ("China's Problems and Christianity"), *Mingbao Monthly*.

19. See Chang, *Zongti Biandaoxue* (*Comprehensive Christian Apologetics*).

Critique of Indigenous Theology

cleanse it from a Western stench, do not realize that they are unable to escape from the bondage of traditional concepts. In addition, they rely on the training they received in liberal Western theology when they were young and the deceptions of Western scholars, and have long been deeply tainted by the Western stench, so that, "having spent so long in the fish market they can't smell the odor." We can therefore say that the problem of indigenous theology, from the standpoint of time, has been around since ancient times, and from the standpoint of space, is the same in both the East and in the West. China is a cultured nation with a very long history that has at the same time experienced all kinds of revolutionary shocks, resulting in two major trends in mainstream Chinese philosophical thinking: One is the old set of traditional ideas inherited from the past; the other consists of the flood of new popular ideas brought in by the incursions of the West. The former can be thought of as a domestic trouble, the latter as aggression from abroad, and the consequence has resulted in China's becoming a battlefield attacked from both Chinese and Western, domestic and foreign thought. Chinese Christians, therefore, should both know about and be cautious towards history and the current times, bring order out of chaos and correct what is wrong, in order to pass on its heritage and open the way for the future. What a weighty responsibility!

Reflection by Chinese Christians

Although most people think that Chinese indigenous theology only has a history of half a century, if we review and examine the Han and Tang dynasties, we find that the "roots and shoots" of indigenous theology go back to that time. For the past two thousand years since the Lord Jesus Christ completed his great work of redemption, God has been constantly watching out for China, standing outside and knocking on its door (Rev 3:20). Sadly, the Chinese people have constantly spurned the gospel of salvation and continually and stubbornly refused to listen to it. Our kind heavenly Father has never forsaken us, however, but, in a truly marvelous fashion, has knocked on the door again and again about every six centuries. The first time came in the first century, in the age of the Apostles. The second was in the seventh century, during the Tang dynasty when the Emperor Taizhong was on the throne (AD 635), when Bishop Alopen of the Church of the East (the "Nestorians") arrived in Chang'an.[20] The third knock came

---

20. Modern Xian. The "Church of the East" is the term frequently used in modern scholarship to refer to the Nestorian church, so called after its founder, Nestorius, who

The Source of the Disaster of Indigenous Theology

in the thirteenth century, when the Church of the East was revived during the Yuan (Mongol) dynasty. The fourth knock was heard in the nineteenth century, with the arrival of Robert Morrison to China as a missionary and his translation of the Bible. In the middle of that century God sent J. Hudson Taylor to China; he founded the China Inland Mission. I shall deal with these events separately in what follows, because we need to reflect deeply on this history.

Most people think that the first knock on the door—the first time that China had any contact with Christianity—came during the Tang dynasty, but there are various ancient traditions that can be traced back to the Apostle Thomas.[21] For example, the Chaldean prayer book has a number of places that say, "Chinese and Ethiopians, at the urging of Thomas, believed the Gospel . . . Christianity was proclaimed through Thomas, as if flying on two wings to China." In the later Han dynasty (AD 65), the Emperor Han Mingdi received a revelation in a dream, and therefore sent emissaries westward to seek the Way. It is said that this dream was prompted by his hearing that in Central Asia a new religion was being preached. According to another tradition, the Apostle Thomas went to the East to preach in AD 67. This is not an entirely unsubstantiated tradition. First, according to a dynastic chronicle record, in AD 65 Han Mingdi sent Cai An and others to the Western regions to look for the Way; two years later Cai and his companions brought back a "monk" from the west. This is about the same time as AD 67, which fits the tradition. In AD 35, it is said that the emperor sent Ma Yuan and others to fight the Qiang Rebellion in Xianling. When Ma Yuan marched to the borders of Tibet, they met a Westerner, who spoke of the miracle of Jesus' virgin birth by Mary.[22] Second, at that time, India and the West already engaged in frequent communications. Through exchanges between East and West, the gospel had already been preached in the northwest regions of India. As for the tradition of the Apostle Thomas in establishing the church in India, at the Asia-Pacific Congress on Evangelism in Singapore in 1968, I personally heard an Indian delegate say that his church, the Mar Thomas Church, was

---

had been declared a heretic by the Greek- and Latin-speaking churches in 431. In recent years, however, Nestorius was absolved of the charge of heresy and the leader of the Assyrian Church of the East, Catholikos Mar Dinkha, signed a joint statement on Christology with Pope John Paul II. The term in Chinese is "Luminous Teaching" (*Jing Jiao*, or *Luminous Religion*). See Charbonnier, *Christians in China: A.D. 600 to 2000*, 51–52.—Ed.

21. For a recent brief discussion, see Bays, *A New History of Christianity in China*, 5–6.—Ed.

22. Qualben, *History of the Christian Church*, vol. 2.

35

Critique of Indigenous Theology

founded by Thomas. According to the research of Dr. K. S. Latourette, Mahayana Buddhism and Christianity share some striking similarities that point to the early influence of Christianity in India.[23] Sadly, the expedition sent by Mingdi resulted not in the introduction of Christianity into China, but of Buddhism. What a tragedy for our race!

Though we had missed that marvelous opportunity, the second knock on China's door came in 635, during the reign of Taizhong in the Tang dynasty, when God, as it were, "called out" to us. When Bishop Alopen brought the Scriptures of the Church of the East to Chang'an (modern Xian), the emperor sent his prime minister to meet him at the outskirts of the city and escort him into his domain. Three years later, the emperor issued a special decree recommending the "Luminous Teaching," permitting it to spread and stating that "it has taken its rise from the establishment of important truths . . . its principles will survive when the framework is forgotten." He also wrote of this new religion, that "its principles are beneficial to all creatures and advantageous to all mankind. Let it be published throughout the Empire."[24] Concerning this, the "Nestorian Monument" says,

> In the time of the accomplished Emperor Taizhong, the illustrious and magnificent founder of the dynasty, among the enlightened and holy men who arrived was the Most Virtuous Olupen (Alopen) from the country of Syria. Observing the azure clouds, he bore the true sacred books; beholding the direction of the winds, he braved difficulties and dangers. In the year AD 635 he arrived at Chang'an. The Emperor sent his prime minister, Duke Fang Xuanling, who carried his official staff to the western border [of Chang'an] and conducted his guest into the interior. The sacred books were translated in the imperial library. The sovereign investigated the subject in his private apartments. When becoming deeply impressed with the rectitude and truth of the religion, he gave special orders for its dissemination."[25]

The five succeeding emperors similarly protected the "Luminous Religion" and built churches in many provinces, including what is now

---

23. See Latourette, *History of Christian Missions in China*, 48–49; and Chang, *Asia's Religions: Christianity's Momentous Encounter with Paganism*, chaps. 13 and 14, and *Zongti Biandaoxue (Comprehensive Christian Apologetics)*, vol. 3, chaps. 13 and 14.

24. See *Tang Hui Yao*, bk. 49.

25. For more on this monument see Bays, *A New History of Christianity in China*, 4–11; Charbonnier, *Christians in China*, 21–38; and Moffett, *A History of Christianity in Asia*, 1: 291–93, 513–17.—Ed.

The Source of the Disaster of Indigenous Theology

Ningxia, Shaanxi, Gansu, Henan, and Sichuan. Later, Alopen himself was given by the emperor the title of Protector of the Nation, the Master of Dharma. He enjoyed a high position and great respect, and everything was going well. Religious persecution broke out in the reign of Emperor Wuzong, however, because Buddhist doctrine was considered to be not good for society. In 845 an order was given to demolish all Buddhist temples. The Church of the East suffered persecution at this time also, and afterward, and never recovered.[26] That was because the Church of the East had become "indigenized,"[27] and had tried to compromise with Buddhism, in reality causing its own destruction. When we inspect the matter, we find that the Church of the East ("Nestorian" Church[28]) comes from Nestorius, whose faith was orthodox. On the one hand, he opposed the Arian heresy, while on the other he opposed Mary's being called the "Mother of God" by the Church of the East. Sadly, his followers went astray, so that when they came to China, they did not bring Nestorius' original teaching, but denied the divine nature of Jesus Christ.[29] On the "Nestorian" Monument itself, the name of Jesus does not appear, only "the Messiah" (the one most revered by the "Luminous Religion"). And the Cross is placed upon the Buddhist lotus.[30] The canon of Scripture for the Church of the East at the time was neither fish nor fowl, and it especially deviated from the truth. Latourette says that the failure of the Church of the East resulted from their compromise with their environment in their acceptance of Buddhist thought, with the consequence that the seed of the Word was devoured by Buddhism.[31] Furthermore, they were seeking to "indigenize"[32] their theology, wrongly employing many Buddhist terms that were incompatible with the Bible, such as calling God Fo (Buddha), Jesus Yishu, Christians Good Knowers, and baptism initiation into monkhood. Thus they retained the

---

26. Ibid.

27. Or *contextualized*.—Ed.

28. "Nestorian" will be placed within quotation marks to preserve both the traditional English designation of this church, which Lit-sen Chang used in his writings, and the modern understanding that (1) this is not the Chinese translation of the name for the "luminous Teaching (Religion)," and (2) the "Nestorians" may not all have held to the "Nestorian" heresy.—Ed.

29. See Chang, *Jidulun (Christology)*, 190–92.

30. Broomhall, *The Bible in China*, chap. 1.

31. Latourette, *History of Christian Missions in China*. This judgment has since been discussed and to some degree questioned by various scholars, including Daniel Bays in *History*, 10–11, and Moffett in *Christianity in Asia*, 305–12.—Ed.

32. Or *contextualize*—Ed.

Critique of Indigenous Theology

name of Christianity intact but gutted it of any real content; this should be a cause for earnest reflection by those who promote indigenous theology.

The third knock on China's door—God would not abandon us—came after about six hundred years, in the fourteenth century, when "Nestorian" Christianity once again revived in China. After the decline of the Church of the East in China proper from the Tang dynasty to the Mongol (Yuan) dynasty, many Christians went into exile along the borders of China, Mongolia, and Russia, and the eastern parts of Central Asia and Western Asia. Therefore, among the Tartar tribes in the north, the faith continued to be propagated, and the lamp of the church was not completely removed. According to the research of modern American, Russian, German, and French archaeologists and explorers, as well as historians of Syria, around the eleventh century, among the Keraits of Mongolia, the Ordus in the west of Suiyuan, and the Turkish Onguts, there were many adherents of the Church of the East. Furthermore, in the region of Yili in Xinjiang, more than six hundred Christian graves have been discovered.[33] As a result, through the rise of the Yuan (Mongol) dynasty, the seed of the gospel was brought once more to central China. Genghis Khan had his son marry the daughter of a Kerait "Nestorian" Christian king; she became the mother of Kublai Khan, and this resulted in the resurgence of "Nestorian" Christianity throughout China.

In 1260, the Italian brothers Nicolo Polo and Maffeo Polo traveled to the East, where they met with Kublai Khan, who expressed great interest and sent them back with a message to the pope to dispatch one hundred missionaries to come and spread the Christian gospel, so that they might notify the people that they must abandon their idols. But the Pope did not catch the vision for this, so that the Khan was totally disappointed, and even doubted whether the pope might really be entertaining ambitions to invade his realms. Marco Polo followed the footsteps of his father to China in 1271 and was given an audience with Kublai Khan in 1275, when he was granted great honor. In 1277, Marco was given a title and the Yuan emperor expressed interest in Christianity, and all this led to another expansion of the gospel. After the death of Kublai Khan, however, the "Nestorian" church again met with misfortune. In the fourteenth century, Timur[34] attacked widely in Central Asia, then in the Indian Ocean region and Northwest China, so that these areas were brought into Islam's sphere of influence.

---

33. Gong Tianmin, *Tang Dynasty Christian Research*.
34. Tamerlane.

The Source of the Disaster of Indigenous Theology

Sometime after 1620, during the Ming dynasty, Roman Catholic Jesuit missionaries arrived in China; among them were Matteo Ricci, Jean Adam Schall Von Bell, and Ferdinand Verbiest. They conversed with the great scholars of China and held important posts in the government. At the same time, they sought to combine the heretical portions of Roman Catholic practice, such as veneration for Mary, with ancient Chinese customs like worship[35] of idols, ancestors, and Confucius, in an effort to indigenize[36] Christian doctrine; the result was a change in the quality of the faith, and even destruction of it.

The fourth knock on the door came after another six[37] centuries, when, in 1807, God sent Robert Morrison to China to translate the Bible and preach the gospel, and then, in the 1850s, J. Hudson Taylor, who later founded the China Inland Mission.[38] We can say that this was the first time that true Christianity was established and began to develop in China. Morrison was steadfast in his purpose to translate the Bible into Chinese. In this way, based upon a solid foundation, Christian truth was able finally to "take root downward, and bear fruit upward" (Isa 37:31). A fresh wind began to blow upon the Chinese people at this time, making possible a change in all facets of the life of the nation, including culture, education, society, politics, medicine, public health, etc. At the time of Morrison's arrival, he was not allowed to live in China proper (he was forced to reside in Macao), and the British East India Company was afraid of his missionary activities, lest they interfere with their business, and would not allow him to travel on one of their ships, thus forcing him to go by way of America. Not only would the Qing government not allow him to preach, they also forbade Chinese to teach him Mandarin. His teachers carried vials of poison in their belts, ready at any time to die! Even more painful was the opposition of the Roman Catholics. Their leaders, in order to protect commercial interests, opposed him, while Chinese slandered missionaries as running dogs of the imperialists. Characterizing Christianity as a foreign religion of Western invaders is truly a baseless slander. In the great famine in 1877 in Shanxi, with millions of half-starved people crowding the roads, and with the government helpless to aid them, foreign missionaries sacrificed

---

35. The author uses the Chinese word *bai*, which usually means to bow and offer prayers, food, and/or incense to an image. It does not necessarily denote inner trust or reliance.—Ed.

36. Or *contextualize*.—Ed.

37. Counting from the Yuan Dynasty.—Ed.

38. The China Inland Mission was founded in 1865 after Taylor had returned to England from his first tour of ministry in China.—Ed.

39

themselves to provide assistance and initiated steps to address the crisis, but who would have thought that the Chinese people would "return good with evil"? In their wicked superstition, the Qing court allowed violent Boxers to kill missionaries, an inhumane action indeed! In 1922, the entire nation was again engulfed in an anti-Christian movement, during which the leading scholars of China, immersed in the Three Teachings,[39] echoed these sentiments.[40] At the time, in the ignorance of youth, I learned to write articles in order to oppose Christianity.

"Do Not Offer Profane Fire [Incense] to God": "Do Not Use Human Hands to Weave a Heavenly Garment."

Proponents of indigenous theology claim that they are true believers; in the name of washing away the "stench of the West," they are trying to mobilize their countrymen. They believe that they are true to the faith. When we study the essence of Indigenous Theology, however, we find that it cannot escape the bondage to the pagan ideas that have been handed down by tradition, and that at the same time it has been stained with the poison of Western naturalism and modernist theology, which means that it is a wolf in sheep's clothing, and its devotees are doing the work of leaving the Way and opposing the truth in the Chinese church. When we talk about others, we should try to put ourselves in their position and forgive their mistakes. It is not their intention or motivation to do wrong. I certainly do not aim to criticize them, but a small misstep at the beginning can lead to great error. "Without vision (prophetic revelation) the people perish" (Prov 29:18).[41] If we look into the future we cannot imagine how great a disaster will be bequeathed by Indigenous Theology. As the famous preacher C. H. Spurgeon wrote, "The heavenly garment of salvation, if sewn by a needle wielded by human hands, will lead to the destruction of mankind!" "There is a way *that seems* right to a man, but its end *is* the way of death!" (Prov 14:12; 16:25). All humanism and world religion is empty nonsense that inflicts disaster on all mankind; it is the way of death.[42] May

---

39. i.e., Buddhism, Daoism, Confucianism.—Ed.

40. Concerning these four eras, see Chang, *Jiu Shi zhi Dao*, vol. 3, chap. 4, and *Liguo zhi Dao*, chap. 4.

41. NKJV: "Where *there is* no revelation, the people cast off restraint."

42. See Chang, *Critique of Humanism* (in this volume); Chang, *Zongti Biandaoxue (Comprehensive Christian Apologetics)*, vol. 3, chap. 2; and Chang, *Asia's Religions: Christianity's Momentous Encounter with Paganism*.

we conduct ourselves with fear and trembling, lest we be foolishly opinionated, seeking to be "counselors of the Lord" (see Rom 11:34); attempting to use human hands to sew a heavenly garment and to "indigenize" theology; leading people to destruction; and destroying ourselves! God will not be mocked, as the Bible repeatedly warns us. Aaron's sons, Nadab and Abihu, taking their censors, but not according to the command of Yahweh, offered "profane fire" before the LORD, whereupon "fire went out from the LORD and devoured them, and they died before the LORD" (Lev 10:1–2; Num 3:4). May proponents of Indigenous Theology not repeat the disastrous blunders of the past. May they "rein in their horses at the brink of the precipice" before it is too late; not offer profane fire (i.e. Indigenous Theology); but come out of death into life. The situation is very serious. Allow me to elucidate it in detail in the chapters that follow.

3

Fallacies of Indigenous Theology

The "Nestorian" Compromise with Buddhism

Although indigenous theology has only come to the attention of the Chinese people in the past fifty years or so, if we inquire into its origins, just as the Lord has said, it can be traced back to basic human nature, which has been stable up to the present and has become much worse recently, since by nature fallen men have always rebelled against God's truth, and have, according to their own private interpretation (see 2 Pet 1:20–21), twisted God's Word so that "the name remains but the reality is lost." From the standpoint of the history of Israel, beginning from the time of the judges, true religion was Canaanized, and indigenized, and then sank into a dark period, with internal distress and external disasters coming thick and fast. From the standpoint of Western history, it resembles the way in which the Catholic Church became Romanized and "indigenized," leading to the Dark Ages. From the standpoint of Chinese history, it resembles the time of the Tang Emperor Taizhong, when Bishop Alopen arrived and the emperor sent his prime minister Fang Xuanling to welcome him and escort him into his domains, and issued a decree to tolerate the Luminous Religion ("Nestorian" Christianity) and allow its propagation, and later emperors conferred on it special protection. Not only in every province of the Central Plains region did they build churches and were they enabled to proclaim their message, but their doctrine spread to the borders of the Northwest, to Gansu, Ningxia, and elsewhere. Their teaching, however, was not the pure gospel, for the missionaries left the correct teaching

Fallacies of Indigenous Theology

of Nestorius and turned his "two natures, one person" Christology into "two natures, two persons." That not only ascribed two personalities to Jesus Christ, but also changed the incarnation of the Lord who came from heaven into the mere union of God with an ordinary human being, thus losing the fully divine nature of Jesus; this tiny lapse led to a huge mistake.[1]

Evidence from the "Nestorian" religion of that time indicates that they not only did not believe in the fully divine nature of Jesus, but also "cut off the foot to fit the shoe," as they tried to accommodate existing circumstances and sought to indigenize the truth. Church historian Kenneth Scott Latourette, diligently seeking to discover the cause for the failure of "Nestorianism" in China, learned that the main reason they neglected to train up preachers was that in their efforts to "contextualize" their theology, they had compromised with the surrounding culture to the point of surrender. They not only sacrificed the truth of the gospel, but also pandered to the great scholars of the day, collaborating with the Buddhists, and as a result allowed the seed of the gospel to be swallowed up by Buddhism![2]

The missionaries, desiring to agree with the Chinese mind and seeking to please others, went to the extent of mixing up and confusing the truth. Thoroughly indigenizing their theology, they did not dare to exalt the name of Jesus: On the "Nestorian" Monument Jesus is only called "the divided Person (body) of our Three in One"[3] and "Luminous Messiah." Although the Cross appears on the monument, it is placed upon a Buddhist lotus blossom, completely obliterating the teaching of the redemption of the world through the Cross![4] The Nestorian Scriptures, furthermore, were not only "neither fish nor fowl," in the cause of indigenizing, but also "sacrificed clarity by the use of the wrong expressions," distorting the truth; especially by calling God "Fo" [Buddha]; Jesus "Yi Shu"; "baptism" "being initiated into monkhood"; Christians and missionaries "*kalyanamitra*" [spiritual friend and teacher]"; and promiscuously using all sorts of other Buddhist and Daoist religious terms that are not compatible with

---

1. See Chang, *Jidu Lun* (*Christology*), all of chap. 4, section 5 of chap. 7.
2. Latourette, *A History of Christian Missions in China*.
3 Or *san fen shen*. Various interpretations have been given of this phrase. The one that Chang seems to accept is that it ascribes two persons to Christ instead of one, as the Nestorians were accused of doing. See Moffett, *A History of Christianity in Asia*, 1:516–17. Recent scholarship has questioned whether the Nestorians were actually "Nestorian" in their teaching, however. See Charbonnier, *Christians in China A.D. 600 to 2000*, 35–38, 50–51. There is no controversy, however, over whether the "Nestorian" missionaries used a great deal of Buddhist, Confucian, and Daoist terminology in all their writings in China.—Ed.
4. Broomhall, *The Bible in China*, chap. 1.

the Bible as adjectives and nouns. Examples include "root of goodness" (*shan gen*); merit (*gong de*); *Yanluowang*,[5] etc. They also shaved their heads, played the "wooden fish,"[6] prayed for the dead, worshiped the saints, and showed reverence to images of emperors. Even more lamentable, of the so-called canon of the "Nestorians," some books were written by Buddhists; because the church had not trained qualified preachers, they had to use an unqualified Persian to do the translation. Not only was the style obscure and unclear, and very hard to understand, but some of their unorthodox doctrines are evident. These led the people astray, while the name of Christian truth was retained but its reality was lost, and was finally assimilated to, and then swallowed up by, Buddhism. In his eighth year the Tang Emperor Wuzong, who was deeply disturbed by the influence of Buddhism upon the country, which he saw as fully harmful and not at all beneficial since it encouraged the people to retire from ordinary life into obscurity rather than engage in productive work, issued a decree to destroy all the Buddhist temples. The Nestorians were also involved in the same evil practices, and so this sort of indigenous theology met with the same disaster.[7] At the beginning of the Yuan[8] dynasty, since there were many Nestorians living in exile in the border area between China, Russia, and Mongolia, their religion experienced another resurgence for a while. Because its doctrine was not pure, however, and they did not possess real spiritual vitality, this proved to be merely a flash in the pan. After the era of Kublai Khan, they disappeared once more.

The Errors of the Roman Catholics

After the Yuan dynasty, during the reign of the Ming Wanli emperor, the Roman Catholics sent more missionaries to China time and again. But the essence of Roman Catholic religion is a combination of "Roman" indigenization and heretical thought—"Romanism," which includes worship of Mary as the "Mother of God" as the idolatry of "Mariology" (Religion of Mary). When this arrived in China, it quite naturally was indigenized with traditional Chinese paganism (such as worship of ancestors, worship of Confucius, idolatry, etc.). Seeking to bring out the best in each, it ended

---

5. Or *Yan-Luo-Wang* [*Yamaraj*], the God of Death and Ruler of the Fifth Court of eng-Du, the Chinese hell.—Ed.
6. A Buddhist percussion instrument.—Ed.
7. *Tang Hui Yao*, bk. 49.
8. Mongol.—Ed.

Fallacies of Indigenous Theology

up in compromise and assimilation. Desiring to cater to the hearts of the ignorant masses, churches stood like trees in the forest,[9] but they had lost the true God of Christianity and the light of the saving gospel.

As a result, I cannot help but think of the recent action of Archbishop Yu Bing in Taiwan when he brazenly promoted the movement of ancestor worship. What he called by the fine-sounding name of "promoting filial piety" was to cater to the leading scholars of the time and to the common people. He said he had a 1939 papal bull as perfect justification for his action, which he said was "following the mandate of Heaven and complying with the wishes of the people." As a result, all the newspapers, with great fanfare, called Yu's action a fine initiative to inspire his countrymen to pay careful attention to the tradition of filial piety, to revive public morality and Chinese culture, and perhaps even benefit the great cause of recovery of the mainland. That even the theological liberals waved the flag and shouted support particularly saddens me. I was deeply upset and thus wrote books like *Refutation of the Ancestor Worship Movement* and *Minzu Xinling zhi Weiji* (*The Spiritual Crisis of a Nation*), to argue with them dispassionately. My grounds for making these charges are two: (1) Yu is not familiar with the Bible and so should be ashamed of himself, since he is a bishop. (2) Yu does not understand the *Classic of Filial Piety* (*Xiao Jing*), and so misconstrues ancestor worship.

In the Ten Commandments, God clearly said, "You shall have no other gods before [other than, beside] Me. You shall not make for yourself a carved image . . . you shall not bow down to them or serve them" (Ex 20:3–5). Moses called heaven and earth as witness when he warned the people of Israel, "See, I have set before you today life and good, death and evil, in that I command you today to love the LORD your God, to walk in His ways, and to keep His commandments, His statutes, and His judgments, that you may live . . . and the LORD your God will bless you in the land which you go to possess. But if your heart turns away so that you do not hear, and are drawn away, and worship other gods and serve them, I announce to you today that you shall surely perish" (Deut 30:15–18).

The *Classic of Filial Piety* defines filial piety (*xiao*) thus: "Filial piety is the root of all virtue, and the stem out of which grows all moral teaching. Filial piety begins with service to one's parents, continues with serving the sovereign, and is completed by the establishment of character."[10] The *Book of Rites* says, "It is not filial piety if one does not rule well his own

---

9. That is, were abundant.—Ed.
10. *Classic of Filial Piety*, chap. 1, author's translation.

house; it is not filial piety if one does not serve his ruler loyally; it is not filial piety if one does not treat his friends faithfully; it is not filial piety if one does not fight as a good soldier." Clearly, being filial has nothing to do with worship of ancestors! So Ouyang Xiu, the Song dynasty Confucian scholar, wrote articles to criticize strongly the evils of his day: "It is more important to provide respectfully and affectionately for the needs of elder relatives when they are alive, rather than worship them [after they have died]." He was imperial censor during the reign of Emperor Renzong, and was honest and sincere in his writings, enjoying a high reputation because his articles were second to none. He belonged to one of the eight most prominent families in the Tang and Song dynasties, so his words should carry authority. In promoting ancestor worship, Bishop Yu proves that he is not yet enlightened. Not being familiar with the Bible, nor understanding the *Classic of Filial Piety*, he wants to lead the people of China to fall back into the ways that the Israelites traversed, as in the days of those evil rulers described in the book of Kings, who "led their people into sin" and brought upon their nation terrible disasters. By his stance, Yu is conducting the people to destruction. He especially does not know that man does not come from his ancestors but from our heavenly Father, the God who created the heavens and the earth. He is "God, who made the world . . . is Lord of heaven and earth . . . He gives to all life, breath, and all things. And He has made from one blood every nation of men to dwell on all the face of the earth . . . In Him we live and move and have our being" (Acts 17:24–26, 28). "For by Him all things were created that are in heaven and that are on earth, visible and invisible, whether thrones or dominions or principalities or powers. All things were created through Him and for Him. He is before all things, and in Him all things consist" (Col 1:16–17). "For of Him and through Him and to Him *are* all things, to whom *be* glory forever. Amen" (Rom 11:36). In sum, God is the "root" (origin) of all things. The true practice of "paying careful attention to filial piety," surely, should be to "revere our heavenly Father," and reverence towards our heavenly Father is the true essence of filial piety, and its greatest righteousness.[11]

---

11. See Chang, *Jizu Yundong Boyi* (*Rebuttal of Ancestor Worship*); *Minzu Xinling zhi Weiji* (*The Spiritual Crisis of a Nation*); and *Liguo zhi Dao* (*The Foundation of a Nation*). According to a friend of mine, Archbishop Yu read my book and had nothing to say in reply; surely he is aware of his errors.

Fallacies of Indigenous Theology

The Violence of the Boxer Rebellion

With the arrival of Robert Morrison in 1807 and of Hudson Taylor in 1853, the Bible was translated and churches were planted. The gospel was preached far and wide, so that the truth of Christianity began to take root in Chinese soil and bear fruit, even deep into the interior of China. They also generously bestowed many benefits upon the people, brought disaster relief, went through "hell and high water," and sacrificed their lives out of love for the Chinese people. When Hudson Taylor came to China, he resolved to give his life, saying, "If I had a thousand lives, I would give them all to China!" But our people put out an evil report, alleging that the missionaries were running dogs of the Western imperialists and calling our heavenly doctrine a foreign faith. The corrupt Qing court, which was confused and ignorant, believing evil superstitions, appointed the Boxers to run wild and destroy churches, murder missionaries, willfully violate all propriety, and perpetrate cruel outrages against humanity.

After the establishment of the Republic in 1911, most intellectuals incited young students to stir up a national anti-Christian Movement. Even more regrettably, on the church side, some "theologians" who went for further studies in the West were not only blinded in their minds by Satan (2 Cor 4:4), but also lost their sense of smell, and were not able to discern the stench of Western liberal theology. From that point they began to promote so-called indigenous theology. Actually, they were intensifying the spirit of the Boxer Movement: though they did not engage in such evil deeds as destroying church buildings or slaughtering missionaries, the woe their teaching has brought is even more worrisome, for if its influence grows, it will cause Christian truth to exist in name only, without the essence. I am not exaggerating or being an alarmist, for their own words supply evidence for what I am saying. Strictly speaking, indigenous theology, as one of their own scholars admitted, "has tried various things many times, and is like soil that has been ploughed and replouged over and over without any objective results." He thinks that "the difficulty lies in not being able to find a proper theological method."[12]

From the foregoing analysis, we see that indigenous theology by no means possesses any brilliant ideas, for those who advocate it are not conversant with the Bible and do not even know what theology is. To repeat what we said before, human nature is basically rebellious, prone to construct theories that depart from the Scriptures and overturn morality. Indigenous

---

12. See Li, *Bense Shenxue—Jiu Geng yi Xin Keng?* (*Indigenous Theology: Previously Plowed Land or a Newly Cultivated Field?*).

Critique of Indigenous Theology

theology reflects and transmits national prejudice; gives way to its feelings and acts impetuously; has a loose tongue; and possesses no theological value. Those among its proponents who have studied theology overseas mostly received a liberal theological education, with its emphasis upon the confusions of Social Gospel. They have "[departed] from the faith, giving heed to deceiving spirits and doctrines of demons" (1 Tim 4:1). They wear the robes of servant of God or theological professor, but are wolves in sheep's clothing, harming the people, and are even more dangerous than the Boxers.

The Taiping Heavenly Kingdom Movement

To take Hong Xiuquan as an example, after reading, quite by chance, Liang Fa's *Good Words Exhorting Mankind*, he began preaching his own "indigenous theology," which he called "Taiping (*peace and tranquility*) Christianity," even going to the extent of calling his movement the "Taiping heavenly kingdom." He made up a canon of Scripture; engaged in far-fetched exegesis; employed ancient Chinese rites in his worship liturgy; built an altar; poured out offerings of tea; and worshiped "Shang Di" as an idol. His so-called Taiping Christianity, thus indigenized, merged with Confucianism into a Christianity that was neither fish nor fowl.[13]

The Heresies of False Teachers

Since Hong Xiuquan had not done formal study, we are not surprised by his theological errors. But when many who are involved in theological circles express views that are even more preposterous than his, we are filled with sorrow. For example, Hu Zanyun, since he dares to take the denial that the Bible is God's word as an "assumption," from that beginning, he presumptuously declares that Chinese Christians should hold to "the third great hypothesis," namely, that "before Christianity was brought to China, what we had was a Chinese Old Testament. God thought that this Old Testament was pretty good . . . Since Christianity has entered China, we need to make a New Covenant with him, a Chinese New Testament."[14] "Simply to rely on the Jewish Jesus of history is not enough!" "It is not sufficient for this New Testament to be based upon the blood that Jesus used to sign it;

---

13. Jiang, *Zhongguo Jindaishr Lunji (Modern Chinese History)*, 178–256.
14. Note: The author quoted here uses the Chinese word for "book" to indicate that the "Chinese New Testament" will not only be a covenant but also a document.—Ed.

Fallacies of Indigenous Theology

each of us must use his own blood to sign the New Covenant." "Let each of us prepare our own blood; build upon the foundation of the Chinese 'Old Testament'; use the New Covenant of Jesus as a reference; and establish a Chinese New Testament concerning China and the relationship of the Chinese to people!"[15] This sort of arrogant nonsense represents a heresy unknown in church history. Not only does it wipe away the redemptive grace of the blood shed upon the Cross by the only Savior; it also shows that there is no God before his eyes. He has made God man's equal, someone who will come at one's beck and call, to whom we stand up as an equal and with whom we draw up a contract. This dishonors and destroys the faith and blasphemes God. Nothing could be worse. May God have mercy, and not allow "the truth to be spoken against because of them," or "false teachers secretly to bring in destructive heresies," or "bring upon themselves swift destruction" (see 2 Pet 2:1–2).

Then there is the case of the former president of Yanjing[16] University, Wu Leiquan,[17] a leftist proponent of the Social Gospel. Though he was a holder of a *Jinshi*[18] degree under the Manchu dynasty, he believed in Marxism, approved of dictatorship, and wanted to employ military force to seize political power. This shows the harmful effect of modernist theology and the baneful seed sown deep in our nation by Yanjing University. He thought that the kingdom of heaven proclaimed by Jesus was a sort of ideal society. For people to misconstrue it as "another world" or "a heaven to be entered only after death" was a harmful and deceptive superstition. We only need to turn to Jesus' clear statements, "My kingdom is not of this world," and also, after his ascension, the promise that he "will come again to take us to be where he is" (see John 18:36; 14:3; Acts 1:11), to see that he is wrong. For Wu thus to attack the Lord Jesus really amounts to massive rebellion and immorality. No wonder he sympathizes with Judas, who betrayed Jesus, and defends him, claiming that "from a patriotic perspective" Judas' action was fully excusable, because "Jesus' plan from the beginning was to gain political power in order to be the Messiah who would restore the nation of Israel." Furthermore, "Jesus planned to obtain power in order to effect a socialistic reform of society." Most of Jesus' teaching can be confirmed with the words of China's ancient philosophers, as in the statement of the Song Confucianist

15. Hu, "Jiuyue yu Xinyue" ("Old Testament and New Testament").
16. Originally spelled *Yenching*.—Ed.
17. Formerly spelled *Leichuan*.—Ed.
18. The highest academic degree granted under the old imperial examination system, comparable to our PhD, though arguably much more demanding.—Ed.

Critique of Indigenous Theology

Lu Xiangshan that "there are sages all over the world with the same heart and doctrine; for thousands of years sages have arisen with the same heart and doctrine."[19] He also holds the Holy Spirit and *ren* of Confucianism to be the same thing.[20] He "fully believes," therefore, that the "truth" of Jesus and the doctrine's of China's philosophers can be "harmonized."[21] There is no God before his eyes; he despises Christ, regarding him as an ordinary person. He thus equates heavenly truth with earthly wisdom, leaving it with the name of truth but without its reality.

Also reflecting the colors of modernist theology is Zhao Zichen,[22] dean of the Department of Religious Studies of Yanjing University, who thinks that Christianity can "help China preserve the ideal of 'the whole world[23] as one community,' and 'the whole world as one family.'" "The church is an instrument[24] that can change with the times ... Besides, many of its teachings are superstitions that can be considered excrescences, and to reject them is entirely proper! ... God is revealed through man; man can reveal God, and be worthy of heaven; indeed, that the sage is worthy of heaven is an ancient and original Chinese idea."[25] "From now on, the Chinese Christian church needs to have a philosophy and a worldview of life that is constructed by Chinese themselves."[26] He criticizes "fundamentalist Christians for making religion into a messy mass of old dogmas." On the one hand, he promotes "accommodation to the spirit of modern science, emphasizing reason and the Social Gospel," and on the other, he seeks to "obtain a way to provide a religious explanation from China's natural experience," urging that we "never forget to repay a debt of gratitude to our forebears for their thought, ethical concepts, and mystical philosophy."[27] Clearly, he is influenced by liberal theology.

Yang Senfu, in his work, *Chinese Customs and Christian Faith*, when discussing the question of "understanding Chinese Christianity," offers

---

19. *Song Shi Ben Zhuan* (*History of the Song Dynasty*).

20. *Ren* is variously translated as "benevolence," "love," "humanity," and the like—Ed.

21. "Harmonized" here could also be rendered, "united," "considered to be the same."—Ed.

22. T. C. Chao.—Ed.

23. Or *all under heaven*.—Ed.

24. Or *tool*.—Ed.

25. Wu, *Jiduyu Zongguo Wenhua* (*Christ and Chinese Culture*), 82–98.

26. See Zhao, *Zhongguo Minzu yu Jidu Jiao* (*The Chinese Nation and Christianity*).

27. See Zhao, "Wo Duiyu Chuangzao Zhongguo Jiaohui de Jige Yijian," ("A few thoughts on the creation of a Chinese church").

Fallacies of Indigenous Theology

several suggestions: "In the history of Chinese thought, or the history of philosophy, Christianity cannot, like Buddhism, occupy a dominant position. Although Buddhism is a foreign import, it has spawned the Tian Tai Sect, Tian Lun Sect, Jingtu Sect, Zen and other forms of Buddhism, all completely indigenous, whereas, on the other hand, Christian thought cannot influence the Chinese intellectual world or become part of Chinese thought." For that reason, he advocates an indigenized Chinese Christianity but, to begin with, he does not know that Christianity and Buddhism are fundamentally different and cannot be "mentioned in the same breath." Second, how Christianity can take root in Chinese soil is a question of strategy; if it were "indigenized" in his sense, the name would remain but the essence would be lost. Furthermore, he wants to eliminate the Western stench of Christianity, not knowing that the Christian faith is a revelation from heaven, not a Western religion. He thus commits the same mistake as other proponents of indigenous theology. Third, he emphasizes that "Augustine created his theology out of Platonism, and Thomas Aquinas re-interpreted Aristotle's *Metaphysics* to build his theology. Why cannot Chinese Christian scholars reinterpret the Confucian, Daoist, Maoist, and other writings?" He doesn't seem to know that after his conversion, Augustine rejected Greek philosophy, warning believers against compromise or comparing incompatible things or joining them together. Whereas, when Aquinas opposed Augustine's doctrine, he trod the old path of Aristotle, using reason to interpret the faith, thus changing its character and causing it to lose its true light, plunging Europe into the Dark Ages. We need not here repeat that which we have already covered in the previous chapter and in my *Comprehensive Christian Apologetics*, where I have already treated this in detail.

To take another example, Li Jingxiong, the chief editor of Hong Kong's Tao Feng Shan publication *Ching Feng*, and other contributors to that periodical, though they have written many articles concerning Chinese religion, culture, and philosophy, hold to a theology that is basically liberal, filled with compromising notions and lacking a pure and accurate position. Li's indigenous theology claims that Christian theology should not only blend with traditional Chinese culture, but also advocate new trends in modern Chinese thought. Furthermore, he states that we should not only preach salvation, but also emphasize social righteousness. Concerning the method of indigenous theology, he thinks it can be based upon Wang Yangming's theory of the "unity of knowledge and practice," and believes that works of Chinese indigenous theology founded on the

Critique of Indigenous Theology

spirit of Wang Yangming's theory would be valuable.[28] It is theologically dangerous, however, thus to mix heavenly truth with human wisdom; it's like using human hands to sew heavenly clothing!

Errors of Theological Liberalism

The authors who advocate Chinese indigenous theology admit that they have no specific literary products and that their writings mostly lack a clear standard, controlling principle, or system. They fail to come to any agreed position or fill up gaps in their theory, so that they cannot justify their opinions. Xie Fuya is the only one who has written much. Sadly, by his admission, the education he received in America, and the teachers he most admires, are vigorous proponents of theological liberalism. In 1924–25, while at the University of Chicago, he came under the influence of that school's social theology. Later, at Harvard, he was inspired by the English philosopher, A. N. Whitehead, who wrote *Philosophy of Religion*, which assesses religion from the standpoint of "particular entities" and pure reason.[29] Everyone knows that the two institutions at which he studied are bastions of theological liberalism. He says, with immense self-satisfaction and pride, "Fifty years ago, I translated into Chinese the famous American preacher Harry Emerson Fosdick's *Manhood of the Master*, which was in a very short time reprinted more than eight times and has been immensely popular ever since." He should know that Fosdick was a proponent of the Social Gospel and caused a great deal of trouble for succeeding generations. This "new theology" was a disastrous departure from the truth that caused the doctrinal foundation of the Chinese church to be transferred from a rock to shifting sand![30] I shall now analyze Xie's theory, as expressed in his writings.

Human Personality Is God

In *Some Principles of Chinese Christianity*, Xie writes, "The doctrine of the Trinity is a universally-accepted fundamental principle of all Christian theology. But, from the standpoint of traditional Chinese culture, the Chinese belief about heaven takes its starting point from "man"; heaven

---

28. See Li, *Bense Shenxue* (*Indigenous Theology*).
29. Xie, *Zonghua Jidujiao Chulun* (*Introduction to Chinese Christianity*).
30. Matthew 7:24–27.

is considered to be a big human personality."[31] In the Chinese mind, a fully complete personality is God. He transcends others in the world, and is equal with God. Not to have God in mind is really blasphemous! When we consider that Satan desired to be equal with God, and consequently fell into hell, we must be careful, lest we follow in the tracks of an overturned cart[32] (see Isa 14:12–14). He says further, "The basic Chinese ethical principle of filial piety and fraternal duty can be extended out to mirror our relationship with the Father and the Son. The Chinese view of human relations can also be called our view of natural bonds [such as family and friendship]; in this way, human personality is elevated to equality with divine personality."[33] He states, "The Holy Spirit is not strange or foreign to the Chinese people, but the traditional Chinese explanation does not start from the Bible, but is explained from the first sentence in the *Doctrine of the Mean*: 'What Heaven has conferred is called "nature."'"[34] Mencius wrote: "The feeling of commiseration belongs to all men; so does that of shame and dislike; and that of reverence and respect; and that of approving and disapproving. The words 'benevolence'[35] and 'conscience' are ethical terms from philosophy; the Holy Spirit is nothing other than the personification of love and goodness." He does not seem to know that the Bible says that human righteousness is "like filthy rags" (Isa 64:6). Xie elevates human righteousness to the level of the Holy Spirit. Being a Christian, he should know that the Holy Spirit is God. He states further: "In the mind of Chinese, God is the Supreme Oughtness, the heavenly principle of which the rationalistic school of Confucianism spoke.[36] And this is the characteristic Chinese concept of God." He thus turns the personal, high and holy Creator of all things into an abstract rational principle. He also advocates, "In addition to the inherited doctrine of the Trinity, we should add 'one essence (substance, *ti*) and two conditions (forms, *tai*),'[37] ('God in action—good—and God at rest—beautiful' as a complementary theory)."

---

31. Xie here plays on the formation of the Chinese characters for "man," "big," and "heaven." "Heaven" is formed from the character "big," which itself builds on the character for "man."—Ed.

32. That is, commit the same mistake and meet the same fate.—Ed.

33. The author plays on words here to compare *ren lun* with *Tian lun*, the former referring to man, the latter to heaven, but also carrying the idea of "natural."—Ed.

34. Translation by Legge, *The Chinese Classics*, 383.

35. *Ren*, also rendered "humanity" or "love."—Ed.

36. *Li xue*.—Ed.

37. Xie, *Zhonghua Jidujiao Shenxue de Jige Yuanze* (*A Few Principles of Chinese Christian Theology*).

Critique of Indigenous Theology

He thinks that this is a humble contribution that Chinese Protestant Christianity can make.[38] He thus rashly seeks to become a counselor to God (see Rom 11:33–36). "Professing to be wise, they became fools" (Rom 1:22).

"Teaching Oneself"[39] Is the Same as "Being Born Again"

In "How to Write 'Chinese' Systematic Theology," Xie Fuya explains, "I have used our Chinese concept of "substance and form" (*ti tai*) to explain the relationship of the Father and the Son: The Father is the essence of the deity at rest, and the Son and the Holy Spirit are God in action." This way of looking at substance and form can be traced back to the ancient Chinese idea of *yin* and *yang*. As the *Great Treatise on the Book of Changes* has said, "The unfathomable interaction of *yin* and *yang* is what we call "god";[40] they derive from the same source, and are not in opposition to one another." He quotes Laozi's words, "We look at it, and we do not see it, and we name it 'the Equable.' We listen to it and we do not hear it, and we name it the 'Inaudible.' We try to grasp it, and do not get hold of it, and we name it 'the Subtle,'" to describe God's unfathomable mystery, according to Confucius' saying, "Nature and the heavenly way cannot be perceived." He says further, "Christianity is very close to China's Northern Zen Buddhism." Further: "Confucius advocated, 'learning without becoming satiated, teaching without becoming wearied'; 'retaining what is old while learning what is new'; 'inheriting tradition, but with critique; preserving what is excellent and good in the tradition, while exercising one's full skill in order to create something new.' This is the real meaning of the declaration of Jesus, 'I came not to abolish to Law, but to fulfill it.'" This comparison is surely nonsense. Thus he goes on to say, "The orthodox Confucian methodology is to 'keep to the center without going to either extreme,' according to time, place, and opportunity; to evaluate the extremes of left and right to identify the center that will form the basis for a creative solution." He goes on, "God transcends history, and yet is housed within history; absolute and relative are really one." He wants God to employ the Middle Way,[41] which is no different from denying eternal, absolute truth.

---

38. See Xie, *Nanhua Xiaozhushanfang Wenji* (*South China's 'Xiaozhushanfang,' A Collection of Essays*), vol. 4, chap. 5.

39. Or *zi xue*: self-study, self-cultivation.—Ed.

40. Or *shen*, which can refer to "spirit," "mysterious power," "the numinous," etc.—Ed.

41. Sometimes translated as the "Golden Mean," a reference to the mathematical ratio considered by many to be the most aesthetically pleasing when used in geometry,

> The sixty-four hexagrams of the *Book of Changes*[42] start with "Heaven" and "Earth"[43] and conclude with "Completed" and "Incomplete."[44] There is the hexagram *Fu* (Return) in between them, which reveals, 'Do we not see in the hexagram the mind of heaven and earth?' This is the same as to say that the ancient prophets of China unconsciously received the revelation of God's mystery and the countless ancient and precious scriptures of India and China also contain God's covenant, which we can even say are precursors of the New Testament. The Israelites had their religious concept of fearing Yahweh and the precious and beautiful writings of their historical prophets, of their Scriptures, responding to and reflecting a part of God's revelation. The Chinese also had their religious concept of reverence and fear toward Heaven,[45] as well as their historical prophets, which they have recorded using their own literary expression, and which they have handed down to us to read and to appreciate. We really feel that they also respond to and reflect part of God's revelation, and see them as a type of the New Covenant (New Testament). Whether it be Confucian or Daoist, or Chinese Buddhism, the excellent parts of this literary corpus are sufficient to merge with the religion of Jesus Christ without any cause for shame or even shyness.[46]

Clearly, he does not understand the difference between general revelation and special revelation; nor does he understand the deficiencies of non-Christian religions, so he commits the common error of thinking that all religions flow together in one great harmony. I have written elsewhere about this, and shall not discuss it in detail here.[47] Xie thinks very highly of Confucius, saying that his teaching, "He who wishes to be established himself, seeks also to establish others; wishing to be enlarged himself, he seeks also to enlarge others," is fully compatible with the "end" of the Law,

---

art, literature, and architecture. But the Chinese term *zhong yong* does not actually refer to this sort of proportion, since it connotes a middle range between two extremes.—Ed.

42. Or *Yi Jing*.—Ed.

43. *Qian* (heaven) and *Kun* (earth).

44. Or *Ji Ji* (Completed), *Wei Ji* (Incomplete).

45. The Chinese phrase uses the same words, but is slightly different from the biblical "fear God."—Ed.

46. The meaning seems to be that they are as worthy of respect as the Christian Scriptures, and not to be considered inferior as vehicles of God's revelation.—Ed.

47. Chang, *Sheng Dao Tongquan* (*A General Interpretation of Christian Truth*), vol. 3, chap. 6; *Zongti Biandaoxue* (*Comprehensive Christian Apologetics*), vol. 2, sec. 3.

Critique of Indigenous Theology

"You shall love the Lord your God," and not a whit different from "You shall love your neighbor as yourself." He clearly does not know that all human righteousness is "like filthy rags" in God's sight (Isa 64:6) or that self-righteousness is a sin. He acts haughtily in God's presence, declaring that "the Chinese character possesses a kind of inborn virtue, 'forbearance,' ... which is a great contribution to Christian ethics and indeed to world civilization." He thus forgets God's kindness and turns his back on him, denying the salvation that was purchased for him by the shed blood of the Lord Jesus, imagining that "with the help of Jesus and the Holy Spirit, one can quickly and completely '"become self-aware,' cultivate oneself, ... and become a virtuous gentleman, like the 'chosen people' of which the Israelites spoke, and the born-again new person of whom Paul wrote. This is the true and ultimate home."[48] This is the great heresy of liberal (modernist) theology, which is a disastrous autosoterism[49] that leads to perdition. As the Scripture says, "There is a way *that seems* right to a man, but its end *is* the way of death" (Prov 14:12; 16:25). I urge my readers not to be misled by such ideas.

Opposing God's Monopoly

In *Christianity's Mission with Regard to China Today*, Xie wrote, "The mission of Christianity in China today is to organize a great revolutionary movement. A people's revolution, social revolution, and spiritual revolution." He thinks that "this revolution has a 'geographical' nature and a 'timing' nature, ... In Rome, it has a mission particular to Rome; in Germany, a mission particular to the Germans; in India or Africa, a mission particular to those places and cultures ... Missions are characterized not only by place, but also by time. In today's China, Christianity must have a new mission. From the standpoint of politics, economics, and culture, the life of contemporary China can really be described as gasping for breath and at death's door. The revolution of Jesus naturally follows in accordance with the revelation of God on the one hand, and on the other hand he secretly listens to the cry of the masses ... For the sake of this revolutionary movement, he gave his life, dying on the cross, calmly offering himself as a sacrifice." He is using a completely secular concept to interpret Scripture, confusing and muddling the truth, and thus totally eradicating the great love of God in sending his only Son, the Lord Jesus Christ, into the

---

48. Prov 14:12; 16:25.
49. Or *self-salvation*.—Ed.

world to die on the cross, shed his blood, and save the world by enabling us to pass from death to life and by overcoming the power of the world, the devil, and sin. Instead, he employs political "old tricks" to stir up the people, saying, "Today's world is a great political era, and Christianity must step up to the forefront and participate in the political movement... The gospel of peace is nothing other than the gospel of struggle; preaching the gospel of peace has already failed. God has come to bring a sword to the earth! (Matt 10:34) . . . The mission of Christianity in China today is to stimulate support for the nation; for her sake to ignite a conflagration; for her to intensify her power to struggle, in order to complete the great revolutionary movement for the independence of the people, social revolution, and spiritual revolution!"[50] Such a statement is worse than the Social Gospel and promulgates liberation theology and revolutionary theology. In the *Mingpao* newspaper he published an absurd article in which he trumpets the vengeful, violent atheistic materialism of Marxism, erroneously claiming that it has biblical justification. He calls for a "Chinese Bible," the creation of a "New Chinese Christianity," and "an independent electorate" to arise and oppose God and establish the kingdom of heaven to break free of "God's monopoly,"[51] in order to expel God from heaven. He thus forsakes the truth and all morality and sets a precedent unknown in ancient or modern history. This is just like the current policy of the Communist government to persecute the church!

Philosophy as the Foundation for Theology

In *Introduction to Chinese Christianity*, Xie writes that "Chinese Christianity does not mean to compromise Christianity with Chinese culture or to merge the two, and even less to say that the teaching of Jesus is the same or even interlinked [with Chinese culture]," and that "to use Christianity to make a far-fetched comparison with Chinese culture is inappropriate." Still, he commits this mistake with eyes wide open, for in his writings and other expressions he does make far-fetched comparisons, compromise, and link the two closely, to the extent that even in that same article he says that writings by two Confucian antireligionists, Tang Junyi and Qian Mu, "contain Christian concepts." He also writes that "Chinese Christianity can be considered as a viewpoint that advocates 'doing your utmost to do what is faithful and loyal.' That is what 'to fulfill the Law' means."

50. Xie, *Nanhua Xiaozhu Shan Pang Wen* (*South China's Xiaozhushanfang*), 121–29.
51. Xie, "Zhongguo Wenti yu Jidujiao" ("China's Problems and Christianity").

Critique of Indigenous Theology

He reveals his compromising attitude in the statement that "Christianity did not come to China to overthrow ancestor worship or the worship of Heaven and Earth." This sort of contradiction proves that his words are not from the heart. Moreover, Xie writes that "God's essence is one . . . and eternally unchangeable," yet denies that theology has a universal standard and is a truth that does not change with time. Thus, he opines that "Chinese Christianity can have different conceptions of God in different ages and in each individual person."

He thus puts the cart before the horse and builds his foundation on shifting sand (Matt 7:24–27), trusting in "philosophy" and "empty deceit, . . . according to the basic principles of the world" (Col 2:8); making philosophy the foundation of theology; replacing the Bible with philosophy; and supplanting God's revelation with human reason. Thus, he says that, "theology is naturally different from science, because science describes truth,[52] but theology merely explains truth.[53] Science does not differ among peoples: You won't hear of English mathematics, French mathematics, or Chinese mathematics . . . But since philosophy is the foundation for theology, and since there are differences among Chinese, German, Greek, Roman, etc., philosophies, theology will also differ according to people and era." He quotes Lincoln's dictum that the government must be "of the people, by the people, and for the people" to assert that "Chinese Christianity also must be 'of,' 'by,' and 'for' the Chinese people." Clearly, he does not believe that "of Him and through Him and to Him *are* all things" (Rom 11:36), for he replaces God with man. As a result, he distorts Jesus' words, "I am the way, the truth, and the life" to mean "the way is the realization of democracy, truth is the goal of science, and human life is the nexus where the highest truth and the ultimate way may be intimately combined," thus turning the incarnate God-man, the savior of mankind, the King of kings and Lord of lords into a ordinary man who promotes science and democracy, and gutting the truth of Christ of its essential meaning. God's Word does not allow "private interpretation" (2 Pet 1:20). Such denial of the Lord's deity and confusion of divine truth will have the most serious consequences.

A Ridiculously Wrong "Philosophy" of Religion

The particulars of Xie's theological thought may be taken as representative of "philosophy of religion." He personally gave me a signed copied of his book.

52. Or *reality*.—Ed.
53. Or *reality*.—Ed.

Fallacies of Indigenous Theology

According to him, he "has gained much from the lectures and writings of Alfred N. Whitehead," and at Harvard University received a great deal of insight from him. If you want an example of the erroneous influence of Western liberal theological seminaries, which disdain the truth of the Scriptures and take the views of worldly scholars as one's standard, Xie fits the description perfectly. To give him his due, Xie was well versed in both Chinese and Western learning, and worked industriously to produce books and articles. If he had been trained in a seminary that held to the truth, he could have become a "vessel for honor," a useful servant of God (2 Tim 2:20–21). We know this from what he wrote in his *Introduction to Chinese Christianity*: He did not intend to "compromise with Chinese culture, much less assert that the teaching of Jesus and the instruction of China's sages were one and the same." But he knew that he was committing just such an error as he wrote. In his *Philosophy of Religion*, he did not express approval of the Social Gospel, but he had been trained in the Social Gospel at the University of Chicago, and his writings are even more violent than the Social Gospel. This clearly results from the deception of evil spirits, so what he wrote did not issue from his true heart. When I critique his writings, therefore, I am not struggling against "flesh and blood, but against . . . spiritual *hosts* of wickedness" (Eph 6:12), not against Xie himself. How I wish that he would come to his senses and join in this struggle!

In the very first line of the first chapter of his *Philosophy of Religion*, Xie writes, "Today, the problems of life are more and more complex, so religion should adjust to this current pressing situation, reflect developments in society, and focus on ethics[54] . . . Western scholars have issued a call for the transformation of theological ethics, . . . from Augustine's *City of God* to a City (Kingdom) of Man."[55] This shows that he is really a humanist, since he wants to discard the theocentric approach of the orthodox theologian Augustine for a man-centered one, transferring the foundation of truth from the Rock to sand, despite Jesus' warning that such a theology will "fall," and that its collapse will be "great" (Matt 7:27).

In the second chapter of his work, *The Religious Thought of Jesus*, he states that Jesus came "not to abolish the Law, but to fulfill it . . . To fulfill it is to instill a fresh rationality into the old law; then the parts that are moribund[56] will naturally dissipate and disappear. The greatest expression of this fulfillment of the Law will be service to society and the extension of God's

---

54. The point is that religion and theology must be turned into the study of society and ethics, as distinct from the study of God and faith.—Ed.

55. Xie, *Zongjiao Jexue* (*Philosophy of Religion*), 15.

56. Or *stiff and frozen*.—Ed.

kingdom. The religion of Jesus is founded upon the firm rock of Reason, and is thus connected with Greek culture, which puts such an emphasis upon knowledge, and views this rationalism as an old friend." This statement further demonstrates that he is a humanist who also falsely states that since Jesus his Lord created a theology that is indigenized Greek thought, his call for Chinese theology to be Sinicized and indigenized will be seen by everyone as perfectly justifiable. He believes that the "Word" that was "in the beginning" is "the same as the fundamental concept of the Greek thinker Philo (25 BC—AD 50)." In order to expand his indigenous theology camp, he praises Clement, who wrote in the third century, saying that he also offers strong support for the harmonization of Greek philosophy and the Christian gospel. Clement's pupil Origen (185–254) even more vigorously employed Greek concepts and thought to interpret Scripture, using the fundamental rationalism of Greek philosophy to explain the biblical notion of the salvation of the soul.[57] In the pursuit of Hellenization and indigenization, Xie turns the truth of the redemption wrought by the body and blood of Jesus into "empty deceit" (Col 2:8); imbibes the poison of humanism and rationalism; puts the cart before the horse; disdains biblical authority while emphasizing "reason" and "critical judgment"; and wrongly claims that the flourishing of Christianity results from "the development and growth of liberalism," while its decline stems from the orthodox theologian Athanasius. Apparently confused in his understanding of church history, Xie seems unaware that Athanasius was the opponent of Arius and a hero of Christian apologetics. In defense of the truth, Athanasius had to endure twenty years of exile from his home, suffering a great deal, but remaining faithful. After a mortal combat with heresy, he emerged victorious. The first Ecumenical Council pronounced Arius a heretic and accepted Athanasius' position as part of its creed.[58] The heretical Arius, who denied the divinity of Jesus, is the forerunner of modern liberal theology and its errors.

Sadly, Xie received training in modernist, liberal theology in America as a young man, thus being tainted with the Western "stench" (the term that the proponents of Chinese Indigenous Theology love to employ). He constantly trumpets the reason of man while despising the revelation of God, distorting the truth and saying that the Deism promoted by Hobbes and Locke rejected traditional notions of revelation,

---

57. Xie, *Zongjiao Jexue* (*Philosophy of Religion*), 92–96.

58. Chang, *Jidu Lun* (*Christology*), chap. 7; and Chang, *Zongti Biandaoxue* (*Comprehensive Christian Apologetics*), bk. 1, chap. 2. (Chang is referring to the Council of Nicaea, AD 321, and to its statement, which eventually, after several other councils, became the so-called Nicene Creed.—Ed.)

Fallacies of Indigenous Theology

thus opening up a new world of thought to Europe. He does not realize that the opposite is true: So-called deism is really "atheism in disguise," which strips true religion of its essence, as I have explained elsewhere.[59] To defend his rationalistic approach, Xie seeks to enlist Jesus Christ on his side, arrogantly blaspheming and bringing Jesus down to the level of an ordinary man. He writes: "When he heard John the Baptist's cry that 'The kingdom of heaven is at hand! Repent!' He suddenly became aware of his divine nature and rushed to John to be baptized; clearly, he felt that a great responsibility had come down to him from heaven." He does not seem to know that Jesus, though by nature God, humbled himself, came down from heaven, and sacrificed himself to save the world. He goes on, "Jesus spent his entire life in constant observation and experimentation in search of the truth demonstrated firm faith, earnestness, and greatness of conduct, all under the leading and control of reason." He apparently does not know that Jesus was eternal and self-subsisting, the omnipotent, omniscient true God, who declared that he himself was "the truth" (John 14:6). Xie writes further, "The rise and fall of religion is directly proportionate to the degree of its rationality," thus opposing the truth of "salvation by faith" as improper.[60] This of course consists in a denial of a fundamental tenet of Christianity. I have already dealt with the absurdity of rationalism in my books; I call it "Practical Atheism."[61]

In the third chapter of his book, Xie deals with "the meaning of religion," approaching it from the standpoint of psychology, following the school of the American pragmatist William James and invoking James' "insuperable authority"[62] in a way that can be termed "asking a blind man to show you the way." Though he is a self-proclaimed Christian, Xie seems to worship those men who do not believe in the true God, secular scholars who oppose the truth. Completely following their lead, he seeks to find answers from their books. Is this not "looking for fish in a tree"?[63] No wonder his thinking is riddled with mistakes. He does not believe in regeneration unto salvation or the marvelous work of the Holy Spirit. He writes, "When Paul suddenly saw Jesus on the road to Damascus, immediately repented, put his faith in Christianity, and zealously proclaimed

---

59. Chang, *Zongti Biandaoxue* (*Comprehensive Christian Apologetics*) vol. 2, chap. 11.

60. Xie, *Zongjiao Jexue* (*Philosophy of Religion*), 92, 95, 96, 100, 101.

61. "Shiji Wushenlun," ("Practical Atheism") in Chang, *Zongti Biandaoxue* (*Comprehensive Christian Apologetics*), vol. 2, chap. 9.

62. Xie, *Zongjiao Jexue* (*Philosophy of Religion*), 109–12.

63. i.e., totally unrealistic.—Ed.

Critique of Indigenous Theology

the gospel that he had previously vigorously opposed, he seems to have become a different person. This sort of extreme change of heart I can't help but call a form of mental illness!"[64] Strictly speaking, for Xie to despise the work of the Holy Spirit and thus to blaspheme God himself is to commit a sin not easily pardoned. Xie seems to have a misplaced belief in the evolution of religion, not knowing that this contradicts the facts of history. Dr. William Schmidt, professor of ethnology at the University of Vienna, demonstrated the primitive nature of the idea of God among all peoples in a twelve-volume work, in which he also dismantled the concept of the evolution of religion.[65] Xie does not believe that man differs from the animals, having been created in God's image and being a living being as a result of God's Spirit being breathed upon him (Gen 1:27; 2:7), and thus possessing an original nature that worshiped and loved God. Religion is the universal character of human nature and is a unique phenomenon of human life.[66] He superstitiously believes secular thinkers who imagine that "the sprouting of the idea of religion must rise from the full development of a society's thought." They "deny that a child has a religious instinct," and assert that "if you force a biblical text upon a child, the result is not to help, but to harm."[67] He approves of the Communist Party's political policy! But "the wrath of man shall praise You" (Ps 76:10).[68] The more the Communists persecute the church, and the more that the anti-Christian "social mindset" develops, the more the church prospers, in effect refuting Xie's silly notions. Since mainland China fell under the control of the Communists, the church has encountered persecution, and the people have no freedom of religion, but in the past thirty years, the number of Christians has grown seventy-fold, from one million to seventy million. The church has also prospered similarly behind the Iron Curtain.[69]

---

64. Xie, *Zongjiao Jexue* (*Philosophy of Religion*), 128–29.

65. Wilhelm Schmidt SVD, priest, linguist, ethnologist, and historian of religions; born on February 16, 1868, in Dortmund-Hörde; died on February 10, 1954, in Fribourg, Switzerland. His grave is at St. Gabriel in Mödling near Vienna. His *magnum opus* was a twelve-volume work (1912–1955) titled *Der Ursprung der Gottesidee* (*The Origin of the Idea of God*). Online: http://www.anthropos.eu/anthropos/anthropos-heritage/schmidt.php [site discontinued].—Ed. See also Chang, *Shengdao Tongquan* (*A General Interpretation of Christian Truth*), chap. 3.

66. See Chang, *Zongti Biandaoxue* (*Comprehensive Christian Apologetics*), vol. 3, chap. 5.

67. Xie, *Zongjiao Jexue* (*Philosophy of Religion*), 125.

68. The Chinese translation which Chang uses says, literally, "The wrath of man shall accomplish the glory of God."—Ed.

69. See Chang, *Shijie Renlei zhi Xiwang—Jiaohui Fuxing de Yixiang* (*The Hope of*

Fallacies of Indigenous Theology

Xie worships human reason, to the extent even of putting God under the control of reason: "The concept of God must be adjusted according to developments in society and in the times. In a totalitarian society, for most people the most powerful thing in the world is the king or dictator, so their concept of God naturally takes on a tint of an evil despot" (note how he blasphemously depicts God, the compassionate heavenly Father, as a tyrant!). "In a socialist society, the most powerful thing is democracy, so their concept of God will be one of equality and cooperation." This egregious error, as even he admits, derives from David Hume.[70] He does not seem to know that all those who have studied the history of Western thought have seen that since the eighteenth-century Enlightenment, because of the influence of Hume and others like him, naturalism has gotten more and more virulent, opposing the supernaturalism that is at the heart of Christian truth and creating a serious threat to the church.[71] Xie approves of Hume's thesis, and is thus an abettor of his cruel error.[72] He puts his trust in "the wisdom of this age ... [which is] coming to nothing," and does not believe in "the wisdom of God" (1 Cor 2:6-7). He thinks that "the wiser men of today, who put into practice the faith of God" are "those who draw their strength from the ontology of Aristotle, Spinoza, and Kant."[73] He mistakenly imagines that the pure Christian faith is nothing but the superstition of foolish people. He has never accepted God's revelation or the authority of the Bible, but goes so far as to quote Nietzsche's statement that "Christianity is the ethic of slaves!" In his opinion, "the religious spirit is learned from society, and is formed gradually from the interaction of the individual and society upon each other." He writes, "In order for it to be of any benefit to us, our faith must submit to the limitations of reason." "A correct religious attitude must come under the rule of reason." True Christian doctrine has never been in conflict with reason, and many eminent philosophers and scientists have also been devout believers,[74] but

---

Mankind: The Vision of a Revived Church), chaps. 12–14.

70. See Hume, *A Treatise of Human Nature*, vol. 1, part 2, chap. 7.

71. See Chang, *Yuan Dao* (*The Way: An Investigation Concerning Divine Truth*), chap. 3, and *Zongti Biandaoxue* (*Comprehensive Christian Apologetics*), vol. 1, chap. 2, sec. 5; and vol. 2, chap. 7, sec. 4.

72. Or *aiding King Jie in his tyrannical rule*, referring to helping an evildoer.—Ed. See Xie, *Zongjiao Jexue* (*Philosophy of Religion*), 137.

73. Ibid., 140.

74. Chang, "Kexuejia de xinyang" ("The Faith of [Christian] Scientists") in *Shengdao Zhenyan* (*A Defense of Christian Truth*); and Chang, "Shijie Mingren Zongjiao Guan" ("Religious Thought of Famous Men of the World"), in *Shengdao Zhenyan* (*A*

Critique of Indigenous Theology

God's mysterious wisdom cannot be penetrated by the blind "wisdom" of worldly men.[75]

In chapter 4 of *The Problem of Religion and Metaphysics* (*Xuanxue*), he begins his discussion of the "question of God" with "naturalism, idealism, realism" (and indeed echoes them), not with the biblical view of God. He goes so far as to take "Yang Zhu's 'I' as a kind of philosophical 'God.'" Further: "Idealism's notion of God" "derives from the *li* (rationality)[76] of human life." "Thus, man is the miniature of God, and God is the completion of man." He opposes the authority of theology, calling it a "bamboo cage world," like a "murky miasma." He therefore adoringly promotes the doubting method of Rene Descartes and John Locke's refutation of revealed religion and Christian doctrine, and substitutes Natural Religion in its place, in a move "from the decree of Heaven to the will of man, from the authority of God to that of reason" as its "primary accomplishment"! He also agrees with the dictum of Whitehead that "to say that God is in all respects unlimited is not true." Finally, he summarizes his view of God: "The Dao is the God of Laozi; the Self is that God of Yang Zhu; conscience is the God of Wang Yang Ming; Chaos is the God of Wu Zhihui; the Brahman is the God of Tagore; 'the Invisible Man' is the God of H. G. Wells; the Prime Mover[77] is the God of Aristotle; "the Absolute" is the God of Hegel; Entelechy is the God of Hans Driech." He does not criticize any of these, nor do you see the God of the Bible [in his summary]. At the end, he says that "Protestant theologians whom we now call 'Modernists' (who oppose the Fundamentalists) are working hard to build a new theology on the basis of reason . . . Their future is very bright."[78] He does not seem to realize that these Modernists are internal enemies in the church who are destroying true doctrine. Xie adds his partisan endorsement of them—what a pity!

He then moves on to the doctrine of salvation and redemption. He first lists various "salvation" practices of primitive religions, then takes such activities as "self-examination, private prayer, meditation, asceticism, keeping [Buddhist] commandments," as "methods of salvation," without any criticism. He also says that "Jesus' so-called statement that

---

Defense of Christian Truth).

75. For more on this, see Chang, *Renwenzhuyi Pipan* (*A Critique of Humanism*); and Chang, *Zongti Biandaoxue* (*Comprehensive Christian Apologetics*), vols. 1, 2.

76. Referring to the rationalism of Neo-Confucianism, not Western rationalism.—Ed.

77. Or *First Cause*.—Ed.

78. Xie, *Zongjiao Zhexue* (*Philosophy of Religion*), 154–220.

you must be born again, or you cannot be saved . . . is nothing other than an emphasis upon the effort of self-cultivation!" The words "so-called" are meant as a depreciation of regeneration, but his own reliance on "the effort of self-cultivation" is the old error of autosoterism, which despises the great love and grace of God the Father, the sacrificial blood of Jesus Christ, his substitutionary atonement, and his redemptive work of bringing men from death to life.

He also raises an objection to the nature[79] of God. He maintains that to say that God is "omniscient, omnipotent, all-loving, omnipresent, one, absolute, infinite, eternal, etc." is to make him "unnatural and unreasonable," "bringing him dishonor while meaning to glorify him"! This is to use human understanding to comprehend God and limit him. "Professing to be wise, they became fools" (Rom 1:22). He thus proves that he is unbelieving and rebellious, despising God, and lacking an awareness of God,[80] unaware that "the wrath of God is revealed from heaven against all ungodliness and unrighteousness of men" (Rom 1:18), a prospect that makes one shudder.

As for man's greatest question, that of life and death, he places undue credence in biology and psychology, rather than in the truth of the Bible and Jesus' statements. He says: "From the standpoint of biology, the traditional view of the spirit and soul is shattered. Today, psychology studies the activities of the mind;[81] the previous word 'soul' has already become extinct." "If what they say is true, then 'the body cannot live forever, and there is no such a thing as the soul.'"[82] "There are two ways for us to be immortal; one is biological and the other is sociological. The former refers to the continuation of [physical] life, and the latter to the eternity of personality." "Though I shall die, I shall have sons and grandsons, who will likewise give birth to other generations, one after another, without end." "Sociological 'death' refers to China's ancient tradition of the 'three incorruptibles,' of 'establish virtue, . . . render meritorious service, . . . leave a heritage of valuable words,' like Plato's 'descendants of the soul.'" "When we read the histories of ancient sages and heroes, it is as if they are still living." Clearly, he is not aware that this is self-intoxication and that he is deceiving himself as well as others; misleading everyone; committing an extreme error; and indulging in self-consoling fantasy.

79. Or *attributes*.—Ed.
80. Or *with no God before his eyes*.—Ed.
81. Or *heart*.—Ed.
82. Or *wu qi wu*.—Ed.

Critique of Indigenous Theology

He adds, "The 'immortality' of philosophy is, as Hans Driech says, 'How do we know that so-called death is not just the change from one form to another?' The 'immortality' of religion is Brahmanism's 'the combining of Atman with Brahman,' 'the Nirvana of Buddhism'; Laozi's 'to devote oneself to the nation and thus to become one with the nation.'"[83] From beginning to end, nowhere do we see a reference to the biblical "way of life." This is astonishing! God's word says, "It is appointed for men to die once, but after this the judgment" (Heb 9:27). But "God so loved the world that he gave His only begotten Son, that whoever believes in Him should . . . have everlasting life" (John 3:16; see also John 11:25, 26; Rom 6:23). God cannot be mocked. Only if people truly repent and trust in Christ can they "[pass] from death into life" (John 5:24). The different "immortalities" of sociology, biology, philosophy, religion are all nothing but the deceptions of Satan. As the Scripture says, "There is a way *that seems* right to a man, but its end *is* the way of death" (Prov 14:12; 16:25). The author has already written extensively on this vital subject.[84]

Chapter 5 is the conclusion of Xie's book. He says, "Of all the world's religions, the one that understands the self and elevates[85] the self is Buddhism. Buddhism's great goal is to annihilate the self, 'possessing a self and yet having no self'[86] as the only way to reach the ultimate goal of Nirvana." He asks, "Does Jesus or Confucius have the sort of active attainment of extinction of individual existence[87] that Buddhism offers?" He seems to be unaware that Jesus said, "If anyone desires to come after Me, let him deny himself, and take up his cross, and follow Me . . . whoever loses his life for My sake will find it" (Matt 16:24–25). The Apostle Paul emphasizes, "God forbid that I should boast except in the cross of our Lord Jesus Christ, by whom the world has been crucified to me, and I to the world" (Gal 6:14). Though Jesus was God, he "made Himself of no reputation, taking the form of a bondservant, *and* coming in the likeness of men. And being found in appearance as a man, He humbled Himself and became obedient

---

83. Xie, *Zongjiao Jexue* (*Philosophy of Religion*), 225–49. Actually, Xie is not here accurately quoting Laozi but is selecting parts of a famous sentence for his own purposes.—Ed.

84. Chang, *Sheng Ming zhi Dao* (*The Way of Life*); Chang, *Yongsheng zhi Dao* (*The Way of Eternal Life*); *Jidutu de Rensheng Guan* (*The Christian View of Life*); and Chang, *Zongti Biandaoxue* (*Comprehensive Christian Apologetics*), vol. 3; see also Moody, *Life after Life*.

85. Or *magnify, promote, praise,* or *emphasize*.—Ed.

86. Or *wo er wu wo*.—Ed.

87. Or *wu wo, anatman*.—Ed.

to *the point of* death, even the death of the cross" (Phil 2:6–8). He came for the express purpose to "destroy him who had the power of death, that is, the devil" (Heb 2:14). He "abolished death and brought life and immortality to light through the gospel" (2 Tim 1:10). When Jesus was nailed to the cross, "there was darkness over all the land." When he breathed His last, "the veil of the temple was torn in two from top to bottom; and the earth quaked, and the rocks were split, and the graves were opened; and many bodies of the saints who had fallen asleep were raised" (Matt 27: 45, 51–52). The record of these earth-shaking events, recorded in the Bible, has been proclaimed throughout the world for the past two thousand years, and is the basic truth of Christianity, its essence. Xie calls himself a Christian and has received a theological education, and promotes his thought through his writings, so how can he not know the truth and still say that some aspects of Christianity are not as good as Buddhism? Is this not the same as declaring that he is only a nominal Christian; a wolf in sheep's clothing; a betrayer of his Lord for his own glory; a false believer and false prophet who has capitulated to Buddhism?

He then discusses "the value of religion." "The desires and searchings of human reason are the origin of religion . . . When a person is thirsty, or discovers his need for drink . . . he finds various ways to satisfy his craving. First, he quenches his thirst by thinking of plums.[88] Then he drinks poisonous wine to quench his thirst. His third expedient is to ladle out unsanitary water from a puddle to drink; finally, he tries sanitary water for drinking." He does not consider Christianity to be "proper sanitary potage," but reflects the opinions of the non-Christian movement that holds that religion is the enemy of progress, a running dog of imperialists, a misleading, intoxicating poison for the youth. It belongs to the second kind of "wine mixed with poison from a bird's egg." He also reflects the rambling speech of atheism, asserting that "to use religion to hold onto the old, thus blocking progress, viewing things only subjectively, and using power purely based on emotional attachment, is like the unsanitary muddy water in the third category above!"

He reprimands, "Some branches of Christianity repeatedly proclaim 'Believe, and you will be saved.' 'Faith is all-powerful' seems on the surface to be vigorous and dynamic, spreading like wildfire, but this sort of intoxication is only temporary, and its state of high-pitched intensity induces a sudden death!" In fact, "The seductions of church leaders show them to

---

88. That is, he feeds on fancies; consoles himself with false hopes.—Ed.

Critique of Indigenous Theology

be world-class criminals!" For this reason, Xie advocates Confucianism, Daoism, and Buddhism, saying,

> Zhuangzi considers that the greatest man has no sense of self.[89] The Confucian sees relieving the needs of the masses as the highest principle of ethics. The Buddhist regards the Bodhisattva as the pattern for mankind. For oneself to enter Nirvana is not enough; Buddhism encourages people to have the spirit that says, 'If I don't go to hell, who else should go to hell?' 'Let all creatures pass to the other shore before I do.' 'You must first rectify yourself and then rectify other officials. When the officials have been rectified, then all the people will be rectified, and thus the goal of establishing the nation and pacifying the world will be attained, and you will have peace of mind.'[90] Wang Yangming clearly and accurately says, 'The Sage seeks to expend all his mental capacity, because he believes that Heaven, earth, and all creatures are of one substance. When there is already affection between father and son in our home, but the same affection does not prevail in all other families, we have not yet exhausted all our mental capacity. If we understand the right relationship between a sovereign and his ministers, but others do not understand, we have not yet exhausted our mental capacity. If we understand the distinction between husband and wife,[91] and the proper order[92] that should exist between elder and younger, and the faithfulness and trust between friends, but others in the world still do not understand, we have not yet exhausted our mental capacity. If in our own home we have enough food and clothing, and there is comfort and happiness, while there is anyone who lacks these things, how can they understand filial affection, marital distinctions, right order between sovereign and ministers, or the faithfulness and trust of friends? As long as that is the case, we have not yet exhausted our mental capacity.'[93]

Judged by this standard, Xie convicts himself of having lost the standpoint of a Christian believer, capitulating to Chinese religions, and consigning himself to divine punishment. What a great pity!

89. "No sense of self" (or *wei wu ji zhi zhi ren*), in that he now identifies himself with nature and does not see himself as having a separate existence.

90. "You must first rectify yourself . . . peace of mind" is actually a Confucian saying, which Xie attributes to Buddhism.—Ed.

91. That is, the different roles and responsibilities of husbands and wives.—Ed.

92. That is, a relationship characterized by justice and appropriate fulfillment of obligations.—Ed.

93. Xie, *Zongjiao Jexue* (*Philosophy of Religion*), 250–68.

Fallacies of Indigenous Theology

Xie's book runs to about three hundred pages, with a reference bibliography of seventy works in English and Chinese, most of which are by non-Christian, secular authors; there are no names of exegetes or theologians. From beginning to end he promotes the ideas of anti-religious writers and scholars of Confucianism, Daoism, and Buddhism. He hardly quotes the Bible at all. There are only one or two biblical quotations in his book, and these are misinterpreted, not examples of "rightly dividing the word of truth." He places his faith in the wisdom of those who are "coming to nothing" (1 Cor 2:6), not believing only in the "wisdom of God" (1 Cor 2:7), but rather arrogantly indulging in preposterous, wanton mockery and calumny. He does not "contend earnestly for the faith" (Jude 3) but "plays the jackal to the tiger," and "gives aid and comfort to evil"[94] by criticizing the saving Christian faith as deadly poison! He takes Paul's concept of salvation to be a form of mental illness (see above). From this standpoint, Xie brags that he is speaking of "Chinese Christianity" and thinks he is creating "Chinese theology," that is, "Indigenous Theology."

I deeply hope that Chinese evangelical leaders will rise up to resist this sort of thinking, strongly rebuking erroneous teaching that amounts to the teaching of Satan. I have heard that some Chinese seminaries have offered courses in "indigenous theology." Would that they had prefaced the words, *Critique of* to avoid misunderstanding and to prevent Christian truth from being corrupted and losing its distinctive nature. I hope they will make common cause to save the Chinese church from danger. In my earlier years, I too accepted the teachings of traditional Chinese religions and opposed the truth. Later, God had mercy on me, revealed heavenly realities to me, and gave me an understanding of the truth. This experience of passing from death to life has led me to rise up and issue a warning. It is like when wind and rain sweep across a gloomy sky and some cocks continue crowing; only some people are sober when the rest of the world is in confusion in this grim and grave situation. I sincerely desire for the leaders of the church to be prominent and worthy of esteem, to rise up as one man for action, raise a loud cry of warning, and do their utmost to stem the raging tide and effect rescue from a desperate situation! I also fervently wish that Xie and his fellows would come quickly to their senses and look at their published works as Paul did: "I also count all things loss for the excellence of the knowledge of Christ Jesus my Lord, for whom I have suffered the loss of all things, and count them as rubbish" (Phil 3:7–8). I pray that they may, like Paul, become mightily used by God, stand erect, advance to the front, and contend for the truth.

---

94. Or *aids King Jie in his tyrannical rule*.—Ed.

4

Indigenous Theology and Philosophy

Introduction

The essence of indigenous theology is humanistic philosophy. Though the self-proclaimed goal of its advocates is to "wash away the stain" of Western influence, they are unaware that they cannot escape the bondage of many ideas that they have inherited from their ancestors. Furthermore, since in their youth they received training in liberal theology, as well as the deceptions of western anti-Christian philosophy, in order to critique indigenous theology we must discuss the question of philosophy.

The Intellectual Crisis of Mankind

Augustine said that man's reasoning ability still contains the toxins of the sin of Adam, which has infected all of us. Theologian Abraham Kuyper also held that, since the Fall, man's will and understanding have lost their normal ability, and thus cannot accurately know the real world.[1] According to the research of the psychotherapist Lombroso, there are countless geniuses in the West, but because of an abnormal lifestyle they degenerate, and become no different from psychotics.[2] When the skeptical philosophy

---

1. Kuyper, *Sacred Theology*, 106–49. See also Chang, *Zongti Biandaoxue* (*Comprehensive Christian Apologetics*), vol. 1, chap. 10.

2. Cesare Lombroso (1835–1909) was an Italian criminologist and physician, founder of the Italian school of positivist criminology, and author of *The Man of Genius*, published in 1889.

Indigenous Theology and Philosophy

of David Hume was inundating the world, J. J. Rousseau wrote articles to argue that science and philosophy were powerful enemies of morality, and were shackles that enslaved mankind; he rebuked contemporary philosophers as a "herd of degenerate animals" because of the corruption of their views about morality.

The Bible tells us that the whole world lies under the power of the Evil One (1 John 5:19) and is enslaved to sin (Romans 6). Every aspect of our being is restricted by the dominion of sin, and what we call conscience and instinct have already completely lost their original healthy condition. The minds of some philosophers have become abnormal, their thinking absurd. Friedrich Nietzsche, for example, was afflicted with serious mental illness. No wonder he advocated heresy, becoming the pestilential source of "death of God" theology. Soren Kierkegaard, the founder of existentialism, was known as "the mad Dane." Even some Chinese who are leading proponents of humanism promulgate such notions. For example, Qian Mu says, "The entire purpose of life derives from man's free choice; and between two different goals there should be no question of higher or lower, right or wrong. There is no real 'good,' only the good of avoiding the not good. Before there is any lesser, the not-good is considered good . . . If it comes to a situation where there is nothing to eat or no clothes to wear, even cannibalism is not to be considered bad."[3] Tang Junyi reprimands Christians for saying that a person confesses his sin and repents and trusts in the Savior; he calls this a "massive overturning of human values." He writes, "Heaven is like our father, hell like our mother; hell gives birth to children, but they take their heavenly father's name, and live on earth."[4] As far as I know, these two authors, who are highly touted by leading scholars in our land, constantly advocate the teachings of Confucius and Mencius. If we examine their thought, we see that they not only do not know God, or the holiness and righteousness of God, but cannot distinguish the difference between heaven and hell. Nor do they realize that to say "there is no distinction between high and low," and go so far as to state that "cannibalism is not wrong," amounts to making man into a beast. This is not my own critique, but the clear implication of their own words, for they themselves are sounding the death knell of humanism and proclaiming the bankruptcy of man-centered philosophy.

The noted English writer C. S. Lewis, seeing the crisis of humanistic philosophy, cried out with a loud voice that intellectuals are the greatest danger to the world. Most people look at warlords who bring devastation

3. See Qian, *Rensheng Shilun* (*Ten Essays on Life*).
4. See Tang, *Rensheng Tiyan*, appendix.

to the nation as those who cause the greatest damage to the world, not realizing that the leaders of the scholarly world of the humanities pose a greater threat, because their thinking is fallacious and in rebellion against the truth, and leads mankind unwittingly to destruction. An article appeared in the *New York Times* in 1950 that listed the so-called most famous philosophers of the twentieth century, of whom ninety-two did not believe in God, and more than half violently opposed Christianity.

Some Christian scholars have faith, but do not add to it knowledge (2 Pet 1:5). They place value upon faith, but not upon thought; they forsake their authority as thought-and-culture leaders, leaving many people in the world at a loss. Since their thinking has no standard based on truth, but only follows the lead of nonbelievers, it thus leaves a foothold for Satan, allowing the power of darkness to create the crisis of "humanistic philosophy."

The Battlefield of Chinese and Western Thought

China is a land with a long history that has also experienced the traumatic shock of all kinds of reforms and revolutionary movements, resulting in two main streams in Chinese philosophical thought: First, there is the old way of thinking that has come down to us from history; then there is the widespread new trend that has come with the intrusion of the West. If the former is an internal sorrow, the latter can be called an external disaster. China can be considered a battlefield on which Chinese and Western ways of thinking are attacking from both the inside and the outside. This is something that Chinese Christians should realize about the pervasive trend of thought that has taken place as a result of their own historical tradition and the events of the world. Caught in this situation of both internal and external intellectual assault, how can we fulfill the responsibility we have from God to proclaim the whole counsel of God? How can we be familiar with all kinds of wisdom, both ancient and modern, and understand the heavenly vision, both that of the past and that which might be, so that we can clarify the mystery that was hidden from ages and generations and present our Chinese kinsmen mature in Christ Jesus (see Col 1:26, 28)?

From the heritage of Chinese history, we can say that the early Chinese believed in *Shang Di*. Sadly, the original concept of *Shang Di* later degenerated into a noun in various schools of philosophy, and an empty, absurd term, an abominable idol, a fatal obstacle to the intelligence of the people, leading to the decline of the nation. This is a cause for great sorrow. The main current of traditional Chinese thought does not stray from

Indigenous Theology and Philosophy

Confucianism, Daoism, and Buddhism. Before I became a Christian, I was immersed—drowned—in these teachings. If we just explore their origins, they do not represent the authentic orthodoxy of China.[5]

To begin with Confucianism: Confucius was a thoroughgoing humanist, who "didn't think about heavenly matters." His theory did not include spiritual teachings, so his early disciples were disappointed, and wrote, "The Master's ideas on human nature and the Way of Heaven—we hardly get to hear them" (*Analects* 5.13).[6] He did not "speak of extraordinary things, feats of strength, disorder, spiritual beings," but emphasized that, "revering the spirits and gods, to keep away from them—this may be called wisdom" (*Analects* 6.22). "The Master would not discourse on mystery, force, rebellion, and deity (*gui shen*)" (*Analects* 7:20). These sayings not only led people away from *Shang Di* (the Supreme Lord), but when mentioning *gui shen* (ghost and god) in the same breath he placed "ghosts" before "god," which amounts to blasphemy.

Second, if we look closely at Buddhism, it derives from Hinduism, which originates from the Vedantas, which express the faith of the Aryans, a Western people! Ancient Buddhism is thus not an Eastern religion. When Chinese accept Buddhism because of its supposed Eastern origin, they are mistaken, even as is their mistake in rejecting Christianity as a "Western" faith. Such an error derives from ignorance of history, for they do not realize that Christianity arose in Asia. As for Buddhist thought, though their slogan is that we should withdraw from the world, even Buddhists themselves say that "Buddhism is an especially atheist religion." With concepts like "five Skhandas" it completely denies the existence of the soul. In sum, Buddhism is really a type of materialistic atheism. It has been a bane to China, as Han Yu, the great scholar of the Tang Dynasty said, "Disorder and subjugation come one after another. Such a dynasty will soon be overturned. People serve the Buddha for blessing, but receive woe instead!"[7] The Chinese people ought to wake up quickly!

Third, consider Daoism. Laozi possessed the lofty conception that "Only when the great Tao was abandoned, was there humanity (*ren*) and righteousness; only when craft emerged was there great deception,"[8] and tried to rebuke Confucius, saying, "You should abandon your pride, desires, pretensions, and unbridled ambitions." Confucius, receiving Laozi's

---

5. See Chang, *Liguo zhi Dao* (*The Foundation of a Nation*), chaps. 1, 2.

6. Unless otherwise indicated, quotations from the *Analects* follow the translation of Chichung Huang, *Tao Te Ching* (*Dao De Jing*).

7. See Han, "Memorial on the Bone of Buddha."

8. See *Tao Te Ching*, chap. 18.

Critique of Indigenous Theology

instruction, was entirely won over, and urged his disciples to promote Laozi's teachings. He said, in great admiration of Laozi, "I feel as if I have seen a dragon riding the winds and the clouds up into heaven."[9] Sadly, Laozi had only a vague and confused concept that "A *tao* that can be spoken about is not the constant *Tao*."[10] Popular Daoism, furthermore, is totally different from the philosophy of Laozi and Zhuangzi. Resorting to alchemy and cultivating oneself in order to become an immortal, and communicating with ghosts and casting out demons, is the superstition of ignorant folk, and leads to obsession and increasing folly.

From the flow of Western philosophy, we can see that indigenous theology is the baneful product of the philosophy of a Western anti-Christian culture. Starting from the New Culture Movement in China, this trend has further intensified.[11] Hu Shi and others like him invited the wolf into the house when they asked the Western philosopher John Dewey to come to China on a lecture tour to inject the poison of materialistic atheism, preparing the way for communism and ultimately causing millions of our countrymen to meet with cruel and unprecedented disaster.[12] Tracing this disaster to its roots, we see that Hu Shi was indeed the nanny of the Communists and should be condemned by Chinese history. He was adored by eminent intellectuals, however, and a bronze statue of him was even erected. Shouting loudly the slogan of anti-Communism on one hand and making friends with the nursemaid of the Chinese Communists on the other hand declares the bankruptcy of Chinese thought. It makes us feel like weeping, but we fail to shed tears. I hope Chinese government officials and the people will be engaged in examining this history in depth and discover the errors that were made.

In the difficult struggle between ancient and modern, Chinese and Western, old and new philosophical thought, all Chinese Christians should clear a path through the wilderness, remove obstacles to the gospel, prepare good soil for the seed of the Word, and enable the Chinese church to "take root downward, and bear fruit upward" (Isa 37:31)—even a hundredfold! (Matt 13:8, 23).

9. By comparing Laozi with a dragon, Confucius is saying that Laozi was no ordinary man who could be fully comprehended.—Ed.

10. *Dao De Jing*, chap. 1.

11. The New Culture Movement of the mid-1910s and '20s. Scholars like Hu Shi had classical educations but began to lead a revolt against Confucianism. They called for the creation of a new Chinese culture based on global and Western values, especially democracy and science.—Ed.

12. See Chang, *Yuan Dao (The Way)*, chaps. 9–12; *Sunwen Zhuyi zhi Shenxue Jichu (The Theological Basis of the Teachings of Dr. Sun Yat-sen)*.

The Revolution in Ancient and Modern Thought

Looking at the entire sweep of human intellectual history, we can see that, regardless of time, in both East and West, philosophers have opposed the truth. They have placed unwarranted faith in the wisdom of this world, believing that "man is the measure of all things." Regardless of many developments, twists, and turns, it always degenerates into the trap of humanism, from which it is unable to extricate itself. After World War Two, when men's hearts were filled with pain, a new school of thought arose, Existentialism. In the name of opposing traditional Western philosophy, though coming from a different direction it really arrived at the same conclusions as Eastern Zen Buddhism, becoming an intensified form of nihilistic, decadent "new humanism."[13] It is evident that, regardless of whether they are ancient or modern, Chinese or non-Chinese, thinkers who disobey God and do not believe Christian doctrine, and who thus have no standard of absolute truth, are all "taken captive" by "philosophy and empty deceit, according to the tradition of men, according to the basic principles of the world" (Col 2:8). Just as the historian Arnold Toynbee said, after only one day of the presence of original sin in human nature, the entire race had lost all hope of moral progress—a fact confirmed by countless examples from history.[14] Hence, mankind's problem does not have to do with whether our systems of thought are new or old, but whether truth is present or absent. The urgent need is for the blood of Christ to cleanse us from our sin and purge out the poison from our thoughts, so that our conscience and natural instincts are freed from the dominion of corruption. Only this can bring us the glorious liberty of the sons of God and, by our submission to Christian doctrine, access to the truth (Rom 8:20–21; John 8:32).

The early church, in contending with the Greek thought of the time, maintained a firm faith and assumed an active posture. Though it employed Greek philosophical methods to explain its own ideas, nevertheless it "used its own principles to guide the process along a path of natural development," to make it easier for Greek philosophers to understand Christian doctrine, for the purpose of transforming Greek philosophical thought by the Christian faith.[15] They firmly believed in the articles of the Christian faith as God's revelation, incomparably great, complete and sufficient, with no need of Greek philosophy to bring it to completion. They also warned people that

---

13. See Chang, *Zen-Existentialism*.

14. Toynbee, *Civilization on Trial*, 21, 248.

15. Or *dao hua*, using the "Dao" of Christianity to transform Chinese culture and thought.—Ed.

Critique of Indigenous Theology

if they blindly followed Greek philosophy, they would perish. In opposing contemporary sects and heresies, therefore, they launched a full-scale attack, absolutely prohibiting them from adulterating the truth of Christianity with alien concepts. Though they suffered persecution because of this, they nevertheless "earnestly contended for the truth," unbowed by threats or violence, faithful and firm to the end, to the point of going through fire and water, for they looked upon death as the way to their heavenly home. "The blood of the martyrs is the seed of the church."[16]

On the other hand, some of the positions taken by early church fathers are not without questionable formulation. I must speak clearly to warn people to learn the lessons of history, so that they do not repeat the same mistake. For example, Justin Martyr said, "the Logos" is the "reason" that moves within the universe, working through the philosophical thought of each nation, illuminating countless Egyptians, Romans, and Greeks. All reasonable men are Christians; all Christians are reasonable, so Socrates and others like him can be considered Christians. Clement of Alexandria believed that before the incarnation of Christ, the Greeks had to receive righteousness through philosophy, which was a tutor to bring them to Christ. He sought to use Greek philosophy to organize his system of Christian philosophy. Because of its long history, Chinese traditional thought has penetrated the hearts of the people, so that some famous Christians, even church leaders, have not avoided mentioning Christianity and Confucianism in the same breath. That is to say, they have not yet broken free from "the aimless conduct *received* by tradition from [their] fathers" (1 Pet 1:18). Bishop Yu Bin has even promoted the worship of ancestors. I have already dealt with this in another place.[17] How many scholars keep calling for Chinese theology and a Chinese Bible, and go so far as to assert that (1) Chinese Christians can, "through the thought of Confucius and Mencius, and the philosophy of Laozi and Zhuangzi, construct a Chinese church." (2) "Chinese Christian intellectuals should not be content to 'rely on the Bible' . . . much less be led by the nose by Western church fathers, or 'gulp down without thought' the creeds and confessions they have passed down to us . . . or even [be bound] by the so-called Latin-based 'Trinity' that we have imported; . . . we should edit another 'Chinese Bible.'" (3) The kingdom of God must be constructed by independent, autonomous voters, not be monopolized by God or an "absolute one." (4) "Marx was a Jew by birth, with an inborn, keen sense of being oppressed. 'He has anointed Me to preach the gospel to *the* poor; . . .

---

16. Tertullian, *Apology* 37, in *The Ante-Nicene Fathers*, vol. 3.
17. See Chang, *Jizu Yundong Boyi* (*Rebuttal of Ancestor Worship*).

to set at liberty those who are oppressed' (Luke 4:18) is the origin of the ideal communist society that Marx envisioned."[18] From this we observe that Xie Fuya, though he suffered from the damage caused by a liberal theological education in America, did not escape from the mindset of traditional Chinese thought, surprisingly ignorant of just what sort of "thing" is Christian doctrine, the Bible, or the kingdom of heaven. Not only does he imagine that Chinese Christians can "construct" another Chinese Christianity and edit another Chinese Bible, but he also intends to encourage an "independent, autonomous electorate to oppose God and build the kingdom of heaven itself" in order to avoid the so-called monopoly of God. He seems as if he wishes to expel God from heaven, and particularly upholds atheistic Marxism, which promotes hate-filled struggle, saying that it has a biblical basis. This sort of absurd thinking, coming as it does from the pen of a so-called scholar of the church, cannot but grieve one's heart. We see from this the recklessness and danger of indigenous theology.

"The fear of the LORD *is* the beginning of knowledge" (Prov 1:7). "Knowledge puffs up" (1 Cor 8:1). Our forbears fell into Satan's trap of "using knowledge to destroy faith." This one false step became the root of ages of mistakes, plunging the human race into empty errors, so that it is taken captive by deceptive words and the elementary principles of the world, forsaking the truth and the source of all wisdom and knowledge (see John 15:6; Col 2:3, 8). Ancient and modern, Eastern and Western, philosophy has opposed the truth and wandered far from revealed Christian doctrine. At the end of the age, people will all the more follow deceptive spirits and the doctrines of demons (1 Tim 4:1). Now, at this critical juncture, when the survival of truth is at stake, it is imperative for all true Christians to arise and engage fully in the conflict, wearing the armor of light, wielding the sword of the Spirit, equipping ourselves with solid theology, reviving our dormant apologetics; and to testify to the truth, "[contending] earnestly for the faith which was once for all delivered to the saints" (Jude 3). We must mobilize an epoch-making revolutionary movement in philosophy, so that "new old" philosophical thought may gain a lofty, holy standard, and thus be transformed into truth, in order to save mankind from this current misfortune and thoroughly destroy the foundation of indigenous theology.[19]

---

18. See "Zhongguo Wenti yu Jidujiao" ("China's Problems and Christianity" in *Ming Bao*, 1974, vol. 107.

19. See Chang, *Critique of Humanism* (in this volume); Chang, *Shengdao Tong Quan (A General Interpretation of Christian Truth)*; Chang, *Liguo zhi Dao (Foundation of a Nation)*; *Jiushi zhi Dao (The Way of Salvation)*; and Chang, *Strategy for Missions in the Orient*.

5

Indigenous Theology and Culture

Introduction

ALTHOUGH CHRISTIANS DO NOT belong to the world, they are not out of the world either (John 17:11, 16), so they cannot remain aloof from the world. China is a great nation with an ancient culture. Its secular culture is very powerful, and proponents of indigenous theology have been deeply influenced by it, with the result that their theological thought has gone far astray.

Adolf von Harnack's research led him to conclude that the Christians in the early church had several different beliefs concerning the world and culture: (1) This world was created by God for us (believers). (2) This world exists for us, and thus its judgment has been delayed. (3) Everything in the world has been arranged by God for us so that it must suit us. (4) Everything in the world, from ancient times to the present, and even to the conclusion of history, is revealed to us, so that we can immediately understand. (5) We Christians shall take part in the future judgment of the world, and we will receive eternal blessing.[1] Their basic conviction was that Jesus Christ is the highest lawgiver and our King, and he has established a new society, a new kingdom, composed of a new race and a new people. This being the case, all who do not belong to his kingdom, that is, all non-Christians, will be controlled by the Evil One. "Therefore there are only two roads for all of mankind: the way that leads to life, and the way that leads to perdition. They are separated by an unbridgeable chasm."[2]

---

1. Von Harnack, *Mission and Expansion of Christianity in the First Three Centuries*.
2. Von Harnack, *The Teaching of the Twelve Apostles*, 1:1.

Indigenous Theology and Culture

The way of life is Christian doctrine, and is totally different from secular society—two kingdoms, two peoples, two roads, two destinies. But from the prayer of Clement we can see that God is not unable to influence the structures of secular culture, its rulers and authorities. We must submit to those in authority but their authority comes from God, and both they and we are under God's authority, and must not disobey God's supreme power and will.[3] We must, therefore, study what should be the church's attitude toward culture. In general, we can divide the responses into three types. First, the rejecters, who think the church should oppose culture. Second, the compromisers, who surrender to culture. Third, the evangelicals, who seek to transform culture. The advocates of Indigenous Theology belong to the compromisers who surrender to culture.

Opposition to Culture

The most prominent representative of those who would oppose culture is Tertullian (150–220 [or 160–240]). He would cry with a loud voice, "What has Athens to do with Jerusalem? What has the Academy to do with the church?" "Those compromisers who would adulterate Christianity and Stoicism, Platonism, and Sophism are anathema!" "Hold fast to the true faith, do not be misled by heresy, so that the truth will shine brightly, and we shall not be only half-comprehending and double-minded." "Only Christianity is the true religion; all others are erroneous, even evil, and without value."[4] He was convinced that the true God was the Trinity. He believed that God appeared through the Lord Jesus, the creator, and also through the Spirit. And Jesus is the Son of God. He therefore holds supreme authority, grants to men the grace promised by God, and enlightens mankind.[5] Tertullian displayed great loyalty to Jesus Christ, believing that he was both truly God and truly man. Because he is fully God, he can completely accomplish God's will. Since he is fully man, he can fully fulfill all the duties of a man.[6] In all things, he honored Jesus as supremely important. He is "God's power, God's Spirit, God's Word (Logos), God's reason, God's Son." He declares: "We say, and in the presence of all we say it, when persecuted, though our bodies are

---

3. *First Clement*, 54.4–51.1
4. Tertullian, *De Praescriptione Haereticorum* (*Prescription against Heretics*).
5. Tertullian, *Apology*, 33.20.
6. Tertullian, *De Praescriptione Haereticorum* (*Prescription against Heretics*), 20.

broken into a thousand pieces and covered with blood, we cry out, 'Worship God through the Lord Jesus Christ.'"[7]

With these convictions, he vigorously opposed secular culture, because human sin was bound up in culture. Tertullian believed that man's original sin was passed on through society. If children of every generation did not come under the influence of evil customs and practices, and were not formed by human education, their souls could perhaps be good. He believed that the world and all of mankind was created by God and thus originally good, but he pointed out that we cannot just look at the situation from one perspective. Although everything is created by God, it has also suffered corruption. "There was an original pure environment, and there is the subsequent corrupted condition, and the two are fundamentally different and cannot be mentioned in the same breath."[8] He believed that the reason for the coming of Christ was not to educate uneducated people, but "to enlighten the world and enable them to know the truth."[9] He violently opposed all evil and encouraged believers to avoid worldliness, especially the paganism of society and of the Gentiles, such as polytheism, idolatry, immorality, and unbridled hedonism.[10] Although he expounded such views, he did not advocate that believers should forget about all earthly affairs. He thought that the superstitious religions of pagans not only led to their moral corruption, but their manner of life also was in opposition to the Word of God, so that Christians should not socialize with them or cooperate with them.[11] He did not approve of Christians' participation in government, for he did not think that the use of political power was consistent with a Christian's faith, "because if Caesar is to turn to Christ, either Caesar has to give up his goal of ruling the world, or Christians will become Caesar. Neither is possible."[12] Nor did he commend a Christian's joining the army, not only because it involved participation in pagan rites, including swearing an oath to Caesar, but especially because of Jesus' command to Peter, "Put your sword back in its place" (Matt 26:52). Believers must not engage in violence or take up weapons.[13] He did not forbid

---

7. Tertullian, *Apology*, 23.20.
8. Tertullian, *De Spectaculis*; *Apology*, 17, "The Soul's Testimony"; and *A Treatise on the Soul*, 34.
9. Tertullian, *Apology*, 21.
10. Tertullian, *On Idolatry* and *Apology*, 10–15.
11. Tertullian, *Apology*, 42.
12. Tertullian, *Apology*, 38.
13. Tertullian, *On Idolatry*, 19, and *De Corona*, 11.

Christians from engaging in business, but thought that covetousness was almost unavoidable for those involved in commerce, and that covetousness, being a form of idolatry, was not suitable for believers.[14]

Tertullian's attitude toward literature and philosophy was even more violent than his convictions about Christians' joining military service, as we have mentioned above. He thought that the faith of the Christian and Greek philosophical thought were as incompatible as fire and ice. To try to integrate Christian thought with Socrates or Plato is to turn it into something that is neither fish nor fowl. "We have the Lord Jesus Christ, and do not need to rely on disputation; having our faith, we need no other."[15] As he saw things, in the sayings of Socrates, there are evil spirits and demons; we are disciples of heaven, and have nothing in common with them. They destroy the truth and win fame by deceiving the world; their words and conduct are not pure; they engage in empty boasting. Even if there is some truth in their writings, it comes from the light of the Bible. Tertullian did not oppose studying pagan literature, but those books will contain many songs in praise of idols, while the dramas and music encourage lust and theft. He was convinced that, when the judgment of God comes, the wise men of this world, the philosophers, poets, actors, and writers, would all suffer the torments of hell, while the Son of a Carpenter whom they so despised would be lifted up in glory. Tertullian loved God with all his heart, and was fully committed to protecting the truth of the gospel; his fame will last forever. But his merely passive antipathy toward culture is, practically speaking, of no help in facing the maladies of this world. It does not enable the church actively to lead or transform society and culture; rather, it leaves the church in another-worldly, independent situation outside of the culture.

There has been another movement in church history that opposed culture—Pietism—which appeared at the end of the seventeenth and beginning of the eighteenth century, whose representatives include Philipp Jacob Spener, August Hermann Francke, Frederick Theodore Frelinghuysen, and Friedrich Christoph Oetinger, among others. With simple faith, they sought to elevate the spiritual life of believers. Sadly, they went too far, over-emphasizing the spiritual and neglecting the rational side of Christianity. They focused on preaching the gospel, explaining it to those within the church without disputing about theoretical matters, to the point of not placing much value upon elegant eloquence. They pursued personal purity,

---

14. Tertullian, *On Idolatry*, 11.
15. See Tertullian, *Prescription against Heretics*, 7, and *Apology*, 46.

and thought that culture and society were impure, convinced that we need not concern ourselves with such matters, lest we be tainted with worldliness.

Aside from the Pietists, in our day we have the Fundamentalists, who faithfully hold to the truth and defend it. Sadly, they are extremely conservative, lack vitality, and are unable to understand essential principles and apply them skillfully to the situation.[16] They pay no attention to social problems, thus relinquishing their leadership responsibility. The result is that they give an opportunity to the devil to inflict "cultural damage" on the church, which is left without power to overcome him in conflict. Not only do they place Christian truth in total opposition to culture, but in education, philosophy, society, and politics they are becoming increasingly dualistic, leaving the church in a spiritual vacuum and placing it in a condition of being under attack from all quarters, so that the truth cannot penetrate society and culture and the gospel cannot be universally proclaimed.

Surrendering to Culture

In total opposition to the Pietists and Fundamentalists are the compromisers, who advocate adaptation to culture, even surrender, "becoming friends with secularity." The earliest representatives were the Gnostics, who were really extreme indigenizers.[17] They appear very early, being attacked by Paul in his letter to the Colossians, where he warned believers: "Beware lest anyone cheat you through philosophy and empty deceit, according to the tradition of men, according to the basic principles of the world, and not according to Christ" (Col 2:8). We see how serious was this error from a famous event: The Apostle John, meeting Cerinthus, who was a Gnostic, in the public baths one day, immediately ran out, crying, "An enemy of the truth is here! Everyone leave quickly, lest you too perish when the building collapses!"

This sect arose in the first century AD, flourished in the second century, and survived right up into the sixth century, popular especially in Greece, Egypt, and Syria. Though it called itself Christian, the Gnostic movement was really a compromise between Christianity on the one hand, and Judaism and Greek philosophy—especially Neo-Platonism—on the other. Gnosticism even employed the spirit/matter dualism of a Persian religion (Zoroastrianism) to establish its theories. The early church considered it a serious heresy and produced many books to refute

16. *Mingti dayong.*
17. Or *contextualizers.*—Ed.

it, sparing no efforts to suppress it, resulting in a major advance in apologetics. Gnostics emphasized "knowledge" and not "faith." They held that the revelation given through Christ and the apostles was for an especially-chosen group of the elite. Belittling traditional faith, they elevated secular wisdom, and defined *salvation* as deliverance from ignorance and folly rather than the forgiveness of sins. In this manner, they accommodated themselves to worldly ways of thinking, believing that Christianity could thus capture the minds of the people and increase its authority.[18] They sought to make Christianity adapt to contemporary culture, employing a so-called scientific and philosophical principle to explain Jesus' person and work. Because the cross of Christ is foolishness to the world (see 1 Cor 1:18) and hard for them to believe (see John 6), they affirmed that Jesus was only a phantasm; he did not really die on the cross. They did not consider Christianity the only truth, but only a kind of doctrine of religion and religious philosophy. Jesus Christ, to them, was not the Lord of all of life. He only dealt with spiritual matters, so they thought that they could follow worldly customs and that it was unimportant whether one bowed down to the image of Caesar or participated in war.

In the Middle Ages, though many advocates of monasticism followed the approach of Tertullian, there was a philosopher, Peter Abelard, adept at debate and dialectic, who adopted the stance of the gnostics. He believed that Jesus was really only a teacher of ethics, different only in degree from Socrates and Plato. In this way he completely obliterated any conflict between Christianity and culture. In his view, the conflict between the Christ and culture arose entirely from the church's misunderstanding of Christ, since they did not realize that he was only a teacher.[19] After the eighteenth century, this type of thinking grew stronger, and in later centuries developed into "the new theology." Notable among these thinkers was John Locke (1632–1704), who once studied theology in a Christian school, but was not content with such a conservative way of thinking. His *Essay Concerning Human Understanding* advocated "the reasonableness of Christianity," by which he meant its conformity to the spirit of contemporary English culture. Following him, Immanuel Kant (1724–1894), who came from a Christian home with very pious parents, and who had also once studied theology, became an agnostic. For him, God and the soul were not objects of experience and did not fall into the category of things that could be known through experience. God's

---

18. Burkitt, *Church and Gnosis*, 8, 29–35, 48, 51, 57, 87–91; McGiffert, *History of Christian Thought*, 1:45ff., and Bowman et al., *Cambridge Ancient History*, 12:467ff.

19. See McCallum, *Abelard's Christian Theology*, 84, 90; De Waff, *History of Medieval Philosophy*, 161–66; and McCallum, *Abelard's Ethics*.

Critique of Indigenous Theology

existence could not be proven through intelligence. In his system, the gospel became a kind of "religion within the limits of reason," "reason" being understood as the ability to analyze and categorize, a characteristic of the culture of that particular time.

Friedrich Ernst Daniel Schleiermacher (1768–1834) was the forerunner of modern theology. He denied the deity of Jesus Christ, seeing him rather as an ordinary man, and as the mature product of perfect human development. Each person could become divine; Christian doctrine can, therefore, be harmonized with science without conflict, each accommodating to the other. Thus, since he was hatched in the nexus of Kant's philosophy, he did not believe in the redemptive work of Christ or the personality and power of the Holy Spirit. He thought that mankind was presented with the law of good and evil, and could be saved by performing more good works than evil deeds, completely following the natural order of things. He not only compromised with secularity, but also considered the Christian faith as only one of the world's religious philosophies.[20]

Aside from Schleiermacher, the greatest influence upon modern theology came from Albrecht Ritschl (1822–1889). He also compromised with secular culture, succumbing to the errors of humanism and refusing to believe in the preexistence of the Word (Christ); the Incarnation; the virginal conception of Jesus Christ; and other similar supernatural teachings of the Bible. Compromising with secular notions, he took Jesus to be a mere man. Any perceived conflict between the church and culture he explained as due to erroneous notions of God, Christ, and the life of the Christ, all being the baneful consequences of the separation of the church from the world advocated by Pietists. Both God and mankind have the same mission: to establish the kingdom of God on earth. Jesus Christ stands between the two, as priest, prophet, and mediator. Sadly, his conception of the kingdom of God came not from Scripture but from Kant; it was not the fulfilling of God's will, but the accomplishment of man's true End (goal). Kant believed not in the "kingdom of God" but in the "Kingdom of [human] ends (goals)." There is thus no conflict between the church of Christ and human culture. "Professing to be wise, he became foolish." He wrongly believed that a senseless and unnecessary conflict had arisen from the ignorance and foolishness of the Pietists.[21]

---

20. See Chang, *Jidu Lun* (Christology), 217–21; Barth, *Schleiermacher: Die Theologie und die Kirche* (*Theology and the Church*); and Brandt, *The Philosophy of Schleiermacher*, 136ff.

21. Ritschl, *Geschichte des Pietismus* (*History of Pietism*), 3 vols.; *Unferricht in der Christlichen Religion*, 5, 35; and Ritschl, *Justification and Reconciliation*.

Indigenous Theology and Culture

This sort of thinking has been the bane of modern theology, affecting Adolf von Harnack, Walter Rauschenbusch, William Temple, D. C. MacIntosh, William Hocking, and others like them. In order to accommodate Christianity to culture, they promoted the "Social Gospel," which today has become "Liberation (Revolutionary) Theology," which not only surrenders to culture, but prepares the way for atheistic Marxism.[22] The librarian of the Yale Missions Library wrote, "In order for Christianity to be welcomed by the masses and to be suitable for the needs and thought of modern men, we need to create a kind of 'great joy,' a single, unifying, universal theology. To achieve this goal, theology must undergo a major transformation. If today's Christians, facing the new world that is coming upon us, hold on to the old doctrines, they will not only fail to make any positive contribution, but also hinder the work that is placed before us." If, "with the arrival of a creative period of theology, a time of 'heresy' must also appear, then there is nothing really wrong with that!"[23] This type of adaptation to culture is in reality a betrayal of the truth, the destruction of Christian doctrine, and a great danger to the faith, a fact of which they should be aware. Sadly, Chinese scholars who promote indigenous theology, having imbibed the poison of rationalistic Western philosophy, employ the same approach in their attitude towards culture.

Transforming Culture

Each of the approaches discussed above has its own distinctive flaw, for too much is as bad as too little. Those who oppose culture, though they love the truth, are complacent and conservative, and are content with staying where they are, and they therefore leave the church in an isolated position; those who accommodate to culture concentrate on the details but lose sight of the big picture, "trying to catch fish in a tree," with the result that they surrender to culture and deprive the Christian faith of its essence. In the fourth century AD, several leaders arose in the church who saved it from error and erected strong bulwarks of doctrine. The earliest was the orthodox bishop of Alexandria, Athanasius (296–374), who engaged in mortal combat with the Arian heresy. Yet those who promote

---

22. Anderson, *The Theology of Christian Mission*; Chang, *The True Gospel vs. Social Activism*; and Hocking, *Rethinking Missions*.

23. Jackson, "The Forthcoming Role of the Non-Christian Religious Systems as Contributory to Christian Theology." Quotation translated by the author and retranslated back into English by the editor.—Ed.

indigenous theology in our country, like Xie Fuya, have called this courageous defender against heresy a "sinner who caused the church to decline."

Next came Augustine (354–430). In his early years he came under the sway of Manichaeism and Neoplatonism; later, he was moved by the preaching of Ambrose of Milan, and became a Christian. He was elected bishop of Hippo in 395. His works include the *Confessions*, *The City of God*, and many books against the Pelagian heresy of autosoterism. Augustine was fully aware of the maladies of pagan culture and philosophy, deeply regretted his previous errors, and rose up to correct them and establish true doctrine. He warned apologists not to submit to or compromise with pagan culture. He played a pivotal role in history, standing on the border between two worlds, and served as a pivot between two cultures, as the classical civilization was undergoing transformation. Just looking at Augustine's conversion gives us a remarkable revelation. As soon as he heard God's voice, he immediately passed from darkness into marvelous light (see 1 Pet 2:9). As a consequence, from the medieval period up to now, every movement in the church, and every transformation of culture, has stemmed from the direction and principles contained in Augustine's writings.[24] In his works he not only dealt with theological theory, but also spoke from his own personal experience. He was convinced that Jesus Christ not only saves the soul, but also transforms human culture. Such a transformation cannot come from human ability, but must issue from a change from being centered upon Caesar to being centered upon Christ. Humanism must be fundamentally changed in order for people's lives to have a new direction, power, and inner vitality. Only thus will man's existence, corrupted and cursed as a result of our fall into sin, be restored from ruin and reveal its good nature as originally created. Early in his life, Augustine went astray into false teachings and immoral conduct. Later, he was awakened from his mistakes, and came to understand himself and his true created nature. From the time that he turned from error and came to know the truth, he was enabled to live for God—Father, Son, and Holy Spirit. In bitter repentance, he penned the *Confessions*, a book known around the world. Indeed, he became a profound critic and an agent of healing and rescue for mankind.

Most people imagine that the troubles in society stem from corrupted systems, unaware that the real cause is mankind's fall into sin, which has resulted in the corruption of human nature and of culture. The corruption of culture flows from the corruption of human nature. Man was created good. Even Satan was not originally evil, but fell because of his rebellion,

---

24. Cochrane, *Christianity and Classical Culture*; also, chap. 3.

whence arose evil in mankind as well. Today, every corruption in spirit, mind, life, and society is a symptom of our fall into sin.[25] Nevertheless, God is redirecting and refining the noble impulses of mankind, enabling the people of "the City of God" to have proper motives and goals as they make their way through the joys and sorrows, trials and tribulations of life. According to Augustine, God initially created mankind to obey him, worship him, glorify him, and rely on him. God is the source of all good; all that he made is good, as is man. The greatest moral good for mankind is to rely upon and obey God, so that the most fundamental sin (the Root Sin) is to rebel against God. To forsake God is the source of all other sins, the spring of all evil.[26] When Adam and Eve succumbed to Satan's deception, refused to believe God, and fell into sin, that was only the first of countless similar steps in mankind's descent into wantonness and corruption. "Through one man sin entered the world, and death through sin" (Rom 5:12). At the same time, man's reason, emotions, and attitude of heart became abnormal. When Adam and Eve walked in the Garden of Eden with God, they were allowed to eat from any tree in the Garden (Gen 2:16). They could do as they wished. As soon as they gave in to Satan and violated God's will, however, by eating the forbidden fruit that would lead to their death in the day they partook of it (Gen 2:17; 3:4,6), they brought disaster upon themselves. God's command was not hard to keep, but they did what they should not have done.

Now all mankind is in bondage to sin, so that we say with Paul, "In me (that is, in my flesh) nothing good dwells; for the good that I will to do, I do not do; but the evil I will not to do, that I do" (Rom 7:18–19). Augustine held that our heart cannot submit to our will, cannot submit to itself, cannot do what it wants to do. Are there not so many things that we want to do, but lack the strength to perform? It is not surprising, then, that effort we put into culture often proves to be in vain. The evil result of original sin is not just that it hinders our moral conduct, but also harms society as well. Augustine says:

> Although there are many groups in society that cooperate with each other, outwardly cordial to each other but inwardly facing in different directions, in reality they are opposed to each other, each one plotting to gain its own advantage, driven by selfish greed, with the result that the strong oppress the weak. When friends get together, they deceive each other; there is no trust or

25. Augustine, *City of God*, 19:6.
26. Ibid., 12:6.

> justice. The home becomes a lair that merely hides evil behavior, not a peaceful abode. The purpose of government was originally to benefit the nation and its people and to cement peaceful relations by upholding good faith, but in reality the government allows the weak to fall victim to the strong and the innocent people to be bullied. There is only might, and there is no right. Never will there be days of peace, because of ferocious soldiers and dangerous wars. Wherever we look, whatever the nation or society, we see the symptoms of corrupted human nature and maladjusted culture. Once mankind turned away from God and rebelled against his truth, we became utterly selfish, seeking only our own profit; all so-called "wisdom," or "benevolence," or "courage," what is called virtue in the world is only a cover for an inner evil deceiving the world in order to gain a good reputation, and a means to cover one's wickedness.[27]

Augustine was confident that God was able to cause all things to work together for good for those who are called according to his purpose. Though men do evil in the name of the good, God is still able to employ human evil to accomplish the good that he has planned. He sent the Lord Jesus to this earth. Though he was nailed to the cross by wicked men, God was able, through what mankind considered the "foolishness" of the cross, to conquer the power of the devil, sin, and death. Through sin, mankind had fallen from original good and had corrupted both human nature and culture. Jesus, however, came to heal, to renew, and to save the world, and even to save culture, so that we could escape corruption and death. The incarnation and substitutionary death of Christ highlight the seriousness of human sin and demonstrate the greatness of God's grace. Through his revelation and teaching, he enables people to turn from the path of destruction; escape Satan's grip; turn to God, the Source of all good; recover the true meaning of love; forsake the love of the world and replace it with the love of God. Mankind has forsaken God and become captive to sin, with no way to escape, no way to save themselves. In his marvelous wisdom God sent his only-begotten Son, who assumed human nature and came into this world as a man, though he remained also in heaven (John 3:13), retaining his deity. In this way only could he, as "God-man," open a new and living way and enable men to return to God. Jesus, therefore, is the only Mediator between God and men. As God, he is the goal of life; as man, he is the way of salvation.[28]

---

27. Augustine, *City of God*, bks. 12, 14, 19.
28. Augustine, *City of God*, 10:24; 11:2; see also 7:31; 9:15.

Indigenous Theology and Culture

On the one hand, he abolishes the pride of men and makes us sacrifice ourselves for others; on the other hand, he manifests God's loving kindness, moving us to seek God's righteousness. Jesus Christ restores the moral character that we had lost, and leads us along the path of righteousness. He also transforms our loves and our moral principles,[29] so that, as we make our way through life, regardless of happiness or sadness, we have proper motives and goals in accordance with God's will.[30] Living in the midst of a rebellious culture, impelled by the love of God, Christians, putting off the old man, which is corrupted through deceitful lusts, and with a renewed mind, conduct themselves in a new way, one according to God's moral standards. They love temperance, self-control, and righteousness; live godly lives; and glorify God. They delight in perseverance, hold to the truth, do not surrender to pressure or waver from their convictions, and seek to please God. They love justice, serve God, and bring blessing to their fellow men. They love to discern the truth, and know what to foster and what to excise, which path to follow and which to avoid; and they clothe themselves in the will of God.[31] Since God has turned the wisdom of this world into foolishness, we must not again be stupid and willful, thinking ourselves intelligent. Our lives must totally change direction as we hold to new fundamental principles, not trusting in ourselves, loving ourselves, or going our own way. We should, rather, trust God, love God, hold to his ways, and thus radically change the direction of not only our lives but also the quality of our culture.

In Augustine's thought, the character of all of our intelligence, wisdom, knowledge, learning, mathematics, logic, science, engineering and technology, and literature must be fundamentally transformed, so that it might be put to the service of God. In this way, every created being will be happy and joyful, mankind will be blessed, and all of our actions and political life, once the nature of culture has been reformed, will reflect the love and glory of God.[32]

On the one hand, Augustine opposed the humanist view of culture, as well as any compromise of Christianity with culture; on the other hand, he did not approve of the total rejection of culture proposed by Tertullian and others like him. He advocated a transformation of the character of a culture that centered on Caesar and opposed the truth, in order to replace it with a culture with God at the center, one that aimed to establish "the City

---

29. Or *qingcao*.—Ed.
30. Augustine, *City of God*, 14:9.
31. Augustine, *On the Morals of the Catholic Church*, 15.
32. Ibid., 19:13; Augustine, *On Christian Doctrine*, 2:25, 26.

of God." For men to be saved, they must be converted to God, so that their wisdom and intelligence might be offered for his use, with the laws ordained by God in the universe as the standard of truth. All the creativity and design of science and art should have the glory of God as their goal. The "city of man" must be converted to Christ and become the kingdom of Christ. The church must inculcate the doctrines of God's kingdom in the hearts of men, so that the truth may be propagated; Christ may rule as king in our hearts; and righteousness may be established throughout the earth.

Like Augustine, John Calvin (1509–64) was a theologian of culture. As Abraham Kuyper has noted, Calvinism is an "all life-embracing system."[33] Calvin believed that the Reformation was not just a simple, superficial movement, but was a total, comprehensive movement to change all facets of human life—in a word, a movement to transform culture. The church's major mission is to proclaim the gospel, but the reformation of the church will also serve as "salt and light." Its necessary and natural outcome, the outward expression of its inner glory, will shine on all of our existence, influencing culture and society. Furthermore, only if human wisdom, intelligence, and cultural systems receive enlightenment from God and conform to his truth, will they have value. In order to put this idea into practice, Calvin emphasized education and opened an academy. The uniqueness of this academy was its organization of "church," "school," and "fortress" all together, so that the freedom of truth could be protected. Learning was God-centered again, and the culture of every country in Europe was greatly influenced.

Calvin believed that everyone on earth receives a calling from God and has a holy cultural mandate. Anyone who had received the Lord's saving grace should live to God's glory by fulfilling this cultural mandate. His view of culture, however, differed from a secular position that regards only this world, for it looked to the next life as its goal. That is because Calvin started with God, not man. Man lives not by bread alone (Matt 4:4). We are citizens of heaven, so we should not make our belly our god (Phil 3:19–20). Culture is not in itself our goal, but should aim to serve and glorify God. If our actions and labor, as well as the creativity and progress of culture do not have the purpose of glorifying God, they are not only worthless, but harmful. Thus, humanism and secularism, which are in rebellion against God, must be transformed, so that God's kingdom will come and his will be done on earth, as it is in heaven.

---

33. Kuyper, *Lectures on Calvinism*. Calvinism is also sometimes called a "world and life view."—Ed.

Conclusion

To summarize, those who oppose culture are faithful servants who love the Lord and hold to the truth, but they are very conservative and cannot employ the "Substance-Use Principle." They leave the church in a vacuum, pull God from his throne, and do not concern themselves with secular matters. On the other hand, those who submit to culture do not appreciate the supernatural character of Christian doctrine or realize that it cannot be put into the same category as secular culture in rebellion against God's truth. They don't see that to become a handmaid to culture is to surrender to it and to turn Christianity into an empty shell, with a name but no essence, thus utterly destroying the "truth" of Christ. Those who only oppose culture forsake the church's authority to lead the world and the culture, almost leading us to abandon the world, and destroying the natural bridge between the church and the world. The church's commission is to preach the gospel to the whole world, but if we are to complete this mission, we must fully understand the all-embracing nature of the work of gospel proclamation and the importance of culture.[34] We must, therefore, guide the church back to the right path and remedy past defects, since we cannot either surrender to culture or completely oppose it, but must take a creative, inspiring, revolutionary, and comprehensive course of action. We must arise and actively lead society and culture, transforming a secular, humanist, and rebellious culture. For this, we must prepare good soil for the seed of the truth and preach the gospel of the kingdom throughout the earth.

Though China is a nation with an ancient culture, because the truth of God has not yet been able to spread widely, the culture lacks impetus. The overthrow of Confucianism of the May Fourth New Culture Movement is only a kind of destruction. In this way, we have imbibed the poison of atheistic materialism, which has brought wolves into the house by preparing the way for the Communists to create an unprecedented and disastrous destruction of culture. The proponents of Indigenous Theology do not know how to transform secular culture, and commit the same mistake as the compromisers who surrendered to the world. We who are evangelicals need to enter this struggle immediately, guide people back to the right path, and remedy the situation, in order to revive the nation and benefit the people.

---

34. See Bavinck, *The Impact of Christianity on the Non-Christian World;* and Chang, *Strategy of Missions in the Orient;* and Chang, *Zongti Biandaoxue* (*Comprehensive Christian Apologetics*), vol. 4.

6

Indigenous Theology and Religion

Introduction

PROPONENTS OF INDIGENOUS THEOLOGY have an inaccurate understanding of God, the revelation of the one true God, the teaching of the Bible, and the true definition of religion (see chap. 3). As a consequence, they fall under the domination of Confucianism, Buddhism, and Daoism, with which they compromise. They even go to the point of saying that Christianity is inferior to these religions, thus eradicating true doctrine and eviscerating the truth, leaving it only a hollow shell. I have written an entire volume on this subject, which I shall briefly summarize in this chapter. My knowledge is not confined to what I have gleaned from books, for I endured fifty years of suffering in the flames of paganism before passing from death to life. By middle age, I was sunk in the darkness of Confucianism, Buddhism, and Daoism, misled by the deception of demons. At the time, I was called "the reincarnation of Ouyang Xiu," and "the reincarnation of Arhat (Luo Han)." Being highly commended by eminent intellectuals, I founded a university to become a center for the revival of Eastern religions, believing that this was the only way to save the world. In 1950, on my way to lecture in India, who would have thought that "because of His great love with which He loved us" (Eph 2:4), God would stretch out his hand from on high to turn me from the way of destruction, cause me to repent, and enable me to believe the truth? I pray for the adherents to indigenous theology to come to a similar sudden enlightenment.[1]

---

1. See Chang, *Asia's Religions*; and Chang, *Zongti Biandaoxue* (*Comprehensive*

The Futility and Emptiness of Confucianism[2]

Concerning the origin of the universe as well as mankind, Confucianism denies the doctrine of creation by God, holding instead to the concept that everything has developed as a result of the interplay and interpenetration of *yin* and *yang*. Simply put, this is naturalism. For example, according to 'Yi· Xi Ci II', "there is an intermingling of the genial influences of heaven and earth, and transformation in its various forms abundantly proceeds. There is an intercommunication of seed between male and female, and transformation in its living types proceeds."[3] The *Book of Changes* and the *Canon of History* say, "Heaven gives birth to mankind, matter, and natural law. Heaven nourishes all and enables everything to flourish" with "no sound or scent."[4] "Vast is the great and originating (power) indicated by Qian! All things owe to it their beginning: it contains all the meaning belonging to [the name] Heaven."[5] But the concept of Heaven is quite confusing, and cannot at all be compared with the idea of a personal God who created heaven and earth as well as mankind. Zhu Xi revived the idea of Heaven and earth, *yin* and *yang*, *li* and *qi*, and expanded these concepts with *Tai ji* (The Supreme Ultimate), as the origin of all things. *Taiji* is fundamentally "limitless," a source that no man can thoroughly penetrate and understand. They identified *Taiji* with *li*, which was a mixture of *li* and *qi*, with no distinction between beginning and end. *Qi* was composed of *yin* and *yang*, with *li* operating throughout both. Heaven and earth were separated as a result of the actions of *yin* and *yang*. The subject of heaven is *yang*, which exercises the control of movement. The subject of the earth is the *yin*, which exercises the control of entire stillness.[6]

The distinction of male and female comes from this interaction, as do the differences between light and dark and the division of life and death, along with the differences of noble and commoner, intelligent and foolish, virtuous and vicious. Human beings are endowed with the entire heavenly principle while things have only a partial heavenly principle.[7]

Christian Apologetics), chap. 3.

2. See Chang, *Asia's Religions*, chaps. 2, 3.

3. *I Ching*, 8., translated by Chiuhwa Liu. Note: Heaven is considered to be *yang* (male), and earth is *yin* (female); so these statements are parallel and complementary.

4. *Book of Odes*, Ode no. 235, (Doyle's translation); that is, effortlessly, with no apparent clue to what is going on.

5. *Book of Changes*, Hexagram no. 1, Tuan Zhuan Qian.

6. Or *quietude*.—Ed.

7. See Jia, *Shen Dao Xue (Systematic Theology)* 2:99.

Critique of Indigenous Theology

As for the fundamental nature of man, and the question of whether it is good or evil, Confucius has only, "By nature men are alike. Through practice they have become far apart";[8] and, "Instruct all and reject none (i.e., in teaching, there should be no discrimination)"[9] to offer us, while Zhu Xi clearly advocated the fundamental goodness of human nature. Most people think that Confucianism promotes the idea that human nature is basically good, but that is not necessarily the case. Xunzi vigorously advocated the evil nature of mankind. He believed that the rise of governmental regulation was meant to prevent evil actions, and demonstrates that human nature is not good. Mengzi emphasized that "human nature is good, as water flows downward; there is no human nature that is not good, and there is no water that does not flow downward."[10] Because Mengzi's status within Confucianism is so prominent, and his debating abilities encountered no rival, his viewpoint was considered the orthodox position, while Xunzi's was deemed heterodox.

In Confucianism, the Way for mankind consists in "illustrate illustrious virtue; renovate the people; and rest in the highest excellence."[11] From "illustrate illustrious virtue" to "the highest excellence" there was a definite order: "Investigate things, extend knowledge, become sincere in thought, rectify the heart, cultivate the person, regulate one's family, order well the state, and thus pacify the whole kingdom." Confucianism holds that "the great attribute of Heaven and earth is the giving and maintaining life." Therefore, "I should try my best in life, and take my life to be a pleasure." "Now the man of perfect virtue, wishing to be established himself, seeks also to establish others; wishing to be enlarged himself, he seeks also to enlarge others."[12] "If poor, we should attend to our own virtue in solitude; if advanced to dignity, we should make the whole kingdom virtuous as well." Though Confucius spoke of the Decree of Heaven, he said that "what Heaven has conferred is called Nature; an accordance with this nature is called The Path of Duty, the Way; the regulation of this path is called Instruction."[13] But, concerning the most fundamental concepts, "human nature and the heavenly way," he acknowledged their existence but would

---

8. *Analects* 17:2; in Chan, *A Source Book*, 45. Translated by James Legge (1815–1897).

9. *Analects* 15:38 in ibid.

10. *Mencius*, 6 A:2.

11. *The Great Learning* in Legge, *The Chinese Classics*.

12. *Analects* 28:2, in Chan, *A Source Book*.

13. *The Doctrine of the Great Mean*, I, in Legge, *The Chinese Classics*.

Indigenous Theology and Religion

not discuss them, since they "cannot be heard or seen. It might be called grasping the shadow instead of the essence."

Confucian scholars, therefore, believed that "the principle of heaven is far from reach, while the procedure of human duty is nearby." "If we don't know about life, how can we know about death?"[14] Their view of life is to be content with what one is and to focus on what is practical. They pour their efforts into "preserving one's mental constitution, and nourishing one's nature," and "making illustrious one's lofty virtue and cultivating one's character." Though they aspire to "build up one's own goals for the world; spend one's entire life on the people's well-being; pass on the heritage of the lost knowledge of the sages; and start the age of peaceful governing in history"; and "stand upright on one's two feet between heaven and earth," they do not know the mystery of the kingdom of heaven, or the way to eternal life. Though they believe in an "imperishable noble spirit," thinking that "one's spirit will never vanish," they are simply indulging in self-delusion and using these theories to console themselves. They cannot solve the huge problems of life and death; we must admit that this is the great shortcoming of Confucianism.

The Emptiness of Buddhism

Basically, the Buddha was an atheist. He held that, "up to heaven, down to earth, only I am the highest." Buddhists hold to such concepts as: man's life is the product of "the three realms and the six degrees of incarnation"; the illusion of the union of causes and conditions; "both the external world and the self do not exist;"[15] and "the five *skandhas* are empty."[16] For example, a chair is nothing but an "image" of the combination of various materials; when it gets old and disintegrates, it no longer exists as a chair. Human life is just like that. Is this not just another type of soul-denying materialism?

Buddhism has two views of human nature. On the one hand, they say that "all life possesses the Buddha nature."[17] "The mind nature[18] of every creature is pure."[19] "The mind nature is as pure as the moon reflected on

---

14. *Analects* 11:11, in Chan, *A Source Book*.
15. Or *fa wo juwu*.—Ed.
16. Or *wuyun jiekong*.—Ed.
17. The Great Nirvana Sutra.
18. Or *xin xing*; "mind" can sometimes also be translated as "heart."—Ed.
19. *Da Ji Jing*.

the water."[20] On the other hand, they also say, "The heart tempts one to do evil."[21] "The mind is the ruler of the five sense organs; it is more dangerous than a poisonous snake or savage beast."[22] Hinayana sutras also refer to the karma produced by ignorance and unbelief as the root of all evil. From this we know that Buddhism teaches that the heart has two doors, one true and one untrue. The former is next to nothing; the latter is evil.

The essentials of Buddhist doctrine are "the three seals of *dharma*": (1) all things are impermanent and in flux; (2) there is no soul (the non-*atman* doctrine); and (3) Nirvana is the realm of quiescence and extinction.[23] They believe that all phenomena in the universe are illusory and impermanent. The life of man is one of the illusions in the universe. Man's perception of himself is merely an illusion. Though every man has the [potential] nature of Buddha in him, and thus all men have sufficient light, because of sins committed in previous existences, and because of the obstacles in this life, desires grow and obscure light. Thus man is entangled in the sorrows of life and death. The great goal in the Buddhist life, therefore, is to be enlightened, and escape from the lure of the three realms (the realms of desire, form and formlessness). There is a great enlightenment as one becomes Bodhisattva, and enters Nirvana.

Since Buddhism is atheistic, it does not believe in any outside source of power or help. Buddhists emphasize that enlightenment originates from within oneself. Strictly speaking, therefore, Buddhism is not a religion, but a school of philosophy. Their own words support this interpretation. Zhiyi, the founder of the Tian-tai Sect, begins his exposition of the "six stages of Bodhisattva development" this way: "The realization that all beings have the Buddha nature." The monk Tai Xu says: "The attainment of man is the attainment of Buddha." The great enlightenment that Siddhartha Gautama attained under the Bo tree is merely that "I have seen the secret of life, the mystery of reincarnation." Under close scrutiny, it is nothing more than a philosophy of life. The Buddhist perspective on life is: the retribution of the illusory world is all sorrow! For example, there is more suffering than pleasure in our bodies. We live, become old and sick, and die; at every

20. *Bao Ji Jing.*
21. *Ba Da Ren Jue Jing.*
22. *Yijiao Jing.*
23. The original term is almost impossible to render accurately into English. The following paragraphs on Buddhism largely follow the translation by Samuel Ling in the *Critique of Humanism* in this volume; in this section on the Three Teachings (Religions) of China, the author repeats much of what he said in the earlier work. Some modifications in that translation have been made, however.—Ed.

Indigenous Theology and Religion

moment, we are subject to constant change. This is sorrow. We are lost because of worries. The evil karma of worries will accumulate bitter fruit for the future. That is what we call the cause of suffering. In order to extinguish this sorrow, we must enter Nirvana, which is extinction. To enter this extinction, one must first cultivate himself in Buddhist doctrine."[24] There are 37 ways to help you attain Nirvana, which are nothing other than ways for the cultivator to discipline his mind. The Eight-fold Noble Path is particularly ethical by nature: (1) right view; (2) right desire; (3) right speech; (4) right conduct; (5) right mode of livelihood; (6) right effort; (7) right thought; and (8) right meditation.

Buddhists believe that the universe is one great illusion. When all creatures remain unenlightened, the wheel of their karma begins to turn, creating "the five *Skhandas*" (form, sensation, perception, character, and mental power) of the realm of sentient beings and the six elements (earth, water, wind, fire, air, and perception) of the physical world.[25] All objects and events in the universe are the result of cause and effect interaction between mental phenomena and physical phenomena in the world. They believe that nothing in the universe can escape from causality. Every sentient being goes through the wheel of incarnation. There are 84,000 kinds of mental distress in mankind; we are all born, we all become old and sick, we all die. All of life is inseparable from sorrow. Thus Buddhists seek to awaken people who are drowning in their dream-world of desire through their philosophy of sorrow and emptiness. But what they seek to attain is an illusory, vague state of *bhutatathata* (genuine thusness, *zhen ru*), not the knowledge of the true God. The end is the extinction of life in Nirvana, and not eternal life. In short, Buddhism is a philosophy that brings suicide to the soul.

The Emptiness of Daoism[26]

Daoism has no firm and clear understanding of the Creator. Of the basic nature of the universe and of human nature, Laozi says, "Nonbeing names the ten thousand things' being; being names the ten thousand things' mother."[27] "All things under heaven are generated from being; being is

---

24. Qiang, *Fojiao Qian Shuo* (*A Simple Introduction to Buddhism*).

25. Chang, *Asia's Religions*, 109.

26. See ibid., chaps. 4, 5; and Chang, *Zongti Biandaoxue* (*Comprehensive Christian Apologetics*), vol. 3, chaps. 11, 12.

27. Unless otherwise indicated, all quotations from the Dao De Jing are from the translation of Huang, *Dao De Jing*, chap. 1. "Ten thousand things" literally translates

Critique of Indigenous Theology

generated from nonbeing."[28] "The Tao generated one; one generated two; two generated three; three generated the ten thousand things. The ten thousand things, carrying *yin* and embracing *yang*, used the empty vapor to achieve harmony."[29]

Daoists' understanding of human nature and of good and evil surpasses that of most secular views. They think that the standard of good and evil does not derive from man, and that the highest good in the world is to recover simplicity and return to one's original nature. Thus they say, "When all under heaven know beauty as beauty, there is ugliness; when all know goodness, there is evil."[30] Again: "Therefore, only when the great Tao was abandoned was there humanity and righteousness."[31] "Man imitates earth; earth imitates heaven; heaven imitates the Tao; the Tao imitates the way things are."[32] "Attain emptiness to the utmost; adhere to stillness indefatigably. The ten thousand things rise everywhere; I thereby observe their revolution. While things grow exuberantly, each will again revert to its root, which means stillness; stillness means reverting to life; reverting to life is the constant."[33] The goal of life is to return to the mandate of Heaven; only in this way can we be re-united with the constant Dao. All that men consider to be etiquette,[34] laws, and government is empty and evil. Thus, "Heaven and earth are unfeeling, treating the ten thousand things like straw and dogs; the sage man was unfeeling, treating the hundred family names like straw and dogs."[35]

Laozi therefore promotes the idea that "eliminate sageness, abandon craft, and the people shall benefit a hundredfold; eliminate humanity, abandon righteousness, and the people shall revert to filial piety and parental love; eliminate adroitness, abandon profit, and robbers and thieves

---

wan wu; it means "the universe and all in it."—Ed.

28. *Dao De Jing*, chap. 40, in Chan, *A Source Book*, 161.
29. Ibid., chap. 42.
30. Ibid., chap. 2.
31. Ibid., chap. 18.
32. Ibid., chap. 25.
33. Ibid., chap. 16.
34. Or *ritual, rites.*—Ed.
35. *Dao De Jing*, chap. 5. Huang's translation here follows his interpretation of the Chinese word *ren*; Lit-sen Chang probably meant to say that "Heaven is not benevolent (*ren*)."—Ed.

Indigenous Theology and Religion

there shall be none."[36] Again, "The Tao constantly does nothing,[37] yet nothing is left undone."[38] These doctrines of "non-action"[39] and "return to the mandate"[40] certainly sound wiser and loftier than the concerns of a secular, this-worldly humanism. Empty talk about "non-action," however, will not necessarily "leave nothing undone." Only if we believe in a God with whom "all things are possible" can we experience "nothing . . . left undone" (see Matt 19:26). Furthermore, mankind is subject to sin, and has lost the freedom and power to "report that we have accomplished our task." It is impossible for us to overcome the "wall of separation" between man and God. Only by relying on the blood of Christ and his redemptive work for us can this wall be "broken down" so that the two can become one, and God and man are reconciled. Only then can we "report that the task is completed" (see Eph 2:14–19).

Daoism considers the happiness of man to consist in purification and non-action, to "return to the truth and recover simplicity," live in harmony with nature, and return to the original condition of nature. They thus think that only if man obeys and submits to heavenly truth can he attain the highest good. The good deeds we try to do, however, are fake. The Daoists call us to "abandon humanity and discard righteousness," and to "abandon sageliness and discard wisdom." With reference to its opposition to human self-importance and self-righteousness, it is superior to Confucianist philosophy, in that it opposes human pride and self-confidence. Christianity, on the other hand, is in some way similar to Daoism at this point. Nevertheless, on the one hand, Christianity warns us that "unless your righteousness exceeds *the righteousness* of the scribes and Pharisees, you will by no means enter the kingdom of heaven" (Matt 5:20), while on the other points us very clearly to the right path: "Seek first the kingdom of God and His righteousness" (Matt 6:33). Christ calls us to imitate God the Father: "Be perfect, just as your Father in heaven is perfect" (Matt 5:48).

---

36. *Dao De Jing*, chap. 19. "Humanity" is Huang's translation for *ren* in this passage; others render it as "benevolence," or even "love."—Ed.

37. "Does nothing" translates *wu wei* in Chinese; this has often been rendered "inaction/inactive," though of course Laozi does not literally mean that the Dao is absolutely inert.—Ed.

38. *Dao De Jing*, chap. 37. This translation is found in the notes of Huang's edition; in his text at this place, he follows the Silk Texts, which he considers to be more authentic. The reading given above is the one most commonly cited in Chinese literature.—Ed.

39. Or *wu wei*.—Ed.

40. Or *fu ming*.—Ed.

Critique of Indigenous Theology

Daoism merely teaches man to model himself after nature: "Man models himself after Earth. Earth models itself after Heaven. Heaven models itself after Tao. And Tao models itself after Nature."[41] But their understanding of nature is that is a mass of uncertainty and chaos. It cannot be clearly described. In short, their frame of mind is exalted, but their understanding is confused. Thus there is no truly noble goal in life; life has no value. Life turns into a sensual, licentious, deadly form of romanticism and nihilism.

Daoism's view of life and death also differs from that of Confucianism. When the wife of Zhuangzi died, Zhuangzi was "squatting on the ground and singing, beating on an earthen bowl."[42] And when one of Zhuangzi's disciples died, "Confucius heard about it and sent his pupil Tzu-kung to take part in the funeral. One of the friends was composing a song and another was playing a lute and they sang in harmony." Confucius said with admiration that Daoists sought only an other-worldly happiness, not one of this world. They are true disciples of the Creator. They consider "life as a burden like a tumor, and death as the cutting off of an abscess."[43] Daoists see heaven and earth as their mother, so death is heeding the call of one's parents to return home. Birth brings hard labor; death brings rest. Birth makes you a slave; death liberates you. Because of self-preoccupation, people cannot see the greatness [of the Dao of life and death]. With regard to life and death, longevity and early death, the more they ponder it, the more fearful they become. They see life as happiness, death as sorrow; they celebrate longevity, and grieve over a premature departure. Daoists, however, regard all these things as trivial. "One who dies in infancy is the most long-lived; Peng Zu[44] is the most short-lived." The hope of life and our ultimate destination is to be united with nature and live together with heaven and earth. They consider life and death as light matters; their concept thus seems elevated and superior.[45]

Sadly, their notion of the Dao is ineffable and illusory.[46] At its best, it amounts to a fanciful form of pantheism—ineffable, empty speculation; at most it can be considered a kind of illusory pantheism, which doesn't know the Triune God and thus cannot give incorruptible, unending life to mankind. "To live together with Heaven and earth" is not eternal life, since

---

41. *Tao Te Ching*, 25; Chan, *Source Book*, 153.
42. Chan, *A Source Book,*, 209.
43. Ibid., 198.
44. Peng Zu is said to have lived 800 years.—Ed.
45. See Zhuangzi, *Xiao Yao You.*
46. It is like trying to grasp the reflection of the moon in a pool of water.—Ed.

heaven and earth alike will be dissolved (2 Pet 3:12). In later generations, Daoism even degenerated into occult practices such as alchemy and the search for the elixir of immortality, and thus has had a very serious, harmful influence upon the life and the spirit of our people.

God's Way of Salvation: The Only Savior

Ever since the rebellion of our forefather Adam, all of mankind has been submerged in sin; because of the influence of sin and man's fallen nature, according to theologian John Calvin, "no one is able truly to know God as heavenly Father or Savior; thus, they need Jesus Christ to save them so that they can be reconciled to God."[47] Because of the corruption of human nature, regardless of whether it is the mind, or emotions, or will, all need to be renewed by the Holy Spirit. Modern philosophers, not understanding this truth, have stupidly used psychology to play down the importance of sin, ascribing it to the contagion of custom or force of habit.[48] They are unaware that sin sinks its roots into the very core of human nature. As the saying goes, "Mountains and rivers are easily moved,[49] but human nature is hard to change." Saving us from sin is not like changing habits and customs, something that could be done by relying on human strength. Only as we trust in the abundant grace of God our Savior can we escape from the disastrous consequences of sin. Calvin says that since the fall of Adam, all mankind is destined to perish. In our flesh, as Paul says, nothing good dwells (Rom 7:18). To think that people on their own can do good is to engage in empty delusion.[50] Augustine maintains that human nature has suffered a serious wound as a consequence of the destruction of sin. Unless men repent, they will cover up their offenses with specious excuses. In short, we must put to death the [evil] deeds of the body, crucify the old self, rise again with the new Adam, Jesus Christ, be renewed in the image of God, and walk in newness of life (Rom 6:3, 11). No longer should we foolishly think that we have the ability to recognize the nature of the mind. This amounts to extreme self-satisfaction, and leads to self-destruction.

Every secular religion contains a plan for saving oneself or a way to escape the troubles of this life. Mankind, however, suffers from a fundamental

---

47. Calvin, *Institutes of the Christian Religion*, bk. 1, chap. 2.

48. Linssen, *Living Zen*, 103ff.

49. In addition to its literal meaning, this can also refer to the ease with which a dynasty can be overturned.—Ed.

50. Calvin, *Institutes of the Christian Religion*, bk. 1, chap. 3.

problem, namely the subjection of our human nature to the corrosive effects of sin; the soul is sunk in the depths of death. It is a vain delusion to think that one can rely on his own strength and extract himself from this calamity; it is only common sense to recognize this.[51] God tells us that grace comes from the Lord and his great love for us. From beginning to end, he seeks to save the lost. God is omniscient; there is nothing that happens unexpectedly or suddenly for him. Even before we had sinned, God had prepared a Savior. Before our forefather Adam had fallen into destruction, God had already prepared a Second Adam to fulfill his plan of redemption. The Lord Jesus Christ, God's only-begotten Son, is the "Lamb slain before the foundation of the world" (Rev 13:8). The way of salvation was prepared by God from all eternity. The entire work of redemption, from beginning to end, issues from God's initiative; he seeks the lost; he calls those who are perishing; he announces the way of salvation to all mankind; and he executes his plan for them. The plan of salvation was formed by God the Father; its cost was borne by God the Son; and its implementation comes from the Holy Spirit. Man contributes nothing to this project; indeed he is obstinate and unwilling to receive advice, and to this day he remains stubbornly opposed to it. But God, because of his great love for us, while we were yet dead in sins, in Christ came down to earth, seeking us out, calling us, and summoning us to turn from the way of death towards God and be reconciled to him. This is God's free gift of grace to mankind. "But as many as received Him, to them He gave the right to become children of God, to those who believe in His name" (John 1:12), because "God so loved the world that He gave His only begotten Son, that whoever believes in Him should not perish but have everlasting life" (John 3:16).

In God's covenant of grace, there are only two elements: One is God's promise; the other is faith. Here is revealed to us the gate to eternal salvation, the road that leads to heaven. "For by grace you have been saved through faith, and that not of yourselves; *it is* the gift of God" (Eph 2:8). The purpose of this covenant of grace is fully to display that great love and mercy of God. He wants his children to grow up in grace, to imitate God, and to enjoy an intimate relationship with him. "Behold what manner of love the Father has bestowed on us, that we should be called children of God! . . . Now we are children of God; and it has not yet been revealed what we shall be, but we know that when He is revealed, we shall be like Him, for we shall see Him as he is" (1 John 3:1–2). The true meaning of the

---

51. Warfield, *The Plan of Salvation*, 16, 33.

Indigenous Theology and Religion

gospel is not a requirement, but a promise; not responsibility, but a gift.[52] Grace originates with God's eternal love. Long before creation, the river of grace flowed from this source, bubbling up with countless delights, so that mankind could be abundantly watered by God's grace; delivered from sin; pass out of death to life; be justified; and be sanctified, all the way to eternal glory. Jesus Christ stands at the center of this merciful plan of redemption. Since "we are children of God, . . . then [we are] heirs—heirs of God and joint heirs with Christ . . . that we may also be glorified together [with Him]" (Rom 8:16–17), because we have been eternally united with Christ.[53] Our salvation and our hope are entirely from God,[54] because "salvation belongs to the LORD" (Ps 3:8). Mankind absolutely cannot save itself; only God has the power to save the world. "Nor is there salvation in any other, for there is no other name under heaven given among men by which we must be saved" (Acts 4:12). All world religions are the vain fancies of men, issuing from "empty deceit, according to the tradition of men, according to the basic principles of the world, and not according to Christ," and end up by depriving us of our reward (see Col 2:8, 18). "There is a way *that seems* right to a man, but its end *is* the way of death" (Prov 14:12; 16:25). Charles H. Spurgeon said that if the fabric of the kingdom of heaven has even one thread sewn by man, it will lead to our ruin! All humanism and worldly religions are pathways to death. We exhort everyone to turn now from the erroneous roads to perdition! We earnestly hope that the promoters of indigenous theology will come to their senses and understand that unique value of Christian truth, rather than making far-fetched comparisons to Confucianism, Buddhism, and Daoism, lest they lose the true way and suffer eternal destruction.[55]

---

52. Bavinck, *Our Reasonable Faith*, 269, 278.
53. Kuyper, *By Grace Alone*, 40–42.
54. Clark, *The Revealed Religion*, 3.
55. See Chang, *Zongti Biandaoxue (Comprehensive Christian Apologetics)*, vol. 3.

7

Indigenous Theology and Humanism

Introduction

INDIGENOUS THEOLOGY IS FUNDAMENTALLY humanistic, whereas Christianity is a religion revealed from heaven. The two, therefore are as incompatible as fire and ice. Those who advocate indigenous theology, therefore, are relying on "the tradition of men [and] . . . the basic principles of the world" (Col 2:8), without regard to the authority and truth of the Bible. We can even say that they are despising the Savior, heedless that they are bringing ruin upon themselves (see 2 Pet 2:1–2). Because the crux of their problem is humanism, I have written this chapter to expound my views on the matter.[1]

Barriers to Christian Doctrine

Christian doctrine is not a system of human philosophy; nor is it a form of man-made natural religion. It is, rather, a saving gospel, the way to life, God's heavenly revelation for the salvation of mankind, an amazing work of God, and a manifestation of his abundant grace. It originates from eternity past and endures to eternity future. In the scope of the progress of human history, it is the guide revealed by God and the motivating force leading to new life, moral progress, and the transformation of culture, a way that mankind cannot afford to be without or to forsake for even a brief moment. The Lord Jesus Christ is both true God and true man. "He

---

1. See also the *Critique of Humanism* (in this volume).

Indigenous Theology and Humanism

is before all things, and in Him all things consist" (Col 1:15, 17). He is from everlasting to everlasting, the center and Lord of all history. He is the only Savior for mankind, one who will enable us to pass from death to life and to gain a life that is both abundant and eternal. He is King of kings and Lord of lords. He rules the nations by his eternal power. He gives new direction, new purpose, and a new way of life to mankind. He eradicates the old and brings in what is new, renewing all things. He will radically remake the world, creating a "race of Christians," and establishing a "holy nation" (1 Pet 2:9). Our ultimate hope is in a new heaven and a new earth, where we shall certainly see the one who sits on the throne, and hear the words, "Behold, the tabernacle of God *is* with men . . . the former things have passed away . . . I make all things new" (Rev 21:3–5).

We have received a commission from the Lord to preach the gospel widely, and we have a very great hope of eternal glory, so we should look to the Lord, the Author and Finisher of our faith, as we move toward such a lofty goal. The purpose of proclamation is primarily to bring about the salvation of souls, but because we are children of God, members of the Body of Christ, and children of light, we should shine like lights in the midst of this wicked and perverse generation (Phil 2:15). The outcome, therefore, will be that all of family life, and all aspects of the life of the nation, will receive power for revival and renewal. Christ is not only the source of our personal life, but also the impetus for the transformation of society, the creation of honest government, the revival of culture, and harmonious relations among nations of the world. The work and basic policy of proclamation are comprehensive. On one hand, we seek to "save souls"; on the other, to "influence the world by the truth of Christianity." On the one hand, we sow widely the seed of the gospel; on the other, we have to remove obstacles to the gospel, clearing away "thorns," removing "stones," and driving away "birds," so that the seed of the Word will not be "choked" by thorns, "scorched" by the sun on stony ground, or "eaten" by the birds (Matt 13:3, 9). In a word, we must attack the "stronghold" of humanism, "casting down arguments and every high thing that exalts itself against the knowledge of God, bringing every thought into captivity to the obedience of Christ" (2 Cor 10:4, 5).

Satan's overall strategy is to tempt mankind to become alienated from God and other men, preventing us from believing in God's existence or his commands. As a result [of his wiles], we see ourselves as wiser than God and establish social regulations, making man the fundamental reality of the universe, the measure of all things. This way of thinking then becomes

Critique of Indigenous Theology

an obstacle to the gospel, a "stronghold" in opposition to God. In the Early Church, Tertullian (165–220) often warned, "What has Jerusalem to do with Athens? The center of one is God, and of the other, man; the two have nothing in common."[2] Martin Luther emphasized that "natural reason is the bride of the devil." We can compare this with Paul's words in: "The natural man does not receive the things of the Spirit of God, for they are foolishness to him" (1 Cor 2:14). If we say that the reasoning of the natural man is humanism, it comes to us as a powerful warning. Luther's words should stir us to heightened vigilance.

When we investigate humanism, we realize it is really the "bride of the devil," the ancient and powerful adversary of the gospel of Christ from the beginning until now. The disciples of humanism transform Satan into "an angel of light" in order to mislead mankind, so that people don't realize that his real face is ugly. Instead, they believe his "empty deceit" and so are "taken captive," with no way to rescue themselves (see Col 2:8). Though people know they should oppose liberal theology, secularism, and atheism, they do not know that all these, in fact, are the rotten fruit of humanism, of which indigenous theology is an example and communism its extreme manifestation. The philosopher O. Spaan said, "Marxism is a mutation of British empiricism." This well-known saying is extremely penetrating and perspicacious. Humanism makes man the measure of all things, which amounts to regarding man as omniscient and omnipotent. How then can we blame someone for making the Party into God? Self-deification follows, then deification of the system, then seeing the leader as infallible, which finally leads to a desire to rule the nation with tyranny and violence, with the leader arrogantly presuming to establish the kingdom of heaven on earth. The ancient and fundamental problem of mankind starts with man himself when we make man the fundamental consideration, so that the truth of God is extinguished and we do not honor God or hallow his name (Matt 6:9, 13). The main foe of Christianity, therefore, is humanism.[3] Dr Hendrik Kraemer, a noted missiologist, in his famous work, *The Christian Message in a Non-Christian World*, makes this statement: "The first battle between humanism and Christianity was in Europe, when God raised up the Apostle Paul to mount a successful opposition to Greco-Roman philosophy. China is a stronghold of humanism in Asia, and will become the second great battleground between Christianity and humanism." Chinese Christians should ponder this very seriously, and be warned. Sadly, pro-

---

2. Tertullian, *On the Prescription against Heresies*, 7.
3. See Chang, *Critique of Humanism* (in this volume).

ponents of indigenous theology have deserted the battleground, causing distress to Christian friends and joy to non-Christian foes.

The True Origin of Science

We cannot, however, group humanism and science[4] together. When we attack humanism, we do not at all mean to "give up eating for fear of choking," completely opposing culture or science as if they were unclean secular matters that we must not allow to taint us. The Pietists committed this error in the sevententh and eighteenth centuries.[5] Even less do we mean to destroy human culture, but rather to save it, by finding a firm foundation for science and opening up a free-flowing stream for it. The whole revelation of God, of course, is nothing other than the root of all things, that on which all things depend, and that to which all things should return.[6] The basic error of humanists is that they have turned things upside down, putting the cart before the horse and running in the wrong direction, by "using knowledge to find faith," which is like "looking for fish in a tree."

According to Plato, man's knowledge is innate; reason is the standard for measuring truth, thus allowing man's mind to usurp the throne of God. In this way, "reality" becomes an empty fantasy. This notion turns philosophy into the slave of one's own nature and thus forever unable to understand the real nature and source of human life.[7] Man-based philosophy, from Plato and Aristotle to Kant, generally takes human reason as its basic principle and does not give priority to God as the ultimate standard of truth. It believes it can find the truth about the world and human life entirely from himself, with no need for God's revelation. This deprives man of the religious relationship he was meant to have with God, so that he has no accurate knowledge of God.[8] Human culture, therefore, having severed all connection with God, also loses its true source and becomes a rootless tree, a "cut flower," producing the danger of disintegration and dissolution.

---

4. Chang uses the term "scientific culture," which I have shortened to "science."—Ed.

5. See Chang, *Shengdao Tongquan* (*A General Exposition of Christian Truth*); *Zongti Biandaoxue* (*Comprehensive Christian Apologetics*); and chap. 5 of this book.

6. It is not clear whether it is God or his revelation that is referred to here, but the meaning would be the same.—Ed.

7. See Cailliet, *Christian Approach to Culture*, 5, 18–19, 29, 131–35.

8. See Gilson, *God and Philosophy*, 1, 34.

Critique of Indigenous Theology

Sadly, this error has also appeared in the church. In the early church, Justin Martyr compromised with the Stoics; later, Origen and Cyprian thought they could integrate Christian faith with Neo-Platonism. This trend of collaborating with human reason was reinforced in the Middle Ages when Scholastic theologians such as Thomas Aquinas and others tried to merge divine revelation and human reason. Aquinas believed that the Bible was God's revelation, but he opposed Augustine's way and returned to the old path of Aristotle, seeking to use reason to demonstrate faith, God's existence, and the accuracy of the Scriptures. He believed that the interpretation of the Bible must conform to the standards set by the pope and the bishops of the church. Unwittingly, therefore, he was basing his theology on man, since he placed the Pope on the throne of God, thus feeding the arrogance of humanism.[9] The advocates of indigenous theology have committed the same error.

Contemporary Western philosophy is confined within the empiricism of Aristotle as a by-product of the Renaissance, which was driven by Greek thought. After the Protestant Reformation began, John Calvin arose in opposition to traditional Greek ideological trends, attempting to correct the error of putting the cart [of reason] before the horse [of revelation]. He insisted that we can only know ourselves after we have come to know God. Sadly, church leaders were unable to develop his ideas and contend for cultural and scholarly leadership, creating the current serious, long-standing problems that are hard for us to solve. As I have said above, Christianity is not an enemy of culture, but a creative force for the formation of a truly elegant culture. As the eminent church historian Philip Schaff said, "The Christian faith, and especially the lofty ideals of its doctrine, with its transcendent nature, furnished the impetus for a new democratic culture in Europe and America. It has been the nursemaid of culture and has provided support for the development of science in the West: its influence is an undeniable fact of history."[10] Though Calvin stood against traditional humanism, he not only did not abandon culture, but had a profound influence upon it. As noted educational authority Edward P. Cubberly stated in his *History of Education*, "The progress we see in the world today, and the development of academic culture, depend greatly upon the broad genius and far-sighted vision of Calvin, who both established it and provided leadership."[11] Calvin himself placed great impor-

---

9. See Chang, *Shengdao Tong Quan* (*A General Interpretation of Christian Truth*).
10. See Schaff, *History of the Christian Church*, 2: 267, 625–26.
11. Cubberly, *History of Education*, 322.

Indigenous Theology and Humanism

tance upon scholarship, affirming that "there is not a good pastor who is not also a scholar." In fact, after the Reformation, the overall cultures of all the European nations touched by it—Germany, France, England, Switzerland, Holland—underwent dramatic development. As Emile Cailliet says, in France and Switzerland at the time, every Reformed church opened a school. In France, the first to promote higher education was Petrus Ramus, a Christian philosopher. In nineteenth-century France, most of the famous educators were Christians. Francis Guizot, a leading politician and historian and a devout Christian, was the first to advocate public schools.[12] In America, education was begun by the Puritans. Both Harvard and Yale were founded as Christian universities, and included theological seminaries. Today they are only nominally Christian, being completely controlled by humanists, and have become "strongholds" of opposition to Christianity. At the fall convocation of the seminary at Harvard in 1966, university president Nathan M. Pusey frankly acknowledged this fact, and called the faculty and students to return to the original faith position of the university. I am grateful for his sending the text of his speech to me.[13]

Furthermore, in our attack on humanism, we are not opposing science. On the contrary, for the development of modern science is a product of the development of Christianity. Nicholas Berdayev, in his well-known book, *The Meaning of History*, wrote, "I increasingly believe that Christian truth is the mother of modern science."[14] Many contemporary scientists, ignorant of God's truth, consider Christianity an opponent of science and earnestly seek to extinguish Christianity; they are totally unaware, of course, that modern science is a product of the Reformation. Suppressing the truth of the creation of the world by God is a major motive driving scientists to explore the mysteries of the universe. In sum, Christianity is the source of natural science; but it now opposes the truth, seeks to dig up its own roots, and destroys the foundations of the scientific enterprise.

God is omniscient, and there is no error in him; the marvels of creation display his wisdom and declare his glory (Ps 19:1, 6). In 1865, the Royal Society of Britain issued a statement declaring that God's Word is written in Scripture and also revealed in the natural order. Thus, nature is rational, not blind. The mysteries of nature can be known. Ancient Greek philosophers, though believing that God was reasonable, did not believe that he was omnipotent, for they believed that outside of God there also

---

12. Cailliet, "The Reformed Tradition in the Life and Thought of France," 349.
13. See Blumenfield, *Is Public Education Necessary?*
14. Berdyaev, *The Meaning of History*, 113.

Critique of Indigenous Theology

existed matter. Thales, Anaximander, Heraclitus and other pre-Socratics thought that matter had its own life and power of motion; which is why their position is called "Hylozoism." This view not only denies that "God created the heavens and the earth and all that is in them," but also posits that natural phenomena cannot be understood by men or by God. By this emphasis upon philosophy, science was not able to develop in ancient Greece. The Christian doctrine of God not only states that God created all that is, but that he is omniscient and totally without error in himself. This conviction becomes the foundation for the faith of the scientist, who believes that since God created the world, it is a knowable, rational order and system. Modern science developed from just this sort of belief.

Furthermore, since the world is knowable and rational, we must study it with great care and attention. The Reformers believed that the created order was a "book" that could be read with understanding, a word that could be heard with comprehension. We must constantly study it, therefore, in order to understand the ways of God, his thoughts, his wisdom, his power, and his glory (Ps 19:1, 6). With such a conviction, early modern scientists, in one discovery after other, by exerting all their efforts to investigate the mysteries of nature laid the foundation of today's science. The first group of these famous men includes Francis Bacon, Isaac Newton, Beechman, Robert Boyle, William Harvey, and others. Humphry Davy, William Thompson, Lord Kelvin, Michael Faraday, James Joule, and James Maxwell followed them. All were devout Christians and outstanding scientists.[15] The noted philosopher Alfred North Whitehead declared, "The result of investigating the natural world is to believe that the universe is rational."[16] Atomic scientist Dr. W. G. Pollard said, "True science cannot be produced in a non-Christian country."[17] Mathematician Charles Hartfield declared, "The natural world is not random, but orderly; behind this order stands God. When we use practical methods to investigate the world, we discover the laws of natural phenomena and begin to build a theoretical model."

From what we have said above, it is obvious that the Christian view of God formed the foundation of the faith of these scientists, and that the development of modern science is the fruit of the expansion of Christian truth. Thus, Christian teaching is not an obstacle to science, but its true

---

15. See Chang, *Shengdao Zhengyan (A Defense of Christian Truth)*, the chapter called "Jidujiaode Kexueguan" ("The Christian View of Science").

16. Whitehead, *Science and the Modern World*, 18.

17. See Pollard, *Chance and Providence*.

Indigenous Theology and Humanism

source.[18] Modern man does not recognize his "mother," but considers her his "enemy," bending every effort to set himself in opposition to the truth. This is truly the suicide of science!

The True Source of Mankind's Troubles

People have been infected with the poison of traditional philosophy, placing too much importance on experience, and have been limited by our bodily senses; they place superstitious faith in science while belittling the truth of God. By doing so, they forget their own origin; eradicate their roots; doubt God's existence; and do not believe the revelation given by the true God. They have thus forsaken the only source of living water and made for themselves broken cisterns that cannot hold water (see Jer 2:13). Today's culture, thus fatally wounded, has become a rootless tree and is in deep crisis. The statement by the English Royal Society in 1865 expressing its view of the relationship between Christianity and science declares:

> That so many men, as a consequence of investigating scientific truth, are losing confidence in the accuracy of the Bible, is indeed regrettable. We believe that God's Word is written, first, in the Scriptures, and then in natural world. Though the methods differ, the two are mutually supportive, and are definitely not in competition with each other. . . . The science of physics constantly progresses, and has not yet reached its perfected condition.[19] At present our understanding is greatly limited: "We see in a mirror, dimly." For some scientists, without really studying the Bible, and relying on a very incomplete knowledge of it, employing a method that claims to be "scientific" but is really not, to doubt the Bible and oppose Christian truth is an attitude that causes us great distress.

This document, signed by six hundred scientists, can be found in the Bodleian Library at Oxford University. We hope that "science addicts" will take the correct remedial action.[20]

---

18. See Berdyaev, *The Meaning of History*.

19. Chang's friend Carl F. H. Henry made this point powerfully in several places, including *God, Revelation, and Authority*, vol. 5, chaps. 5–8. It is possible that Henry influenced Chang.—Ed.

20. See Chang, *Shengdao Zhengyan (A Defense of Christian Truth)*, the chapter called "Kexuejiade Xinyang" ("The Faith of [Christian] Scientists").

Critique of Indigenous Theology

Furthermore, the realm that science investigates is limited by space and time; the mission of science is only to enable people to understand the order of nature. The Bible, however, can enable us to know the mysteries that transcend space and time.[21] To a contemporary humanist, Nicodemus, Jesus said, "If I have told you earthly things and you do not believe, how will you believe if I tell you heavenly things?" (John 3:12). Clearly, then, scientists are not omniscient, for they do not possess a comprehensive understanding of earthly things; their understanding of heavenly things is even more uncertain. With regard to these matters of which they are ignorant, today's humanists yet dare to oppose them; this is not only a blind jumping to conclusions, but entirely unscientific.

Humanism, being based upon man, is earthly, not heavenly; it relies on feeling, not revelation; upon reason, not faith; what can be seen now, not on invisible things of the future. It is temporary, not eternal, belonging to this age, not the age to come. Death is its terminus, for it has no hope of an eternal glory after death. Jesus said, "For what profit is it to a man if he gains the whole world, and loses his own soul? Or what will a man give in exchange for his soul?" (Matt 16:26). If life is centered only on man, with death as its destination, what use is all learning and knowledge? "The fear of the LORD *is* the beginning of wisdom, and the knowledge of the Holy One *is* understanding" (Prov 9:10). The really wise person, therefore, will discard what is "limited" for that which is "unlimited." His utter purity[22] and natural kindness will lead him to fear God, seek the things that are above, and long for the boundless, mysterious, heavenly wisdom, and the life and inheritance with are eternal and incorruptible. Only thus can the boundaries of our life be liberated from their narrow-mindedness. Only then can we come to our senses; hold on to God's sovereignty, which is from eternity past to eternity future; experience his infinite love; and see his matchless glory.

"The LORD by wisdom founded the earth; by understanding He established the heavens" (Prov 3:19). "For I know that the LORD *is* great, and our Lord *is* above all gods. Whatever the LORD pleases He does, in heaven and in earth, in the seas and in all deep places" (Ps 135:5–6). "Blessed be the name of God forever and ever, for wisdom and might are His. And He changes the times and the seasons; He removes kings and raises up kings; He gives wisdom to the wise and knowledge to those who have understanding. He reveals deep and secret things; he knows what *is* in the darkness, and light dwells with Him" (Dan 2:20–22). He "made the

---

21. Pollard, *Chance and Providence*.
22. Or *innocence of childhood*.—Ed.

Indigenous Theology and Humanism

world and everything in it . . . He gives to all life, breath, and all things." (Acts 17:24, 25). Furthermore, "according to His great mercy," he "has begotten us again to a living hope through the resurrection of Jesus Christ from the dead, to an inheritance incorruptible and undefiled and that does not fade away, reserved in heaven for [us], who are kept by the power of God through faith for salvation ready to be revealed in the last time" (1 Pet 1:3–5). "According to His good pleasure which He purposed in Himself, that in the dispensation of the fullness of the times He [will] gather together in one all things in Christ, both which are in heaven and which are on earth" (Eph 1:9–10; see 1:22). "God has highly exalted [Jesus] and given Him the name which is above every name, that at the name of Jesus every knee should bow, of those in heaven, and of those on the earth, and of those under the earth" (Phil 2:9–10).

This is precisely the Christian view of the universe, human life, and history.[23] Sadly, "the whole world lies *under the sway of* the wicked one," having lost "the glorious liberty of the children of God." Men have become under the dominion of the "basic principles" that have "taken us captive" (Rom 8:21; see Col 2:8). We have a very narrow perspective.[24] We are caught in a web that we ourselves have spun, but we still arrogantly presume to transcend the supernatural, arrogating to ourselves the position of rulers of the universe. We have turned the positions of "God" and "man," of "first" and "last," upside down, fashioning a warped view of the world and of life, and bringing all manner of disaster and suffering upon mankind.

The American president Abraham Lincoln used a good story to express something in a way that anyone can understand: One day a farmer was teaching his son how to plow a field. He put the yoke on the ox, and got everything ready. He told his son to go in the direction of another ox in front of them, and the furrow would then be straight. After saying this, the father turned around and started on another task, thinking that if the goal is clear, there will be no chance for a mistake. When he returned, however, to his disappointment, though his son was obedient to what he had said, the other ox had moved, so the furrow was not straight. This story points to a fundamental flaw in mankind, namely, that we do not glorify God or give thanks to him, but have "worshiped and served the creature rather than the Creator, who is blessed forever" (Rom 1:21, 25). We do not believe in that immutable and eternal Word that is settled in

---

23. See Chang, *Shengdao Tong Quan* (*A General Interpretation of Christian Truth*), chaps. 4, 5, 8, 9.

24. Or are "looking at the sky from the bottom of a well."

heaven and abides forever (see Ps 102:26, 27; 119:89; 1 Pet 1:25). Instead, we believe in the "empty deceit" that is "according to the tradition of men . . . [and] the basic principles of the world" that are "here today and gone tomorrow" (Col 2:8).

The ancient Greek philosopher and engineer Archimedes said, "Give me a fixed point[25] and I will move the world." As the Chinese saying goes, "A tiny lapse can lead to a huge mistake," and, "One wrong step can lead to a thousand hatreds." A position and starting point affects not only personal success and failure, but the well-being or disaster of mankind as a whole. With an incorrect starting point, proponents of indigenous theology have become confused about the truth, and their form of Christianity is only nominal, with no substance.[26]

The greatest tragedy of the human race results from our first ancestors' initial error, when they followed Satan's philosophy and imagined that not to trust God but to doubt his will was really the "beginning of wisdom" (see Gen 3:4, 6). Immediately, the "god of this world blinded the eyes of men so that they could not see the true light of the gospel of God." Groping about in the dark, they rush into apostasy. The pre-Socratic philosopher Protagoras (480–410 BC) wrote, "Man is the measure of all things." Man then becomes the standard of truth and sovereign lord of the universe. The modern philosopher affirms, "I think, therefore I am," taking doubt as the first rule and way to learning. One seeks all knowledge only from within oneself. Further, one posits infinite perfectibility in human nature. Chinese Confucianism "seeks knowledge" from "examination of particulars," believing that the "heavenly way is distant, but the way of man is near." Therefore, they try to "establish human regulations"; "set up a theory to make clear the truth of heaven and earth; find a way to ensure the livelihood of the people; pass on the heritage of earlier sages; establish peace for future generations." Both Chinese and Western philosophers, do not know that "the fear of the LORD *is* the beginning of wisdom" (Prov 9:10). They are not aware that the beginning and measure of all things is not man but God, "for of Him and through Him and to Him *are* all things" (Rom 11:36). And Christ is "the image of the invisible God, the firstborn over all creation. For by Him all things were created that are in heaven and that are on earth, visible and invisible, whether thrones or dominions or principalities or powers. All things were created through Him and for Him. And He is before all things, and in Him all things consist" (Col 1:15–18).

25. i.e., fulcrum.—Ed.
26. Chang again uses the phrase "the name is present but the reality has been lost."

There is a saying, "When what is fundamental has been established, then the Dao grows naturally." But only God is the root of all things, the Way of all things, the fount of every blessing. He is the fundamental principle of all principles, the Lord of lords, King of kings. The source of the Ancient Way is God, not man. Since today that order has been reversed, to try to "cultivate oneself, establish one's family, govern the nation, and pacify the world" is to look for a fish in a tree. No wonder, then, that in recent years we have seen so much chaos and civil war; no wonder peace has been elusive. In the face of mankind's multiple catastrophes, which are worsening by the day, people should search for the source of the trouble and the root of these disasters, repent quickly, and return to the true Way.

I used to be an extremely ardent humanist. I was distressed in mind and perplexed in my thoughts, though I practiced what the ancient sages taught and firmly believed that their ideals would be fulfilled one day. Hence, I founded a university to serve as a major base for humanist education. How grateful I am for the great mercy of God, who redeemed me "from [my] aimless conduct *received* by tradition from [my] fathers" (1 Pet 1:18). He delivered me "from the power of darkness" and transferred me "to the kingdom of His beloved Son" (Col 1:13 NASB), calling me "out of darkness into His marvelous light" (1 Pet 2:9). Having come to my senses, I "counted all things as loss," and forsook my previous studies of the "empty deceit" that is "according to the traditions of men, [and] . . . the basic principles of the world" (Col 2:8).[27] May the advocates of indigenous theology also come to a similar understanding and repent.

The Last Chance for Mankind to Awake from Sin

Humanists, not believing that God is the Creator of all things and the Lord of life, make "man" a product created from blind mechanistic matter and causal processes. How could they imagine that such a blind thing could ever fulfill the great and holy commission that God has given to establish a millennial Golden Age and ideal world that is purposeful and planned? This is like an idiot speaking out what he is hearing in a dream, whose words are nonsensical and inconsistent. Even one of their own, an atheistic psychiatrist, Sigmund Freud, said, "A man is not even master of his own home." How then, can he be the "measure of all things," lord of the universe, and savior of the world?

---

27. See Chang, *Jiushi zhi Dao* (*The Way of Salvation*), vol. 1, chaps. 1, 2.

Critique of Indigenous Theology

The disaster of all the various problems in the world can be traced to humanism. Christian people only know that they should oppose secularism as the cause of the overflow of human passion and the moral degradation that lead to broken hearts, but they don't realize that secularism is just the inevitable product of humanism. They see the threat of communism to the nation, and are daily more and more worried, but they don't realize that communism is only the extreme expression of humanism. They realize that they should oppose modernist and liberal theology, since it causes the decline of the church, and they are grieved at the movement to "destroy God," but they don't realize that this also is the final expression of the apostasy of humanism.

Human history approaches its end point; a disease has penetrated its vital organs. Reality has long since demonstrated that all of man's schemes to save himself are merely "pie in the sky." According to the analysis and diagnosis of eminent historians and sociologists, the emptiness and failure of humanism are undeniable facts. The reason for this is that mankind's real crisis stems from the fundamental corruption of human nature, which is extreme (Jer 17:9). All political and social problems are the fruit of sin. Any way to save the world, therefore must address the basic root rather than continuing to plaster over the surface by trying to improve the environment. Instead, people need to have a radical awakening and must ask God to "create in [us] a clean heart . . . and renew a right spirit within [us]" (Ps 51:10, KJV). Only thus will we implement radical reform and create the most thorough and effective movement for change.

Sadly, the leading humanistic thinkers are blind to this truth, and do not realize that to lower the intensity of a fire, they should pull out the wood from the stove; instead, they are "pouring out the water from the boiling pot and then pouring it back into the pot." They seek to apply only temporary and ineffective measures. Thus, their efforts are unavailing; the more they try to unravel a twisted skein, the more tangled it becomes, thus causing mankind's crisis to become more and more serious. Because of the basic, unconquerable, and unfounded pride of men, not only are they unwilling to come to their senses, but they hide their fatal illness, by every possible means seeking to prolong their last gasp and engage in the final struggle. Satan takes advantage of men's weakness and their bored and curious heart to fashion all sorts of slogans and strange teachings that capture people's attention, attract the masses, and bewitch the world. At present, he seizes on the pretext that modern philosophy and culture have developed, saying that mankind has arrived at the stage of mature manhood to which Confucius

Indigenous Theology and Humanism

referred when he said, "At thirty I was fully established." They conclude that we should be given freedom to govern ourselves, since we do not need God's help or interference in our lives. Christianity—so this argument goes—is a crutch that should be cast aside to enable us to stand on our own two feet and advance. The traditional view of God, it is said, is old-fashioned thinking and out of step with the trends of the times. If we want mankind to be free, culture to develop, and society to progress, we should proclaim the death of God! Traditional humanists only knew that the greatest offense was to kill "man" but today's humanists believe that to "kill God" is a righteous action, one that "obeys the mandate of Heaven and complies with the wishes of the people," and is the real way to save the world! Thus to go against what is natural and destroy fundamental principles and to sear the conscience and rebel against righteousness is a supremely wicked offense; there is nothing worse. It is like a deranged man who has already arrived at the point of trying to "reign in a galloping horse on the edge of a precipice"! They should know that God is the Lord of life, the source of all blessing. Today's humanists' "death of God" movement is actually a project that despises its source and cuts off the root of one's life. It is not only an unprecedented heresy, but Satan's sorcery. It is a peril for all mankind, one that could lead to eternal perdition, with no hope of recovery.[28]

As a result of the fundamental error of the humanists, which has increasingly led them to leave the true God, the people of this world are like a herd of lost sheep that is rushing off in defiance of God's Word, each person going his own way (Isa 53:6). Now it's not just a matter of having "gone a thousand miles in the wrong direction," but of "reining in a horse at the brink of a precipice." They must rein in this horse at once and correct their mistake. But, having forsaken the revelation of God, they are totally unable to see the light; they cannot of themselves recognize the truth, know God, understand the world, or even know their own nature. "To enlighten the mind and realize the Buddha-nature immanent in all things"[29] is nothing but a self-deceptive daydream. If someone truly repents and believes the gospel, he will have the starting point for a new life, a correct direction, a bright future, and a glorious hope. Only when we believe in Jesus Christ and acknowledge the redemptive work that he accomplished for us by shedding his blood on the Cross can we "return to the truth and come back to honesty." Only in this way can we return to our heavenly

---

28. Consider, for example, the existentialist Jean-Paul Sartre's belief that for man to be free, God has to die. See Chang, *Zen-Existentialism*.

29. i.e., find one's true self.—Ed.

home, enter the bosom of the Father, be reconciled to God, and fulfill the supreme degree of filial piety. (Honoring our parents is the beginning of filial piety, while fearing our heavenly Father is its highest expression.) We seek reconciliation with other people, not realizing that reconciliation with God is the only way to correct our relationships with other people in a fundamental and lasting way, and bring about peace and happiness on earth.[30] For God, "in the dispensation of the fullness of the times . . . [will] gather together in one all things in Christ" (Eph 1:10).

When Christ Jesus was born, God was entering into human history in order to create a new humanity (the "race" of Christ). This was the most "violent" revolution in the history of mankind, one that enabled a lost and fallen humanity, just when it was about to perish, to be granted an opportunity for renewal and to enter into a higher stage of existence and a more exalted realm.

When Jesus Christ came into the world, it was not just a turning point for individuals to pass from death to life, but also a pivotal transition from the incurable, destructive way of all mankind, from extreme adversity to high felicity, thanks to the abundant saving grace of the one true God. Our salvation is all due to God's grace, but it comes "through faith" (Eph 2:8; John 3:16; Rom 1:17). This "faith" is a "choice" that we make. God's great saving grace comes to us freely, but if we stubbornly resist and are unwilling to receive it, we shall "drift away" (see Heb 2:1). Our "faith," our "choice," is actually the most dramatic kind of revolution in our life, and the starting point for revolution in the world. It is an irrevocable inner revolution, an experience of passing "from death to life." It requires that we give up hope in ourselves, other people, society, the nation, the world, all of mankind, and [thus] humanism, and in our despair believe in God's saving power from the depths of our heart. It brings complete liberation from the chains that bind us to sin and death, from the "old Adam," the "old world," from humanism, from empty deceit, and the strongholds of Satan.

"There is a way *that seems* right to a man, but its end *is* the way of death" (Prov 14:12; 16:25). For millennia, people have followed this "way of death" so long that it now seems right to them, and appears to be the correct path for men to take. Following the crowd without thinking, people have blindly accommodated to this way of living, and have now come to the brink of destruction. Life and death, happiness and misery, all derive from the heart. All true Christians should consider others' desperate plight as their own; help others fulfill their desire to establish themselves just as

---

30. See Chang, *Shengdao Tong Quan* (*A General Interpretation of Christian Truth*).

Indigenous Theology and Humanism

we want to establish ourselves; return to our source; "not be ashamed of the gospel;" raise a "cry in the wilderness;" and preach the saving "gospel of the kingdom to all nations" to awaken the world and turn it from error to understanding. We should rely on our Savior, believe in the truth, and turn from the path of destruction to the road that leads to eternal life. May God's mercy enlighten the proponents of indigenous theology, enabling them to reject man and turn to God as the basis of all things, and to cease from distorting the truth and turning Christianity into a hollow shell. May they not continue to give forced and far-fetched interpretations of Christianity, but "rightly [divide] the word of truth" (2 Tim 2:15), so that the doctrines of Christianity might "take root downward, and bear fruit upward" (Isa 37:31) in China and lay a solid foundation of truth for the future of our people and our nation.

8

Indigenous Theology and Indigenous Church

The Test of True and False Believers

TEN YEARS AGO, I repeatedly read an article in the China Evangelical Seminary journal by Dr. James Taylor, who was president of that seminary in Taiwan. Addressed to the Chinese church, this "earnest explanation" made a profound impression upon me at the time, and I have not been able to forget it since then. It reminded me of when I was in Java and read the biography of the founder of the China Inland Mission, J. Hudson Taylor (who is James H. Taylor's great-grandfather), in which he said, "If I had a thousand pounds, I would give them all for China." Hot tears flowed down my cheeks as I read these words. Though thirty years have passed, I cannot forget this incident. At a time when foreigners were restricted entry to China, Taylor left his family and home, risked many dangers and difficulties and, regardless of his own health and safety, resolutely came to China. This kind of sacrificial, magnanimous spirit fills my heart with not only the deepest admiration, but also a sense of great shame. Hudson Taylor was willing to sacrifice his life for Christ and for the Chinese people—not only one life, but a thousand lives—but we are usually not willing to give up even one hair on our head to benefit the entire world. We mouth empty talk about "self-sacrifice," but are really deceiving ourselves. The reason I broke away from what I had studied before, counting everything as rubbish, and even now, at about eighty years old, am writing day and night to promote the gospel, not daring to let up for a moment, is that I was so moved by the Holy Spirit through the example of Hudson Taylor.

Because of the Holy Spirit's work in my heart over the past thirty years, since reading the "simple explanation" that President Taylor wrote out of the depths of his heart, I have felt a heavy responsibility to speak about the indigenous church and ask fellow believers and leaders of the Chinese church their opinions. Taylor explained that his vision was for the day when "the responsibility for proclaiming the gospel would rest upon Chinese Christians." He felt that "in this developing process, he had been assigned a role that was 'excessive.'" Clearly, he had no ambition to exceed his proper responsibilities. He was completely faithful to God, working so hard that he had no time to catch his breath, forgetting himself for the common good, with little time to take care of his own children, making them almost like orphans. President Taylor has thus been faithfully serving, going on despite hardships, including never being recognized by the Chinese as one of their own. His children have been educated in Chinese schools, where they were made fun of, so much so that they didn't dare to go to school. What preyed on his mind was the incomprehension and criticism of his fellow missionaries.

I am not at all trying to defend Dr. Taylor or make a case for missionaries, for in his article he never denied the "errors of mission societies, or the failings of the missionaries." Furthermore, from my earliest youth I was an extreme nationalist, putting all my efforts into opposing Christianity because of my enmity towards the West. My earliest written works were motivated by a desire to contradict the Christian religion. After I believed in Christ, however, God's love supplanted my former hatred and prejudice and gave me "the same care for [fellow members of the Body of Christ]. If one member suffers, all the members suffer with *it*" (1 Cor 12:25–26). "He who does not love *his* brother abides in death." "If someone says, 'I love God,' and hates his brother, he is a liar; for he who does not love his brother whom he has seen, how can he love God whom he has not seen? ... He who loves God *must* love his brother also" (1 John 3:14; 4:20–21). For me to have this sort of response to a brother with sincere faith who faithfully serves God is surely the true test of a believer.

A Misunderstanding of the Indigenous Church

Let us take our investigation to another level. Many Chinese Christians object to foreign missionaries, including J. Hudson Taylor, in order to promote the development of indigenous theology. This poses a major question for the great task of spreading the gospel in the context of China's process

Critique of Indigenous Theology

of transformation. For "Chinese to feel increasingly responsible for themselves" is a positive sign for the future of the Chinese church. On the other hand, only to "have zeal for God, but not according to knowledge" will always entail acting too much out of emotion and feeling, and thus to fall into Satan's trap. "To feel responsible for ourselves" deals mostly with getting rid of a sense of "dependence on others," but that is not the same as developing a drive to "expel the other."

As I have said earlier, we do not deny the "errors of the mission societies or the failings of the missionaries," much less do we seek to shield them from all criticism. To be honest, however, we must admit that some missionaries suffered and sacrificed for China. Take Ruth Brittain of China Evangelical Seminary, for example. In order to save money to help the Chinese church, she not only skimped on food and clothing, but also often bought fruit that was going rotten. It is impossible for us to be unmoved by her deeds. Others who willingly sacrificed their lives are heroic, and their examples move us to tears. Furthermore, with regard to errors and failings, Chinese believers should not absolve themselves of responsibility and put the blame entirely on Western missionaries. As President Taylor says, "These are waiting for Chinese believers to correct and to make up for." What a pity that most proponents of indigenous theology only know how passively to "expel the other," and not actively to "correct" and "make up for."

Over the past thirty years, when I have been preaching in Chinese churches in America, I occasionally have had to speak in English, or to interpret into English, because the listeners did not understand Mandarin or Cantonese. Many also are proud of being able to understand English and not ashamed of not being able to understand Chinese. Sometimes I have received letters in English from Chinese preachers whose education in Chinese took place long ago. By contrast, some of those missionaries whom they wish to reject can not only speak beautiful Mandarin, they can also quote the classics and write books in Chinese to convey their thought. Their ability in Mandarin surpasses that of some Chinese. Dr. W. M. Hayes, president of the North China Theological College, is an example; his knowledge of Chinese studies was deep and rich, and he has many published works to his credit, enough to make a Chinese person ashamed! Language is an essential tool for the proclamation of the gospel, and a key factor in the development of an "indigenous church." For a proponent of an "indigenous church" not to study Chinese assiduously, to the point of not being able to speak, much less write in it, is a contradiction. When the door to China opens, if "Chinese" preachers enter speaking English and needing interpreters, may I ask, "What will come next? Is this not ridiculous?" Recently, I read an article by Chen Chung Dao, the editor of the *Sheng Jing Bao* (*Bible Times*), about Christian literature work among the Chinese, in which he expressed his concern that in the future it would be hard to find Chinese authors, or even Chinese readers. All who discuss the "indigenous church" should reflect deeply upon this statement.

A true Christian is a citizen of the kingdom of God, and should not harbor any notion of boundaries between East and West, much less racial prejudice. "The members should have the same care for one another" (1 Cor 12:25), offering mutual help and pulling together. If, in the name of an "indigenous church," we reject and despise those foreign missionaries who truly love our people, sacrifice their lives for China, acquire a deep knowledge of Chinese language and culture, and have an orthodox faith, that would be ridiculous. Such an action does not lead to the development of an indigenous church; rather, it opposes Christ himself. A real indigenous church is able to "take root downward, and bear fruit upward" (Isa 37:31), not remain in a state of dependence and waste the land on which it stands. It can stand on its own two feet, walk erect with its head held high, take the offensive, and win a great victory for the sake of the kingdom!

The Foundation for an Indigenous Church

The commission to preach the gospel is not just a religious one, but also has to do with culture. We are not just to engage in private devotions within a monastery, but should imitate Paul, who debated with the philosophers on Mars Hill (Acts 17:22). Asia is a great fortress of non-Christian culture. If we want to establish a truly "indigenous church" that will take root and never be eradicated, we must shake up this anti-Christian cultural structure and philosophical system. If we cannot challenge these and enable the gospel to penetrate deeply into the anti-Christian culture and philosophical system, then we will not be able to extend and firm up the boundaries of our battle line. Then the idea of preaching the gospel to the ends of the earth is only fantasy, since more of the world's population lives in Asia than anywhere else.[1]

The Reformation movement had another sense of mission, one that has to do with culture. John Calvin, one of the leaders of the Reformation, not only possessed a profound understanding of the theological

---

1. See Chang, *Strategy of Missions in the Orient*.

teaching of the Bible, but also of the "Substance-Use Principle,"[2] and so was able to elucidate the truths of Scripture from a cultural and academic standpoint. Sadly, the church did not fully put into practice Calvin's principles, and did not fully understand the comprehensive nature of his understanding of the work of proclaiming the gospel. In a word, the church merely emphasized the subjective nature of Reformation teaching on the salvation of the soul, while it neglected the objective side, which is its power to transform the world. This includes the "vertical" application of God's sovereignty to the entire world, as well as the "horizontal" application of the truth of the Bible to society and the nation. Overlooking these truths has ever been the principal legacy produced by the failure of evangelistic endeavors, and should be something carefully considered by those who wish to establish an "indigenous church."

If we are to establish an indigenous church, we must employ a new strategy of proclamation, in order to create a new social and cultural environment that will both be advantageous for evangelism and enable the gospel to take root in pagan nations. That is not at all to say that such a comprehensive strategy for proclaiming the faith will change the goal of evangelism, so that it focuses on society and culture and neglects the greatest motive for evangelism, the reconciliation of men to God and their being saved from death to life through the work of the Cross. To the contrary, only if we adopt such a strategy will mankind be able to walk the way of Golgotha most actively. In a word, the power of the Cross not only saves lost souls and changes individual lives, but also makes "all things new" (Rev 21:5). This new kind of strategy is all-embracing, and is not confined to the limits of the individual as its final goal. Justification by faith, regeneration of the individual, the salvation of the soul—these belong to the essence of the gospel, and comprise the supreme message that must be preached by the church. To proclaim the gospel is one thing, however, and to cause the seed of the gospel to take deep root and grow is quite another. That is to say, if we want pagan nations to discard their native religions, we must first sweep away obstacles to the gospel by thoroughly transforming and renewing a culture's philosophical system and ideology.[3] This is not at all to preach a "Social Gospel," to which I am most vehemently opposed. I believe, however, that merely to resist this error passively is useless. Only if we adopt a comprehensive strategy can we knock out the Social Gospel,

---

2. Or *Mingti dayong*; i.e., to be clear on the substance [essence] and to use [apply] it effectively.—Ed.

3. The author uses two words that are translated "system" in English; I have rendered the second one as "ideology."—Ed.

and keep the seed of the true gospel from being eaten by "birds" or choked by "thorns" (see Matt 13:3, 7). Only thus will pagan nations receive the message of Christ and believe in the truth. Only thus will their cultures be enlightened by Christ and be renewed and thoroughly transformed, becoming "good soil" so that the seed of the gospel can be deeply embedded in the soil and bear fruit, "some a hundredfold, some sixty, some thirty" (Matt 13:23). Only in this way can a truly "indigenous church" be established on a firm foundation.

The Mission of the Indigenous Church

Furthermore, the even greater significance of establishing an "indigenous church" lies in mobilizing believers in every region of the world. From the standpoint of the long history of the East, the development of [Protestant] Christianity has taken place in only the past 150 years.[4] Measured by the number of believers and the proportion of them in the total population, some areas are less than 5 percent Christian. Clearly, our past efforts at evangelism have not yet been characterized by a whole-scale and vigorous mass movement. That is absolutely not to say, however, that Christianity is a foreign religion unsuited to the East. I must re-emphasize that the origins of Christianity are in Asia; it is not at all a Western religion, but a movement raised up by God in the center of the globe to save people from all over the whole world.

God's truth is "settled in heaven" and endures forever; it is universal and everlasting, and will not mislead; it is not limited by time and space. Most people, not possessing real knowledge and without vision, see so many doors to the gospel slammed shut and the scattering of the local church and of missionaries, and conclude that the work of missions has come to a dead end. Sadly, they do not realize that "closed doors" are really "open doors" in disguise. They are God's way of arousing us, causing us to see new vistas, grasp a new opportunity, adopt new strategies, open a new front, and actively develop an indigenous church.

An "indigenous church," therefore, is not the "death of missions," but "new life" for the church universal. It is a new opening for the proclamation of the gospel to the world, and a new offensive by the church on a "second front." It is a chance for the mobilization of believers all over the world, from every place, people, and nation to take part in a movement

---

4. Chang must have been composing this sentence in the mid-twentieth century.—Ed.

for revival. The retreat of foreign missionaries from China, therefore, does not amount to "rejection of the other," but a rejection of our own "sense of dependence." In other words, this is not the abandonment of the work of evangelism and missions, but the ending of our past "professionalism," and "servant/master" relationship, which reversed the relationship between what is primary and what is secondary. Only thus can the universal church, composed of saints in every nation, strive together and accept the mission given us by God, each taking his own battle-station, with all of us fighting the good fight for the kingdom of God on every front so that the gospel of the kingdom can be preached to every creature under heaven.[5]

By nature, the work of Christian proclamation is a global, total, and comprehensive "war." The major goal of establishing an "indigenous church" is to awaken the self-awareness and sense of responsibility within the universal church, so that the church in every nation can take its place in the line of battle, and every believer might become an elite soldier of Christ and participate in the glorious army of the Lord of hosts, all with one Lord, one faith, one hope, under one banner following our Commander, the King of kings and Lord of lords, in a worldwide, total, and comprehensive war. Then we can introduce Christ the Savior to every country in the world and enable the gospel to penetrate the heart of each person. The "nations of the Gentiles" will then believe the truth, become saints, and stand firmly, erect, going into battle against Satan as stalwarts for the truth and messengers of the gospel. This is the uncompleted work of the Reformation. May God have mercy on us, expel all our racial, national, and denominational prejudice and error, open the eyes of our hearts to see this new "vision" and take up our part in the formidable and urgent mission of these last days.[6]

The Transcendent Nature of the Church

Furthermore, Christian truth is God's way of salvation for the world. The Christian church, therefore, is a worldwide, spiritual society, not limited by nation or race. To use nationalism, whether of the East or the West, to turn the church into an organization that is narrowly national and uniting it with a local culture, not only eliminates the universal and spiritual nature of the church, but also rebels against God's will and the royal authority of Christ. To promote indigenous theology, or overemphasize an

5. See Chang, *Strategy of Missions in the Orient*.
6. See Chang, *Shijie Xuandao Zhanlue Zhongxin* (*Strategy of World Mission*).

Indigenous Theology and Indigenous Church

"indigenous church," therefore, is to distort the nature of Christian truth, which is from heaven. There is a danger of turning the church into something merely human, or even pagan, and thus losing its transcendent, heavenly nature. This is an important matter that requires detailed discussion. I plan to write another book to deal with the subject in more detail.

Historian Arnold Toynbee wrote, "The Western Christian nations are products of Christianity, but Christianity did not arise in the West, but in the East, in the nations that are now Muslim."[7] In the history of missions, the authoritative teachings of the Early Church Fathers do not represent the West, nor do they represent the East. Although many of the Western church fathers employed Western terminology to express their ideas, they all had African and Asian backgrounds. For example, Greek theology was developed in Alexandria and Antioch, and the founders of Latin theology were the Africans Tertullian, Cyprian, and Augustine of Hippo. They all wrote in Latin, but it was not the Latin of Rome, but a Christian Latin developed in Tunisia, replete with Eastern influences. This demonstrates that Christian doctrine is not a religion of the West.

The essence of the church should not be limited by human nature. If we turn it into a national organization,[8] we shall strip it of its heavenly, transcendent character, a danger that results from an over-emphasis upon an "indigenous church." The church transcends human culture, and is not restricted by any kind of cultural prejudice. It can, however, be fully inclusive by absorbing eminent cultural institutions and fine cultural elements resulting from common grace to construct a new whole to express its own spirit for the benefit of worldwide proclamation. For example, every language has its beautiful and distinctive expressions. When we write, we can't just be "neither Chinese nor Western," but must use idiomatic expressions and literary quotations, as long as they are not in opposition to the truth, to render our style elegant to glorify God's name. That being the case, our question, then, is only whether the elements of the whole that we construct are consistent with Christian truth and the heavenly goal of the church, not whether they are Eastern or Western. They must transcend the limits and prejudices of any national government or culture. The church is a holy, heavenly organization with its own internal, spiritual life-force, so that it is able to break through these limitations and

---

7. Toynbee, *Civilization on Trial*, 154–55.

8. Chang refers here to the idea of creating a Chinese church, with distinctly Chinese theology and characteristics, implying also a rejection of Western theology and characteristics.—Ed.

prejudices and "Christianize" every kind of element[9] and bestow upon it a holy image. The church, therefore, represents a transcendent principle that is completely different from the ordinary, and represents the coming into the world of that which belongs to the kingdom of heaven. It is therefore incompatible with many secular notions, and will arouse powerful hostility from secular society. At this time, the most evident and challenging manifestation of that hostile power is a narrow nationalism, of which indigenous theology is one form which this sort of spirit takes. This kind of conflict is not a battle between East and West, but arises from the ancient, original conflict between the power of "the spiritual and the worldly." At present, the conflict engulfs the entire world, so the church, both East and West, must actively participate in this universal spiritual warfare and remove obstacles to the spread of the Word of God, so that the gospel of the kingdom of heaven might be spread throughout the earth. We must dispel Eastern and Western prejudice and limitations and pray for the kingdom of heaven to come, so that "the nations of those who are saved shall walk in its light, and the kings of the earth bring their glory and honor into it" (Rev 21:24). This is the greatest vision of mankind and its ultimate hope.[10]

---

9. Or "to make every element subservient to Christian truth."—Ed.
10. See Dawson, *The Historic Reality of Christian Culture*, chaps. 12, 13.

9

Christian Doctrine and the "Substance-Use [Essence-Application] Principle"[1]

"Essence" cannot be change: It is a universal standard, immutable throughout the ages

"Application" can change: It should adapt to place and time

The Penetration of Christian Doctrine: Tearing Down Strongholds

AFTER I BELIEVED IN Christ, as I was reading 1 Pet 3:15, God's Word seemed to explode in my heart with the force of an atomic bomb, causing me to seek, night and day, to *"give* a defense" of the "reason for the hope that is in" me and to expound the truth through my writings, even forgetting to eat and to sleep.[2] In 1968, God sent me to lecture in seminaries in Taiwan, Hong Kong, the Philippines, Singapore, and Indonesia, as well as Greece, England, France, and other nations. Everywhere I preached, I emphasized the "Essence-Application Principle" with fellow theologians.[3] In the same year, I worked day and night to compose *Zongti Biandaoxue (Comprehensive Christian Apologetics)*, a four-volume work that runs to almost a million

---

1. Or *mingti dayong;* i.e., be clear on the essential principles, and apply them effectively. Sometimes translated as Substance-Use Principle, as in Samuel Ling's translation of the *Critique of Humanism* in this volume.—Ed.

2. See Chang, *Jiushi zhi Dao (The Way of Salvation)*; and Chang, *Qimiao Jiuen (Amazing Grace)*.

3. See Chang, *Dongzheng Ganhuai Lu (Remembering My Eastern Journey)*.

words, in order to "contend earnestly for the faith" (Jude 3).[4] I call apologetics "theology at war," in an attempt to mobilize the church to a total spiritual warfare that would tear down the strongholds of the devil.[5]

I read accounts of the persecution of the early church and how the early church fathers rose up to contend against Greek and Roman pagan religion and philosophy; they gained widespread fame and prestige; their deeds were heroic and inspiring; their strong sense of righteousness will shine forever. Cherishing their memory, I was deeply moved and filled with a new strength to enlist in the same cause. Some theologians in certain denominations of the Chinese church, by contrast, do not follow the example of their forebears to do battle with spiritual forces in the heavenly places, but rather "giving heed to deceiving spirits and doctrines of demons" (1 Tim 4:1), they promote so-called indigenous theology, confuse their countrymen, slander Christian truth, and even defame the name of the Lord.[6] Recently, even among evangelicals, there are some who do the same, agreeing with what the indigenous theology proponents are saying. This causes me to feel a burning, consuming zeal (John 2:17). At this point, having just finished my *Zongti Biandaoxue (Comprehensive Christian Apologetics)*, and hardly stopping to catch my breath, I began to compose the present volume, hoping to share with those of like mind. (If Chinese seminaries offer a course on this subject, they should add *Critique* to the title, so as to avoid misunderstanding and join the battle as allies.)

Christian doctrine is "forever . . . settled in heaven" (Ps 119:89), but we must not "sit at the bottom of a well,"[7] holding on to something that is incomplete; close our eyes and engage in idle musings; or simply think without applying what we know, content with our narrow scope and not eager to "press on toward that which lies ahead." It is essential to apply the "Substance-Use Principle"[8] and to adapt our theology to the local situation (so-called indigenization, or "contextualization"). We must apply our theology to the current trends of thought, the situation of each nation. Engaging in a flexible strategy and going on the offensive against humanism, we should seek to penetrate society and culture [with the truth]. Of course, we must actively preach the gospel in order

---

4. See Chang, *Zongti Biandaoxue (Comprehensive Christian Apologetics)*. Part of this work has been issued in English as *Asia's Religions*.

5. See Chang, *What Is Apologetics?* for an explanation of this concept.—Ed.

6. See chap. 3 of this book.

7. That is, "have tunnel vision."—Ed.

8. Or *mingti dayong*.—Ed.

Christian Doctrine and the "Substance-Use [Essence-Application] Principle"

to bring salvation to individual souls, but we must also create an environment that is advantageous to the spread of the gospel. "Adapting to the local situation" does not mean surrendering to the environment, but preparing the soil for the seed of the gospel in order to go on the offensive against secular culture and philosophy and every kind of social science, and to wage a comprehensive campaign of proclamation.[9] The non-Christians now occupy the schools, bookstores, and newspapers; we barely have a foothold. The classic Chinese dictionaries are full of Confucian, Buddhist, and Daoist terms and concepts, with hardly any Christian flavor. The academic culture is dominated by non-Christian scholars. Even sadder, a so-called Christian university, Peking University (formerly Yanjing)[10] is a base for the Social Gospel. The president and dean both promote indigenous theology. The dean of the school of religion, T. C. Chao (Zhao Zichen), opposes orthodox Christian doctrine. He writes, "Theological doctrines are mostly superstitions that should be discarded." President Wu Leichuan veers even further to the left, for he believes in Marxism, approves of revolutionary tyranny, and sympathizes with Judas, who betrayed Jesus. He promotes social revolution and the present rule of China by the Communists. The persecution of the church can in several ways be called the baneful fruit of this school. It pains me even to think of it. This sorry situation has resulted from neglect of cultural education by the church, allowing the devil to gain a foothold. We should take to heart lessons painfully learned, and reflect carefully on what has happened. We cannot remain satisfied with our current narrow scope, hold on to that which is incomplete, or rely on outworn slogans to deal with the world, using "gospel platitudes" to propound the truth of Christianity. Rather, we should "be distressed in mind and perplexed in thought,"[11] study hard and think deeply, and actively, intentionally, and boldly rise up to engage in battle with secular scholars, traditional culture, and those false prophets who have come into the church as "wolves in sheep's clothing." Their base must be shaken to its foundations; their strongholds must be torn down, leaving them no place to stand, rendering them silent and unseen and unable to continue to be an obstacle to the truth of Christianity. Further, we must consider whether the inability of the truth to be propagated widely and of the gospel to flourish might

9. See Chang, *Shijie Xuandao Zhanlue Zhongxin* (*Strategy for World Missions*).
10. Formerly Yenching.—Ed.
11. Or *kunxin henglu*, from the *Mencius*, referring to the testing that must first come to every man who is to be given a great responsibility by heaven.—Ed.

not be only because people don't believe, but might perhaps lie with the coldness and indifference of ordinary believers—their superficial study of the truth; their not seeking for deeper knowledge of the faith; their weakness and incompetence. We need true and sincere faith, as well as unwavering resolution, firm and assertive courage, and a spirit of learning and reflection. Having faith, we need to "add to [it] . . . knowledge" (2 Pet 1:5). We must love God not only with our heart, but our mind as well (Matt 22:37). Only thus can we take up our daunting mission and assume leadership in cultural scholarship.

Christianity is, essentially, spiritual, so I have always completely opposed the heresy of the Social Gospel. That does not mean, however, that because of "giving up eating for fear of choking" we completely ignore our responsibility to society and culture.[12] Especially in an age in which the culture rejects the truth and has become a major threat, we cannot mouth empty slogans and repeat worn-out "gospel platitudes," but must actively formulate a counterstrategy. A major significance of the Reformation was cultural. The great theologian John Calvin not only understood the truths of the Bible, but also took a fresh look at the many implications within Scripture that bear upon culture. The Reformation was a great movement, not a flash in the pan; and it has not yet reached its ultimate stage. As the great Dutch theologian Dr. Abraham Kuyper said, "We have not yet brought this great movement to complete victory, to comprehensive fulfillment. Martin Luther only looked at the subjective aspect of individual salvation, but did not completely emphasize the objective aspect, which pertains to the world. His starting point was to rely on the saving grace of Christ (Soteriology), especially the doctrine of 'justification by faith.' Calvin, however, expanded the horizon further, emphasizing God's sovereignty and the comprehensive and universal principles that apply to the world as a whole (the Cosmological Principle). Lutheranism is limited to the essence of church and theology. Calvinism penetrates every aspect of human life, emphasizing the total transformation of human thought and worldviews." Many faithful Christians only focus on their relationship with God (vertical relationship), but neglect the broad application of Christian truth to life in this world (horizontal relationship). They do not understand the "Substance-Use" principle and do not penetrate every aspect of human life with the sovereignty of God and universal principles of Christian truth. That is, they do not construct an "all embracing life system."

---

12. See Chang, *The True Gospel vs. Social Activism*.

Christian Doctrine and the "Substance-Use [Essence-Application] Principle"

When we examine the history of Christian missions, we learn a deep lesson: there has been a lack of a comprehensive strategy, and a failure to pay attention to "theological penetration" of society and culture. When a people abandons its former religion and begins to accept a new faith, they will always encounter many cultural, religious, and similar problems, which they must thoroughly resolve. China is a nation with an ancient culture, so for us this matter is even more pressing. We have neglected this aspect, even to the point of some so-called "Christians" not being clear about the truth, so that those who advocate indigenous theology propound many ridiculous things, leaving Christianity an empty shell with no core. If we really want to propagate Christianity widely, we cannot ignore matters of culture and religion. Only thus can we achieve maximum results with less effort. This is not to neglect the individual soul, nor to approve of the Social Gospel, which merely pays attention to trivial things while neglecting what is essential, as I have said already and so do not need to repeat myself. My goal is to transform the nature of humanistic culture and the structures of secular society, and thus remove obstacles to the gospel by attacking Satan's strongholds. Only in this way can we prepare the soil for the sowing of the seed of the gospel. In this matter "the sons of this world are more shrewd in their generation than the sons of light" (Luke 16:8). They are able to carry out a comprehensive strategy, so the "elements of this world and "the doctrines of demons" seep into every nook and cranny. Our countrymen, therefore, are scrambling for humanism, rationalism, materialism, and communism. They consider the pure gospel, including the Trinity, the deity of Christ, the mystery of the Cross, the power of the resurrection, the return of our Lord, the new heaven and new earth as superstition. Proponents of indigenous theology even follow secularism, abetting wicked men as they perpetuate wickedness and thus causing mainland China to fall under Communist control. As a result, the church has become the target for unprecedented persecution!

History tells us that religious and moral persuasion is not enough for an entire nation to change its religion beliefs. The scribes and the Pharisees were sharply rebuked by Jesus: "You travel land and sea to win one proselyte, and when he is won, you make him twice as much of a son of hell as yourselves" (Matt 23:15). We should reflect deeply on this accusation. This kind of "success" in evangelism "only consists in quantity, and does not penetrate the hearts of men."[13] Missions scholar Hendrick Kraemer writes, "Eastern culture is thousands of years old. From

---

13. Buck, *Christianity Tested*, chap. 5.

Critique of Indigenous Theology

beginning to end, its peoples have expressed their firm self-respect. They have held to their beliefs, and will not meet their disputants half way in order to reach a compromise. "[14] Orthodox theologian Charles Hodge wrote that "Hindus are a highly intellectual race. Their language and literature are on a par with those of Greece and Rome. Their philosophers nearly 3,000 years ago anticipated the highest results reached by Schelling and Hegel in our day. Hindu philosophy occupies an original and important position in the history of thought. The Rig-Veda is older than the Old Testament, the Upanishads antedate Plato, and the Vedanta exerts world-wide influence. It has always been a challenge."[15] After World War II, Indian religious philosophy began to launch a violent assault on the West, prompting some Western church leaders to ask me to write a refutation.[16] The damage done by Indian religious philosophy to China was already talked about during the Tang dynasty. Han Yu, the great scholar, appealed loudly to the emperor, saying, "Chaos and subjugations are coming one after another; the dynasty cannot last much longer."[17] The declining condition of our nation and the low spirits of our people today can be said to resemble that period in our history.

In Hudson Taylor's era, when a missionary conference was held in Shanghai, Dr. Joseph Edkins declared that "The three religions of Confucianism, Buddhism, and Taoism are obstacles to the advance of the gospel, and are fortresses erected by Satanic art that must be captured and destroyed," but they exist to the present day as strong as ever.[18]

The literature of Confucianism, Buddhism, Daoism and Hindu philosophy is vast, and they place prominent advertisements in the newspapers. The works of Christian systematic theology and apologetics, on the other hand, are as "few as morning stars," and popular Christian publications are

---

14. Kraemer, *The Christian Message in a Non-Christian World*, 57.

15. Hodge, *Systematic Theology*, vol. 1.

16. See Chang, *Zen-Existentialism*. In my early years, I studied abroad in France and did not learn much English, but later I began to compose books in English, even receiving commendation from eminent scholars and church leaders, one of whom said my book was "the work of a first-rate scholar" and a "light to the world." This is also a miracle; may God receive the glory.

17. See Han, "Memorial on the Bone of Buddha," 1:372–74.

18. *Records of the Shanghai Missionary Conference*, 1877. Joseph Edkins, a careful and sympathetic student of Chinese religions, held that Buddhist beliefs could serve as a point of contact when preaching to the Chinese. This comment reveals, however, that he nevertheless held to the necessity of faith in Christ for salvation. See articles on Edkins in *The Biographical Dictionary of Chinese Christianity* (www.bdcconline.net) and *The Ricci Roundtable* (ricci.rt.usfca.edu).—Ed.

Christian Doctrine and the "Substance-Use [Essence-Application] Principle"

mostly shallow tracts, almost nothing in comparison. When I was young, I studied law and government, and because of the perils of our nation, I was assigned by the central government to administrative duties. After the Second World War, I left government and returned to the academy, establishing a university. Against my will, I was made president. I would have preferred to shut myself up in my study with my books, but could not fulfill my original desire to do so. All my writings were composed during stolen time in my office, and are really not the products of deep research. After I was saved in my later years, I counted them all as refuse, and devoted myself to the study of Christian doctrine, night and day, burying myself in the work of composing Christian literature in defense of the faith, such as my first work, *Shengdao Tongquan* (*A General Interpretation of Christian Truth*) and other volumes. I felt as if I were singing a song for elevated tastes and thus could find few to join in concert with me. My more recent work, *Zongti Biandaoxue* (*Comprehensive Christian Apologetics*), in four volumes, amounts to almost one million words. It was considered too expensive to publish, but the Christian and Missionary Alliance Church and the president of China Evangelical Seminary, Dr. James H. Taylor, thought that apologetics was what China needed most and lacked most. "However, we speak wisdom among those who are mature, . . . the wisdom of God in a mystery," relying on the Holy Spirit who "searches all things" (1 Cor 2:6, 7, 10). Christian truth is "the mystery which has been hidden from ages and from generations, . . . we preach . . . in all wisdom" (Col 1:26, 28). In our proclamation of the gospel, we must not rely on emotion or upon little tracts filled with "gospel platitudes." Orthodox theologian J. Gresham Machen said, "By supernatural power God can overcome the intellectual obstacles, but this happens very seldom and divine power is generally exerted by appeal to the faculties of the mind. There must be intellectual labor as well as religious emotion. The modern world is dominated by ideas that ignore the gospel and make it seem irrelevant. This fact not only prevents the acceptance of Christianity; it blocks Christianity from even getting a hearing. To a very large extent the students of secular universities are not Christians. That they are not believers is often just because they are students."[19] (Note that Karl Marx was born in a Christian home, and when he was young he wrote an essay on the theme of the union of the believer with Christ, based on John 15. Nietzsche studied theology in his youth, preparing to enter the Christian ministry. Both of them came under the influence of secularism while at university and abandoned the

---

19. Machen, *What Is Christianity?*, chap. 12.

faith. Nietzsche mocked Christian ethics as an expression of hypocrisy and a scourge of mankind. Marxism has become the source of a flood of disasters for the whole world.) As Machen also wrote, "The thought of the day, as it makes itself most strongly felt in the universities, is profoundly antagonistic to Christianity. The chief obstacle to saving faith today lies in the sphere of the intellect. Unfortunately, our labor in this arena has been neglected, and the Church is now reaping the fruit of her indolence."[20] Looking back on the anti-Christian movement in China, we see that it was led by intellectuals and young college students. Actually, at the time I myself blindly agreed with them, and submitted an article to a newspaper as part of the attack.

China is not only a nation with an ancient culture, but also one whose culture has been impacted by the trends of Western academic culture as a result of the New Culture Movement. On the one hand, there is the cultural, philosophical, and religious heritage that has come down to us from our forebears over the past millennia; on the other, there are varieties of anti-Christian theories and viewpoints from the West, all of which are the devil's attempts to oppose the truth. We must resolutely attack these strongholds so that the gospel may penetrate the entire culture. The mission of today's Christians is therefore doubly difficult.[21]

The Mission of the Christian Church

"Don't hold on to that which is anachronistic."

When I was young I opposed the church and objected to Christianity. In my middle age, being deceived by Satan, I was addicted to the three Chinese religions, so much so that I was called a "re-incarnation of Ouyang Xiu," and "a re-incarnation of Luo Han." People said that my physical body was still on Mt. Tai.[22] As a result, I was commended by my peers and superiors in the government and undertook to establish Jiangnan[23] University. I was also chosen to be president of the new university. At the time, because of the troubles that our nation was facing, people

---

20. Ibid.

21. See Chang, *Strategy for Missions in the Orient*; *Shijie Xuandao Zhanlue Zhongxin* (*Strategy for World Missions*); and *Critique of Humanism* (in this volume).

22. Mount Tai (*Tai Shan*) in Shandong is the foremost of the Five Sacred Mountains and has been a place of worship for at least three thousand years, serving as one of the most important ceremonial centers of China.—Ed.

23. Formerly Kiang-nan.—Ed.

Christian Doctrine and the "Substance-Use [Essence-Application] Principle"

with ambition were encouraging others to take to the streets in protest in an effort to overthrow the government. The central government, therefore, did not allow the formation of private universities, to the extent that when the former minister of education, Chen Lifu, thought of establishing a university for the reconstruction of the nation, even that proposal was not approved. But because my university cherished the lofty ideal of not only reviving Eastern religion and culture but also of using this to save the entire world, they made a special exception in our case, which people at the time considered almost a marvel in Chinese education history. Wang Shijie, the former Minister of Education, and others strongly endorsed me. Right after that, I was recruited by a university in India to go there to lecture on the topic, "Asia's Destiny: The Hope of the World." Our intention was to link up leaders of both India and China in the endeavor to revive Eastern religion and culture as the way to save the world, indeed, the only way. Midway through the journey, however, God, out of his great mercy and love, hindered my rebellion. Seeing that I was "a child of wrath," he closed the door to India. Reaching out his hand from heaven and bridling this wild horse, he turned me from the way of destruction. I received revelation from on high, which enabled me to understand the truth and caused me to shed tears of remorse and to trust in Christ. Treating all else as rubbish, I devoted myself to studying Christianity and dedicated myself to his service.[24]

After I believed in Christ, I began to write books. Upon the publication of my first works, *Yuan Dao* (*The Way: An Investigation Concerning Divine Truth*) and *Shengdao Tong Quan* (*A General Interpretation of Christian Truth*), a number of pious and orthodox believers thought that I was promoting indigenous theology because I had quoted from many Chinese classics and employed many phrases and terms from Confucian, Buddhist, and Daoist writings. Little did they know that I was actually opposing indigenous theology and was in absolute disagreement with it. Though both indigenous-theology proponents and I use similar sayings and terminology, Indigenous Theologians are making far-fetched comparisons, compromising with pagan views, and even surrendering to them, while I deploy such terms so that the leading intellectuals of our country might understand the truth and be saved in a more natural way, by building on what they already know. Towards those theories that are opposed to biblical truth, however, I engage in sharp critique and even refutation,

---

24. See Chang, *Qimiao Jiuen* (*His Amazing Grace*); Chang, *Chongsheng Aomi* (*The Mystery of Rebirth*); and Chang, *Jiushi zhi Dao* (*The Way of Salvation*).

Critique of Indigenous Theology

so that they might thoroughly repent, forsake emptiness, and believe in the gospel. The proponents of indigenous theology and I are, therefore, as incompatible as fire and ice, and totally antithetical to each other. Some want to engage in conflict with them that will lead to mutual destruction, but I want to seek to lead them from death to life. When dealing with unbelievers, we should put ourselves in their position, sympathize with them, and care for them, not being prejudiced against them just because they are different from us. We should share the gospel with them in love. When it comes to the defense of the truth, however, we cannot make any accommodation or compromise, or we will commit the same fatal error as do the advocates of indigenous theology.

Now we must consider further the question of what sort of attitude we should take towards Chinese culture, philosophy, and religion.[25] Although we must persevere and hold fast to orthodox Christian teaching, we cannot just separate ourselves to maintain our purity, or hold on to what is inadequate; confine ourselves to old ways; live in an ivory tower, enthralled with ourselves, unconcerned with what is happening in the world and completely ignoring the culture, philosophy, etc., of our nation. Nor can we imagine ourselves to be spiritual and think that we must not be tainted by secular studies, being excessively scrupulous and refusing even to discuss such matters. The church does not live in a spiritual vacuum, for God has placed us in the world; we live in various different cultural environments, so that we cannot be indifferent to what is going on around us. Church historian Philip Schaff has written, "Christianity at first had to do with highly civilized nations. The Apostles planted churches in the cities of (highly cultured) Jews, Greeks, and Romans."[26] Christian scholars must not "hesitate to pelt a rat for fear of smashing the china vase," imagining that the world consists of dirty things to be despised and ignored, for this will only give Satan a foothold.[27] God had a special purpose for selecting the Apostle Paul. He debated with "Epicurean and Stoic philosophers" on Mars Hill at Athens (Acts 17:16–31). Our missions strategy should follow the principle, "If you want to capture brigands, first seize their chief." We should begin by contending with Gentile cultural and philosophical leaders. We should imitate the example of our fore-runners, inheriting their spirit, in order to pull down "strongholds"

---

25. See chaps. 4–7 of this book.
26. Schaff, *A History of the Christian Church*, vol. 4.
27. See Chang, *Zongti Biandaoxue* (*Comprehensive Christian Apologetics*), vol. 4, Culture.

Christian Doctrine and the "Substance-Use [Essence-Application] Principle"

and cast down "arguments and every high thing that exalts itself against the knowledge of God" (2 Cor 10: 4–5).

At the end of the seventeenth century and the beginning of the eighteenth century, the Pietist movement arose. With pure motives and hopes, they sought to liberate Christians from the scholastic formalism into which the church had fallen. They pursued a recovery of pure biblical teaching and emphasized the spiritual life of the believer. They not only looked down on philosophical theories, but even went to the point of rejecting church doctrines, only emphasizing faith, believing that religion was only a spiritual matter and had nothing to do with reason. The goal of preaching was to establish the spiritual life, so sermons should avoid theoretical disputes and not strive for rhetorical elegance. Culture and society were considered unclean. One should not get involved with the world, lest one become tainted. They possessed pure motives and high spirituality. They deserve to be admired, but they clung to what was incomplete, disregarding what was going on in the world around them. They were thus unable to "give a defense . . . for the hope that [was] in" them (1 Pet 3:15), or to lead others to wholehearted acceptance of the gospel or a sudden conviction of sin and understanding of the truth, and thus receive God's grace. As a result, the enemies of the church and proponents of the Social Gospel had much to criticize in them, saying that our faith is of no use to the world, but is useless garbage and thus should be rejected. We should mount a counteroffensive and "contend earnestly for the faith" (Jude 3). The prominent English writer C. S. Lewis wrote that "our efforts should be to force people to confront reality and to realize that their questions can only find their answers in Christianity."[28] Noted biblical scholar R. A. Torrey once said, "To read the Bible only is not necessarily to understand the Bible." In other words, we must not only study the Bible and understand it, but must put it into practice, using biblical truth to solve current problems. Reformed theologian Louis Berkhof, criticizing Schleiermacher, the father of liberal theology, said, "In our study of theology, to use only the biblical method is insufficient. The value of doctrinal theology is that it can speak to the current situation, explaining the mind of God in concepts that people can understand and employing the scientific style of contemporary theologians to express the will of God," in order to show the practical application of biblical principles.[29]

Dr. J. Gresham Machen wrote,

28. Lewis, broadcast message, *British Broadcasting Company*.
29. Berkhof, *Introductory Volume of Systematic Theology*.

Critique of Indigenous Theology

> Modern culture is a gigantic force; to make this force submit to Christianity, it is not enough to rely only on religious fervor. We also have to employ our intellect. The influence of Christians upon civilization today is very weak. Intellectuals are the greatest barrier to the Christian gospel. We are holding on to what is inadequate and hiding in our foxholes, which is safer, but will not lead to victory. If we remain on the defensive, and do not go on the offensive, we cannot defeat the enemy win the battle. Unfortunately, today's Christians are not able to be 'distressed in mind and perplexed in our thoughts' or engage their minds. Most Christian workers are not willing to study hard or do the work of serious thinking, but only do easy and routine work. We are now eating the bitter fruit of our laziness and neglect. If today's church wants to survive, it must hoist the flag and enter the fray.[30]

Dr. Emile Cailliet adds, "After the Reformation, Christian thinkers lost the leadership role they had played in culture, so that the church seems to have burned its bridges to the world. They serve God but neglect the world that God created. Because the church cannot lead the development of culture, Christian doctrine and culture have become opposed to one another, so that in education, society, philosophy, and government, they have gradually become two separate worlds, and are now sharply in conflict with each other."[31] My colleague at Gordon Seminary, Dr. Burton L. Goddard, once challenged graduating students with these words: "Have you ever thoroughly studied the culture and mysteries of the world around you? Can you put into practice the truth that you know, applying biblical truth to the society in which you live?" This is an extremely important question, which Chinese theological students should thoroughly ponder, so that they might put truth into practice and benefit the people of our nation.

We must not stay in our own little circle, cling to things that are incomplete, and simply oppose liberal theology and indigenous theology. We must leave our lovely little ivory tower and go with Paul to debate with the pagan philosophers on Mars Hill (Acts 17:22).[32] Chosen and sent by God, Paul sought out the pagan Gentiles. He neither compromised nor assumed an inflexible posture, but moved by God's love he used methods that enabled him to speak to the current situation, leading the Gentiles to

---

30. Machen, *Christian Faith in the Modern World*; and Machen, *What Is Christianity?*
31. Cailliet, *The Christian Approach to Culture*.
32. Or the Areopagus.—Ed.

Christian Doctrine and the "Substance-Use [Essence-Application] Principle"

conviction of sin, understanding of the truth, and trust in the Savior. From Acts 14, 15, 17 and Romans 1, we can glean several key points and see the measures he adopted in speaking to pagans:

1. Through general revelation, especially his works in the created order, God has revealed himself to you and demonstrated his existence.
2. You must forsake folly and turn to the eternal Maker of heaven, earth, and the seas and all of creation, for we have no excuse to do otherwise.
3. But you considered yourselves wise, and count the truth as falsehood, not worshiping the Creator, who is the living and true God, but worship idols instead.
4. Furthermore, you constantly oppose the truth, rejecting God's testimonies and his grace.
5. Though you are stubborn and rebellious, God has not forsaken you, but constantly seeks you out, stretching out his hand and calling to you.
6. So, you must repent, hear and heed his call, accept his saving grace, and submit to the Savior, so that you may pass from death to life.
7. Finally, Paul warns them, urging them to repent, saying, "Truly these times of ignorance God overlooked, but now commands all men everywhere to repent, because he has appointed a day on which He will judge the world in righteousness by the Man whom He has ordained" (Acts 17:30–31).

We should imitate Paul and his spirit, employing his methods, not clinging to what is inadequate, but adding "to [our] faith . . . knowledge" (2 Pet 1:5). We ought to study deeply and understand our nation's culture, philosophy, religion, and similar matters, so that we can apply the truth to today's situation and "dispense the right medicine to the disease" when preaching the gospel to our countrymen, especially to intellectuals. We should advise the proponents of indigenous theology to see clearly the differences between Chinese traditional culture, philosophy, and religion, and Christianity, so that they do not try to compare things that cannot be compared or compromise the truth. They must not think that "all paths lead to the same destination," lest they all lead to the same destruction, because "There is a way *that seems* right to a man, but its end *is* the way of death" (Prov 14:12; 16:25). We need to have a heart that sees others' loss as our own, as Moses did when he called upon heaven and earth, making

Critique of Indigenous Theology

clear the path of life and the path that leads to death and urging them to turn back from the brink of the precipice and not to "offer profane fire before the Lord" (Lev 10:1, 3; Num 3:4). We must beware of using human hands to weave a heavenly garment, lest we ourselves perish.[33]

Strategy for Comprehensive Apologetics

Most advocates of indigenous theology are intellectuals who are unwilling to spend much energy studying the Bible. They quote out of context to suit their own purposes; make far-fetched comparisons; willfully distort facts; confuse the truth; and have a high opinion of themselves, thinking that their ideas are innovative, thereby foolishly imagining that they can be counselors to God. It is possible, of course, for the power of the Holy Spirit to grant enlightenment and heartfelt repentance to these intellectuals. St. Augustine, for example, was misled by Greek philosophy in his youth; it poisoned his mind, and he carried on a degraded lifestyle. During a period of discouragement and loss of purpose in life, he was weeping under an olive tree when suddenly he received a revelation from heaven as he heard a voice saying, "Take up and read! Take up and read!"[34] As he opened the Bible and read Rom 13:12, 14, which says, "The night is far spent, the day is at hand," a shaft of light entered his soul. God called him from darkness into his marvelous light, and he received new life. Thenceforth he was a different man, as his doubts were dispelled, his faith confirmed, and he became a path-breaking theologian.[35] Readers of my books have similarly offered remarkable testimonies. For example, one stubborn anti-Christian college student, by chance opening one of my books, was thrown to the ground by a strong power, repented of his sins with bitter tears, and afterwards testified to the truth of the gospel. Another youth, a Westerner, while deep in meditation, was possessed by an evil spirit, and was struck by panic. When he opened and read one of my books, he saw a bright light, and was delivered from fearful darkness into marvelous light. After that, he dedicated his life to preaching the truth of the gospel. There was even a man who had preached for several decades who, when he read some of my books, received the joy of real rebirth and spent night and day kneeling before the Lord and praising him. As the orthodox theologian to

33. *The Collected Works of Charles S. Spurgeon.*

34. Actually, Augustine says he thought he heard the voice of a child, but could find no one nearby, so he concluded that God had spoken to him.—Ed.

35. Taylor, *Augustine, Wayward Genius*, chap. 5.

whom I referred earlier, Gresham Machen, said, however, "God can use supernatural power to sweep away obstacles to the gospel, but he does not ordinarily do so because he does not want us to enjoy the fruits of others without having toiled ourselves. His power usually employs our minds to manifest itself. We must not rely only on religious fervor but must engage in hard intellectual labor. The greatest barrier to the saving faith is the intellectual class. It is a pity that we have evaded the crucial point and attended to what is less important. The church is now suffering the consequences of this neglect." With many years of experience in sharing the gospel with intellectuals, Dr. Francis Schaeffer warned the church, saying, "In this age of doubt and unbelief, people have stereotyped ideas about religion, thinking that it has lost meaning. Most evangelicals only mouth slogans, and have no real message to proclaim. Even worse, these Christians have come under the influence of this age's irrationalism."[36] (Rationalism, of course, has many deficiencies, which I have critiqued in volume 2 of *Comprehensive Christian Apologetics*, but we must not "give up eating in order to avoid choking," and abandon reason entirely). They believe that reason cannot answer the questions asked by mankind, thinking that we should rely instead on piety or zeal to gain spiritual victories. There are also those who "cherish the outmoded and preserve the outworn"; repeat platitudes; and can only passively resist the enemies of the church. They are unable to use creative biblical theology to mount an offensive and overcome foes of the truth.[37]

In our offensive against non-Christian ideas, if we go for their weak points we shall be "more than conquerors." If we examine the works of proponents of indigenous theology, we shall see that they are all humanists and have not been born again, but are merely natural men. As the Bible says, "The natural man does not receive the things of the Spirit of God" (1 Cor 2:14). With this fundamental weakness, though they speak at length about Chinese religion and Christian theology, they are completely ignorant of the true meaning of religion, and lacking even the simplest knowledge of theology. With this in mind, we should take the following three approaches in confronting them:

---

36. Or "antirationalism."—Ed.
37. Schaeffer, "The Evangelical Outlook."

Critique of Indigenous Theology

Man-Based Philosophy

According to the definition of the Greek philosophers, humanism takes "man as the measure of all things." Man, therefore, is the center of their system; God is not Lord of all. Man is the wellspring of all value; God is not the source of righteousness and holiness. Thus, "human nature" and "God's nature" are disconnected, and man has no part in divine attributes such as righteousness and holiness. Although they seek to "cultivate virtue, exercise self-discipline, and regain one's original nature," they are finally still under the control of the power of sin, and have not "escaped the corruption *that is* in the world through lust" (2 Pet 1:4). There is no way to transcend worldliness and attain holiness, or attain to the realm of perfection. Even more dangerously, they do not believe in the existence of a personal God, but philosophize him, turning him into a concept of their own vain speculation, such as "the social ideal," "the spirit of mankind," "the Great Ultimate," "the Infinite," "the nature of the universe,"[38] and other symbols. In this way they completely sever the relationship between God and man. They seek to gain knowledge through observation, and earnestly desire the truth, but merely investigate the universe and the purpose of life, and fail at the very source of truth. "They want to imitate the holy sages," and "understand virtue and cultivate themselves," but they do not know that "men are not what they were in ages past"; "human nature is hard to change"; or that, as Paul wrote, in our flesh "nothing good dwells; for to will is present with me, but *how* to perform what is good I do not find" (Rom 7:18). Knowledge is not united with conduct, a fact which even Confucian scholars admit is "the tragedy of the sage."[39]

Man's fundamental mistake is to rebel against the true God, to go his own way, not heeding God's commands, but constantly being enticed by the devil and imagining that if he eats the forbidden fruit his eyes will be opened and he will have wisdom and intelligence, just like God. This first fatal misstep is the root of the awful tragedy of human history (see Gen 3). The rotten root of humanism can be found at just this point.

Today's humanists become worse and worse, and are pompous and insolent. There is no God before their eyes. They elevate the value of man,

---

38. *Zhen ru*, *Tathāta*.—Ed.

39. See Chen Gong, "Shengren zhi yu Tiandao" ("The Heavenly Course and the Sage"), *Rensheng* (*Life*), issue 224. One passage says that "no matter how sublime a personality the sage can rise up to, it cannot demonstrate (show) fully and completely the heavenly course or God . . . This is what Mr. Mou Zongsan called 'the tragedy of the sage' (*shengren de beiju*)."

Christian Doctrine and the "Substance-Use [Essence-Application] Principle"

but degrade God's position. They erroneously create God in man's image. Comparing him to 'the spirit of man," "the social ideal," even "self-deification," they replace God with man. They also impose their understanding on the Scriptures, misinterpret the Bible, and make a forced comparison of the revelation of the true God with the hollow sayings of their sages and men of virtue. They equate Christian doctrine with human philosophy, not realizing that the two are totally different. The former is revealed, the latter is from reason; the former is supernatural, the latter is of the world; the former is absolute, the latter is relative; the former is complete, the latter is limited; the former is eternal, the latter is temporary; the former is God-centered, the latter is man centered. So these two systems really can't be mentioned in the same breath. I have discussed this at length elsewhere.[40]

"The message of the cross is foolishness to those who are perishing, but to us who are being saved it is the power of God. For it is written: 'I will destroy the wisdom of the wise and bring to nothing the understanding of the prudent.' Where *is* the wise? Where *is* the scribe? Where *is* the disputer of this age?" (1 Cor 1:18–20). Where are the ancient sages? Where is the prolific scholar? Though it is said, "Establish your speech and your virtue," what we call "being remembered for a thousand generations" is really narcissism and self-consolation; we cannot change the fact that these people are dead and gone. As the Scriptures says, "A man can receive nothing unless is has been given to him from heaven" (John 3:27). Again: "Whether *there is* knowledge, it will vanish away" (1 Cor 13:8). This is God's very solemn warning to those who falsely trust in worldly wisdom, and is the ultimate sorrowful condition of humanists, who will eventually return to nothingness. The Way is "not far from each one of us" (Acts 17:27). Repent and be saved! "God so loved the world that He gave His only begotten Son, that whoever believes in Him should not perish but have everlasting life" (John 3:16). The one who believes in Jesus, "though he may die, he shall live. And whoever believes in [Him] shall never die" (John 11:25–26). God "desires all [sorts of] men to be saved and to come to the knowledge of the truth" (1 Tim 2:4). May God's infinite mercy move in the hearts of proponents of indigenous theology, that they may abandon humanism, which amounts to "empty deceit, according to the tradition of men, according to the basic principles of the world" (Col 2:8); turn from error to understanding; and "turn around and allow faith to arise." May the glorious light of the gospel shine in their hearts (see 2 Cor 4;4) and bring them "from darkness to light, and *from* the power of Satan to God" (Acts 26:18),

---

40. See *Critique of Humanism* in this volume.—Ed.

so that they might see "the hope of His calling, . . . the riches of the glory of His inheritance in the saints" (Eph 1:18), a hope that is "living," and brings "an inheritance incorruptible and undefiled and that does not fade away, reserved in heaven for" those who believe (1 Pet 1:3–4).

The Real Definition of Religion

Proponents of indigenous theology prattle about religion, but they are completely at a loss when it comes to distinguishing between true and false religion. They don't know how to make important distinctions: They imagine that the sense of justice and rationality is the same for everybody. "All paths lead to the top of Mt. Fuji." Some of them take religion as philosophy, but do not know that true religion is not philosophy, and is not worldly knowledge, but is the revelation of God and the salvation of God. The Bible says, that our "faith should not be in the wisdom of men but in the power of God" (1 Cor 2:5) and that "the kingdom of God *is* not in word but in power" (1 Cor 4:20). Therefore, "beware lest anyone cheat you through philosophy and empty deceit, according to the tradition of men, according to the basic principles of the world, and not according to Christ" (Col 2:8). Or they mistake religion for ethics, not realizing that true religion is the marvelous grace and love of God. The gospel of the Lord coming to earth to save men is not an ethical teaching for advising and regulating people. To be sure, Christianity is an ethical religion; it has a supremely holy and good model, with a goal that saints should always honor, but ethics and salvation are inseparably connected with each other, with salvation as the root and ethics as the fruit. Only a true religion of redemption can become a true ethical religion. "When what is fundamental has been established, then the Dao grows naturally." "We must know what is prior and what should follow." We must repent and turn to the Lord; that is the key issue, for holiness and righteousness are attributes of God. The words of the sages are replete with good words and beneficial sayings and the teaching of virtue and ethics. Even Laozi said, "When the Great Dao was demolished, benevolence and righteousness appeared. Only when craft emerged was there great deception."[41] Thus, Confucius received Laozi's rebuke, "You should abandon your pride, desires, pretensions, and unbridled ambitions. These are not good for you." Entirely won

---

41. See *Dao De Jing*, chap. 18. Quotations are from Huang, *Tao Te Ching*. An alternative translation would be "When wisdom and shrewdness appeared, there ensued great hypocrisy."—Ed.

Christian Doctrine and the "Substance-Use [Essence-Application] Principle"

over, he felt inferior to Laozi and urged his disciples to promote Laozi's teachings. In great admiration of Laozi, he said, "I know that birds can fly; I know fish can swim. I know that beasts can walk. We can use a net to catch beasts; we can use fishing poles to catch fish; we can set a trap for birds. As for dragons, they can ride the winds and the clouds up into heaven. Seeing Laozi today, I felt as if I have seen a dragon."[42] What flattery of Laozi this is! Human ethical teaching is only "great deception," not "the great Way"! Furthermore, the righteousness of men is like "filthy rags" in the sight of God (Isa 64:6), and does not comply with God's holy standard. "Unless your righteousness exceeds *the righteousness* of the scribes and the Pharisees, you will by no means enter the kingdom of heaven" (Matt 5:20). Third, human goodness is only the self-righteousness of the old man. They say, "Preserve virtue in one's heart and cultivate oneself." "Abandon what is evil, evince what is good."[43] All this comes only from God's common grace. We can pretend that all is going well in society and "apply ointment" for a while. Only when we are empowered by God's special grace, which comes through the redemption wrought by the death of Christ, and by relying on the sprinkling of the shed blood of Jesus, the transforming work of the Holy Spirit, which causes us to be born again and sanctified, can we constantly "[escape] the corruption *that is* in the world through lust," and become "partakers of the divine nature" (2 Pet 1:4). Our salvation is from God, not our own self-righteousness. Human autosoterism[44] is the heresy of Pelagius, and the common malady of secular religion and indigenous theology. Now the whole world is noisy and confused, like a cauldron boiling with dissension. It is extremely wicked and ripe for punishment, which is clear proof of man's refusal of God's salvation and of the failure of self-righteousness.

Real religion is revealed religion, God's way of salvation. It is tragic that the whole world is ignorant of this religion. Foolish men and women worship idols, which is ignorant folly. But even intellectuals, including proponents of indigenous theology, do not understand the real meaning of religion.

In the area of moral conduct, some explain religion in their own way, taking it as a way to cultivate their character or accumulate virtue to make up for their faults, not knowing that "the heart [of man] *is* deceitful above all *things*, and desperately wicked" (Jer 17:9). "Can the Ethiopian change

---

42. Sima Qian, *Historical Records*, "Laozi."
43. *Great Learning*, in Chan, *A Source Book*.
44. "Salvation by one's own efforts."—Ed.

his skin or the leopard its spots?" (Jer 13:23). It is said that "it is easier to change rivers and mountains than to change human nature"; how much more true is it that in the eyes of God, human righteousness is like "filthy rags" (Isa 64:6). Jesus declared to his disciple, "Unless your righteousness exceeds *the righteousness* of the scribes and the Pharisees, you will by no means enter the kingdom of heaven" (Matt 5:20).

Or, in the area of reason, some are trying to gain understanding by themselves, using religion to gain clarity about their own nature to turn from error to understanding, to be enlightened, and to be liberated from existence. They don't know that the mystery of the Way[45] is "hidden . . . from *the* wise" (Matt 11:25). Our "faith should not be in the wisdom of men but in the power of God" (1 Cor 2:5), "but God has revealed [His mysteries] to us through His Spirit. For the Spirit searches . . . the deep things of God" (1 Cor 2:10).

Or, in the realm of emotions, seeking relief and consolation by themselves, some make religion into an emotional crutch that will relieve the troubles of their heart. They do not know that the pain of mankind issues from the sin of our original parents (see Gen 3:16, 19). The whole world lies in the power of the evil one (1 John 5:19). We must rely on God's grace to "be delivered from the bondage of corruption" so that we may gain "the glorious liberty of the children of God" (Rom 8:21) and be "raised . . . up together, and . . . sit together in the heavenly *places* in Christ Jesus" (Eph 2:6); be eternally protected and kept by the Lord (John 10:28–29); and receive "an inheritance incorruptible and undefiled and that does not fade away, reserved in heaven" for us (1 Pet 1:4).

The true meaning of religion is a mystery hidden from eternity, but now revealed to believers through the Holy Spirit and disclosed in these last days by the incarnation of the Son of God. It was also "confirmed to us by those who heard *Him*, . . . God also bearing witness both with signs and wonders, with various miracles and gifts of the Holy spirit, according to His own will" (Heb 2:3, 4). Most people don't believe, because "the god of this age has blinded" their minds, "lest the light of the gospel of the glory of Christ . . . should shine on them" (2 Cor 4:4). May God "give a spirit of wisdom and revelation" to those intellectuals and superstitious pagans and indigenous theology advocates, that they might "know Him" (Eph 1:17) and believe in him. Would that they would "count as loss for Christ" all the things that "were gain" to them before, "for the excellence

---

45. Or *Dao*.—Ed.

of the knowledge of Christ Jesus [the] Lord" (Phil 3:8) and join me in bearing testimony to Christ.

I myself once indulged in Confucianism, Daoism, and Buddhism, and intended to revive Eastern religion and culture. I didn't expect that in later years I would receive God's grace by coming to a sudden understanding of the truth. Therefore, with all my heart "when I saw someone else drowning, I felt as if I myself were drowning." I began to speak the truth straight from my heart and to share my testimony. I deeply hope that the advocates of indigenous theology will come to an understanding of what I am saying.[46]

From the standpoint of God's revelation, there is a fundamental question concerning the relationship between theology and revelation. The advocates of indigenous theology talk a lot about theology, and think that they are making a unique contribution, but in fact they barely have any understanding of theology. It is like a person with no medical training who tries to be a physician. There is nothing more dangerous. "The task of systematic theology is to make a systematic and logical exposition of God's revealed truth."[47] "Theology is suitable for all men, and is not limited by time."[48] The fundamental teachings are universal, and do not change over time. Indigenous theology advocates, however, are "tossed to and fro and carried about with every wind of doctrine" (Eph 4:14), since they believe that truth will change according to the preferences of men, and that everyone will disagree with everyone else. "Theology is the science that concerns God, and if it is not correctly explained, error will result."[49] Proponents of indigenous theology, however, interpret God according to their own thinking. "Theology differs from most sciences in that it has the special characteristic of being absolute and unchanging."[50] God's word is "forever . . . settled in heaven" (Ps 119:89). "Heaven and earth will pass away, but My words will by no means pass away" (Matt 24:35). Scientific theories, on the other hand, can be overturned by new discoveries, and cannot be guaranteed of absolute accuracy. The "assured results" of a previous generation are often merely ephemeral.[51] A state-

---

46. I have written in more detail elsewhere on the subject of religious issues.

47. Shedd, *Dogmatic Theology*, vol. 1, chap. 3, "The Nature and Definition of Theological Science."

48. Coleridge, "Table Talk."

49. Shedd, *Dogmatic Theology*, vol. 1, chap. 3.

50. Ibid.

51. Or, "The infallible law of yesterday is now a dead letter."—Ed. See MIT Professor Vannevar Bush, *Fortune* Magazine; Chang, *Shengdao Zhenyan* (*A Defense of Christian Truth*), chap. 2, "The Faith of Scientists"; and other works by Chang.

Critique of Indigenous Theology

ment by the Royal Society of England declared that "the science of physics has not yet reached perfection; it is still in a state of constant progress. Our limited present understanding is like looking into a mirror; the image is still quite blurred. Many scientists today do not take the trouble to study the Bible, and yet raise doubts about it. This sort of attitude evokes nothing but pity!"[52] It is really not right for the proponents of indigenous theology to criticize and oppose Christianity in the name of science.

In short, according to the Lutheran and Reformed definition, "Theology is the science that concerns itself with God."[53] Or, "Theology is the science that deals with God and the universe."[54] Again, "Theology is the science that deals with God; it speaks of the relationship between God and the universe."[55] Charles Hodge writes, "The goal of theology is to search out, organize, prove, and expound the truths and facts of the Bible, and their relationships with each other."[56] Abraham Kuyper and Herman Bavinck, though mostly agreeing with this statement, do not approve of the use of the term "prove," because "this is to come under the control of natural theology."[57] Kuyper especially points out that, "the object of theology is the knowledge that God has already revealed."[58] Bavinck believes that "the object of theology is God. Theology is the scientific systematic knowledge of God."[59] "Theology is entirely based on the Bible; it takes the Bible as its sole source to speak of God, and of God and his relationship with the universe."[60] All major orthodox theologians have the same view. Sadly, not only do proponents of indigenous theology not only ignore the Bible, but also vilify Christian truth. In their works, besides sometimes quoting out of context and twisting the Bible to suit their purposes, they never quote the Scriptures, but kowtow to our Chinese sages. Even more ridiculously, they deceive our people by saying that they are only seeking

---

52. Statement of the Royal Society, 1865, signed by 167 noted scientists. See the works by the Chang cited in the previous note.

53. See Berkhof, *Introductory Volume to Systematic Theology*, chap. 3.

54. Shedd, *Dogmatic Theology*, vol. 1, chap. 3.

55. Strong, *Systematic Theology*, 1.

56. Hodge, *Systematic Theology*, 1:1.

57. See Kuyper, *Encyclopaedie der Heilige Godgeleerdheid* (*Encyclopedia of Sacred Theology*), vol. 2; Bavinck, *Geneformeende Dogmatick* (*Reformed Dogmatics*), vol. 1.

58. Kuyper, *Encyclopaedie der Heilige Godgeleerdheid* (*Encyclopedia of Sacred Theology*), vol. 2.

59. Bavinck, *Geneformeende Dogmatick* (*Reformed Dogmatics*), vol. 1.

60. Warfield, "The Idea of Systematic Theology"; introductory note to Beatties, *Apologetics*.

to promote indigenous theology and remove the stench of the West, but they are only deceiving themselves, since they worship the most offensive sort of anti-Christian secular Western scholars and liberal theologians, obsequiously accepting their views in opposition to the truth. They "secretly bring in destructive heresies, even denying the Lord who bought them" (2 Pet 2:1–2). For example, Yanjing University[61] president Wu Leichuan follows the materialistic atheism of Marxism and supports revolution and dictatorship, as well as gaining political power by force.[62] Xie Fuya also advocates the hatred and struggle of materialistic, atheistic Marxism. He says, "The concept of a God who is an evil tyrant does not accord with a democratic, republican society," and urges an "independent, autonomous electorate" to "rise up and oppose God, building the kingdom of heaven ourselves, rather than allowing God to monopolize power."[63] The reason for these devilish doctrines, the root cause of their disease, is that they despise the Bible and do not believe in God's revelation. Their indigenous theology, therefore, abandons the rock and builds on shifting sand. The Lord long ago knew this, and therefore solemnly warned of "wolves in sheep's clothing" who are false prophets. Although they establish Christian universities and write books to propound their theories, they "cannot enter the kingdom of heaven." The Lord will rebuke them, saying, "I never knew you; depart from Me, you who practice lawlessness!" (Matt 7:23). "He will also say . . . 'Depart from Me, you cursed, into the everlasting fire prepared for the devil and his angels'" (Matt 25:41). God is a consuming fire, who may not be mocked. He is also loving, however. As long as we repent and believe, we can pass from death to life. His Word cannot ever be abolished, for the Bible is God's revealed Word, the rock on which theology is built. May God have mercy and lead the proponents of indigenous theology from the sand back to the rock so that they also may obtain the incorruptible inheritance that is reserved for us in heaven.

God's revelation can be divided into two categories. The first is called general revelation and the second, special revelation. This distinction is extremely important. Because they do not understand its meaning, proponents of indigenous theology commit a serious error. A small mistake at the beginning has enormous and deleterious consequences. The recipients of general revelation (or natural revelation; but the latter term is not as suitable as the former, so we shall use the former) are ordinary people,

---

61. Formerly Yenching.—Ed.
62. See chap. 3 of this book.
63. See chap. 3 of this book.

Critique of Indigenous Theology

not necessarily those who have been born again. These would include also heretics, nominal Christians, liberal theologians, and proponents of indigenous theology. The purpose of general revelation is to enable people to know that there is a God (so that they are without excuse; see Rom 1:20–21) and thus to seek God. By relying only on general revelation, however, it is difficult to gain a complete insight, and we cannot know the correct way to life.[64] This sort of revelation, therefore, can only provide us with very unclear knowledge, but cannot offer an accurate, much less infallible, knowledge of the Triune God, who is the only true God. That is why liberal theologians do not know Jesus as the Son of God, for they deny his deity. Proponents have many ridiculous theories and cannot understand the spiritual things of God, which "are foolishness" to such people (1 Cor 2:14). Secondly, general revelation cannot provide an understanding of the true meaning of sin, which they take to be merely a shortcoming that can be overcome by cultivating ourselves and thus saving ourselves. They thus fall back into the heresy of autosoterism.[65] Some pagan religions only speak of human suffering (such a Buddhism's *ku di* and *kong ku*—"emptiness-suffering" philosophy), but do not know that the root of suffering is sin (Gen 3), so their teachings cannot save people from suffering and pain, take away the sins of the world, or become a means of salvation. Third, because they are ignorant of God marvelous grace and cannot know the only way to salvation, and are therefore misled by the Chinese idea that "the different religions do not contradict each other," they think that all ways lead to the same destination. They therefore promote the movement to fuse all religions together, but end up leading all men to the same destruction.[66]

Let us now look at the means and effect of general revelation. The means of general revelation include natural phenomena, human history, and the human heart. As for natural phenomena, as it is written in the *Book of Songs* (*Odes*), "Heaven, in producing mankind, gave them their various faculties and relations with their specific laws." "The doings of Supreme Heaven have neither sound nor smell." In the *Yijing* it is written, "Vast is the great and originating power, indicated by the hexagram *qian*. All things owe their beginning to it. It contains all the meaning belonging

---

64. Calvin, *Institutes of the Christian Religion*, vol. 1, chap. 3; 5, p.14.

65. See chap. 3 of this book.

66. See Berkhof, *Introductory Volume of Systematic Theology*; and Chang, *Jiushi zhi Dao* (*The Way of Salvation*).

Christian Doctrine and the "Substance-Use [Essence-Application] Principle"

to 'Heaven.'" "Heaven is the origin of all things."[67] "The great attribute of Heaven and earth is the giving and maintenance of life. Heaven and earth exert their influences, and there ensued the transformation and production of all things."[68] "The benevolent person considers Heaven and earth and all things as one."[69] "The wind blows, the rain falls, there is thunder and lightning, the flower blossoms and falls off—how could this be without a God?"[70] The Bible also tells us, "The heavens declare the glory of God; and the firmament shows His handiwork. Day unto day utters speech . . . Their line has gone out through all the earth" (Ps 19:1–4). Paul spoke of "God, who made the heaven, the earth, the sea, and all things that are in them, who in bygone generations allowed all nations to walk in their own ways. Nevertheless He did not leave Himself without witness in that He did good, gave us rain from heaven and fruitful seasons, filling our hearts with food and gladness" (Acts 14:15–17).

> God, who made the world and everything in it, since He is Lord of heaven and earth, does not dwell in temples made with hands . . . And he has made from one blood every nation of men to dwell on all the face of the earth, and has determined their pre-appointed times and the boundaries of their dwellings, so that they should seek the Lord, in the hope that they might grope for Him and find Him, though He is not far from each one of us; for in Him we live and move and have our being. . . . Truly, these times of ignorance God overlooked, but now commands all men everywhere to repent, because He has appointed a day on which He will judge the world in righteousness by the Man whom he has ordained. He has given assurance of this to all by raising Him from the dead. (Acts 17:24–31)

Paul also wrote, "What may be known of God is manifest in them, for God has shown *it* to them. For since the creation of the world His invisible *attributes* are clearly seen, being understood by the things that are made, *even* His eternal power and Godhead, so that they are without excuse" (Rom 1:19–20).

As for human history, the *Book of History* says, "God withholds his blessing, but bestows all sorts of benefits to those who do good, and all sorts of bane on those who do evil." "Great Heaven has no partial affections; it

---

67. Dong Zhongshu.
68. Chen Mingdao.
69. Chen Yichuan.
70. Zhu Xi.

helps only the virtuous." "If Heaven allows him to prosper, who can ruin him? The one who disobeys the mandate of Heaven will bear a great punishment." "The ones who commit many acts of unrighteousness are bringing death upon themselves." "God is wise, just, and consistent"[71] and he alone. The Bible says, "All our fathers were under the cloud, all passed through the sea, . . . but with most of them God was not well pleased, for *their bodies* were scattered in the wilderness. Now these things became our examples, to the intent that we should not lust after evil things as they also lusted. And do not become idolaters, . . . Nor let us commit sexual immorality, . . . nor let us tempt Christ, . . . nor complain . . . Now all these things happened to them as examples, and they were written for our admonition" (1 Cor 10:1–11). In 2 Peter we read, "God . . . did not spare the ancient world . . . bringing in the flood on the world of the ungodly; and turning the cities of Sodom and Gomorrah into ashes, condemned *them* to destruction, making *them* an example to those who afterward would live ungodly" (2 Pet 2:4–6). Old Testament prophets were the earliest philosophers of history. They not only narrated historical events, but added God's revelation, so that we can see God's action behind the happenings in history and can understand the meaning of history. Even the great powers of Egypt, Assyria, and Babylon, though they seemed to be enemies of Israel, were in reality instruments in the hand of God. "The wrath of man shall praise You" (Ps 76:10). In fact, God used these nations to carry out his purposes. The prophetic books in the Old Testament are definitely not just about yesterday and useless now, but communicate abiding truths and inspire us to think deeply.[72] God is the Lord of history, governing the affairs of men; even at the darkest times he does not "take his hands off the controls" or leave his throne. He will reward good and punish evil and execute just judgment. He "changes the times and the seasons; He removes kings and raises up kings; . . . He knows what *is* in the darkness, and light dwells with Him" (Dan 2:21–22). Both good and evil work together for good (Rom 8:28). Man's unbelief and disobedience will bring severe consequences. "Do not be deceived; God is not mocked; for whatever a man sows, that he will also reap" (Gal 6:7–8).

With regard to the human heart as a locus of general revelation, John Calvin said that the Lord "placed the idea of God" into man's mind, and causes it to increase, constantly protecting it and not allowing to be extinguished. The deepest reason that people hunger for righteousness,

---

71. *Spring and Autumn Annals (Zuozhuan)*.
72. See Chang, *Jiuyue zonglun* (*Studies in the Old Testament*).

Christian Doctrine and the "Substance-Use [Essence-Application] Principle"

searching for truth and propagating it, is that there is a "seed of religion" in their hearts. God's infinite mercy is demonstrated by the fact that all nations have religion, for God has placed that seed within their hearts. Because of our sin and corruption, however, we do not cherish or hold on to God's grace, but destroy it or find other things with which to replace it, creating many idols in our own image (Note: even atheistic communists turn their leader into an idol). God has not only sown the seed of religion in our hearts, but has also, through created things, demonstrated his wisdom and honor, as well as his "eternal power and Godhead" (see Rom 1:19–20). Sadly, though God constantly reveals himself, we constantly degrade and corrupt this concept of God and the "seed of the Word"—this is truly the tragedy of human history![73] Dr. William Schmidt, the first professor of anthropology at the University of Vienna, filled twelve volumes to discuss "the origin of the idea of God" (*Der Ursprung der Gottesidee*), demonstrating that there is real evidence for Calvin's view, for the earliest peoples all had faith in a "God," and only changed later to worship material objects and spirits, mythical creatures, superstitious belief in various ghosts and similar beings. The famous evangelist Billy Graham said, "Conscience is the clearest evidence of the existence of God."[74] "What ten eyes behold, what ten hands point to [should be held in reverence]." "When a man is driven to an impasse, he will cry out to Heaven." Plato also writes, "Atheists appear strong on the outside, but when danger approaches, not one of them does not call upon God." French philosopher Voltaire began by opposing Christianity, predicting that the Bible would be extinct within one hundred years, but at the end of his life he cried, "God! Save me! Jesus! Save me!" What a terrible pity! Sigmund Freud claimed that religion is a childish mental illness, but in reality the opposite is true: Atheists Nietzsche and Thomas Paine both fell prey to serious mental illness. So, Feud's disciple Carl Jung disagreed with him, saying that the more educated and civilized men are, the more they succumb to mental disorders. According to the well-known sociologist Dr. Sorokin, 50 percent of all unbelievers suffer from serious mental illness. As Augustine's famous saying goes, we are created in the image of God, and unless we find him, our hearts will not know rest. According to his daughter, as he approached death, Stalin, who was an atheist, pointed towards heaven in an expression of unspeakable regret. Behind the Iron Curtain, though the church encountered unprecedented persecution and children were from earliest years indoctrinated in atheism, yet young people still turned to God

---

73. Calvin, *Institutes of the Christian Religion*, bk. 1.
74. Brown, *Day-by-Day with Billy Graham*, reading for November 9.

Critique of Indigenous Theology

with enthusiasm. God revealed his reality in men's hearts through the prospering of the church under persecution.[75]

As we have said earlier, however, we can have no hope of salvation through natural religion of general revelation. The reason is, first, that men do not have a correct knowledge of God, so they turn to self-deification or make their own god, turning the living God into an empty and imaginary philosophical concept. The advocates of indigenous theology believe that human personality can be equated with God's personality; they regard God as nothing more than "conscience," even to the point of identifying him with Yang Zhu's *I*, demoting the Lord Jesus to the status of a mere man, and the Holy Spirit into Mengzi's "heart of compassion."[76]

Second, they do not have an accurate understanding of sin, and so become conceited, self-righteous, and unwilling to repent of their sins. They ignore the horror of human sin, and cannot break free of the sting of death (which is sin; 1 Cor 15:55–56). Finally, they do not understand salvation correctly, so they wrongly try to save themselves, thus rejecting the Lord and denying the gospel, which is actually the most serious crisis facing mankind. Like most scholars of religion, liberal theologians and indigenous theologians do not at all realize the essential difference between general and special revelation, and utterly disbelieve in special revelation, so that they are unwilling to repent and be saved. Allow me to explain this further.

Special Revelation

The object of special revelation is the born again believer, the child of God. By his Spirit, God grants him revelation that only the spiritual person can fully comprehend. The natural, fleshly person, which includes all varieties of pagans, "Christians" who have not been born again, liberal theologians, and proponents of indigenous theology, cannot understand the gospel, and even consider it as foolishness. Nor do they comprehend special revelation, which only those who have the Holy Spirit can understand (1 Cor 2:14). One proponent of indigenous theology, as we have seen, goes so far as to say that Paul's sudden and radical change of heart was a symptom of mental illness.[77] Not to believe or repent and be born again, and to despise the miraculous work of the Holy Spirit, is especially foolish and even blasphemous.

---

75. See Chang, *Shijie mingren zongjiaoguan* (*Religious Thought of Famous Men of the World*); and Chang, *Jiaohui Fuxing zhi Yisyang* (*The Revival of the Church*).

76. See chap. 3 of this book.

77. See chap. 3 of this book.

Christian Doctrine and the "Substance-Use [Essence-Application] Principle"

The content of special revelation falls into three categories. In biblical history, starting with Abraham, God, through the Law, the prophets, and his judgments, made human beings realize three truths: First, with respect to God, we understand the Trinitarian nature of God, his omnipresence, omniscience, omnipotence, holiness, righteousness, and incomparable glory. Second, with respect to men, we see the horror of original sin, our total depravity, and our utter inability to save ourselves. Third, with regard to the *Dao*,[78] we are enabled to know the great wonder of God's saving grace, which is completely dependable and irresistible. Those who believe gain life; those who do not believe perish (John 3:16).

The manner or means of special revelation can also be divided into three categories: First through the prophets. There is a fundamental difference between Christianity and pagan religions. The former is the revelation of the true God, and does not issue from man's thought or traditions. If the Confucian classics do not say, "the Book of Songs says," or "Book of Rites says," or "Confucius says," then they will say, "It is said by Yao, Shun, Yu, Tang, Wen Wu, or Zhou Gong."[79] As for the Buddhist Scriptures, they will use "This is what I heard" to pretend that they are being objective. In the Bible, however, "No prophecy of Scripture is of any private interpretation, for prophecy never came by the will of man, but holy men of God spoke *as they were* moved by the Holy Spirit" (2 Pet 1:20–21). When the prophets saw visions or heard the voice of God, they wrote down the words of God. That is why the often say, "This is the word of the LORD." Jesus referred to "all the prophets" (see Matt 11:13). The climax of revelation came with Jesus Christ, so he is the greatest prophet.

Second, through miracles. Miracles are the "revelation of fact"[80] and go hand in hand with God's verbal revelation, each one complementing and completing the other. According to his own will and purpose, God uses supernatural power and acts to verify his words and promises as well as the greatness of his saving grace (see Heb 2:4). The incarnation of the Lord Jesus was the climactic miracle, for in this way God revealed himself in the flesh, as "the Word became flesh, and dwelt among us ... full of grace and truth" (John 1:14), so that we can say that, "No one has ever seen God at any time. The only begotten Son, who is in the bosom of the Father, He has declared *Him*" (John 1:18), so that men could see him with their eyes

---

78. Or *word*.—Ed.
79. These are the Sage Kings of ancient China.—Ed.
80. Or *reality*.—Ed.

and touch him with their hands (1 John 1:1). As theologian J. Gresham Machen said, this is the greatest and highest blessing for mankind.

Third, through theophanies. In the Old Testament, the "Angel of the LORD" is the "bodily presence and speech of God." His climactic "presence" took place when God became incarnate in Christ. Through the Lord Jesus and his Holy Spirit, "Immanuel" —God with us—becomes a spiritual reality through the followers of Christ, the perfect manifestation of which will come when Jesus returns and the New Jerusalem descends from heaven. "For now we see in a mirror, dimly, but then face to face. Now I know in part, but then I shall know just as I also am known" (1 Cor 13:12). "Though now you do not see *Him*, yet believing, you rejoice with joy inexpressible and full of glory" (1 Pet 1:8). "Now we are children of God; and it has not yet been revealed what we shall be, but we know that when He is revealed, we shall be like Him, for we shall see Him as He is" (1 John 3:2).

"When Christ, *who is* our life appears, then you also will appear with Him in glory" (Col 3:4). When the Lord became flesh and was born in a manger, he took "the form of a bondservant." "Being found in appearance as a man, He humbled Himself and became obedient to *the point of* death, even the death of the cross" (Phil 2:6–8). This was his state of humiliation; his return will be in a state of glory.[81] "When the Lord Jesus is revealed from heaven with His mighty angels, in flaming fire taking vengeance on those who do not obey the gospel of our Lord Jesus Christ" (including the Indigenous Theologians, who wrongly explain the Scriptures), they "shall be punished with everlasting destruction from the presence of the Lord and from the glory of His power" (2 Thess 1:7–9). At that time, "the sun will be darkened, and the moon will not give its light; the stars will fall from heaven, and the powers of the heavens will be shaken. Then the sign of the Son of Man will appear in heaven, and then all the tribes of the earth will mourn, and they will see the Son of Man coming on the clouds of heaven with power and great glory. And He will send His angels with a great sound of a trumpet, and they will gather together His elect from the four winds, from one end of heaven to the other" (Matt 24:29–31). "Though He was rich, yet for your sakes He became poor, that you through His poverty might become rich" (2 Cor 8:9). He was God by nature, but for us became man; because of his humiliation in dying for us on the cross, he has caused us to "pass from death to life" and become children of God. "Our citizenship is in heaven, from which we also eagerly wait for the Savior, the Lord Jesus Christ, who

---

81. See Chang, *Zongti Biandaoxue* (*Comprehensive Christian Apologetics*), vol. 3, on religion.

Christian Doctrine and the "Substance-Use [Essence-Application] Principle"

will transform our lowly body that it may be conformed to His glorious body" (Phil 3:20–21). Now he is seated at the right hand of God, "far above all principality and power and might and dominion, and every name that is named, not only in this age but also in that which is to come" (Eph 1:20–21). Because he has completed the work of salvation, "God also has highly exalted Him and given Him the name which is above every name, that at the name of Jesus every knee should bow, of those in heaven, and of those on earth, and those under the earth, and *that* every tongue should confess that Jesus Christ *is* Lord, to the glory of God the Father" (Phil 2:9–11). Though we were dead in sin and "were by nature children of wrath, just as the others," God, "who is rich in mercy, because of His great love with which He loved us, . . . made us alive together with Christ, . . . and made *us* sit together in the heavenly *places* in Christ Jesus" (Eph 2:3–6).

The Apostle John received a great revelation of God on the island of Patmos, seeing Jesus appear to him in glory: "His head and hair *were* white like wool, as white as snow, and His eyes like a flame of fire; His feet *were* like fine brass, as if refined in a furnace; . . . out of His mouth went a sharp two-edged sword, and His countenance *was* like the sun shining in its strength. And when I saw Him, I fell at His feet as dead" (Rev 1:14–17; 21:1–8). The proponents of indigenous theology, not believing in God, say, "Man is the miniature of God; God is the perfection of man." They do not believe in the Bible or in God's revelation, but put their faith in non-biblical theories, "the elementary principles of this world," replacing the Bible with philosophy and replacing revelation with man's knowledge. Not believing in Christianity, they take it to be "inebriating poison for the youth and unsanitary water." They consider preachers of the Word to be "world-class criminals." They do not believe in eternal life, but in the "immortality of philosophy" or the "immortality of sociology." Not believing in regeneration, they claim that Paul's sudden conversion was a "symptom of mental illness." They do not believe in the kingdom of heaven, considering it "a terribly misleading superstition."[82] By the mercies of God, I urge them to "rein in the horse before it plunges over the precipice"; to forsake their own superstition and come to their senses; to turn from darkness to light, from the dominion of Satan to the rule of God. May God be gracious to them, granting them "the spirit of wisdom and revelation, . . . that the eyes of their heart may be [quickly] enlightened," that they may believe in and submit to the truth, receive grace, and be given the hope of glory. This is my fervent prayer.

---

82. See chap. 3 of this book.

10

Conclusion

Paul's Example

The Author's Own Bitter Experience

I DID NOT HEAR the gospel until late in life, at the age of fifty-three, when I became like an infant again and began afresh as a student.¹ When I opened the Bible and began to read it, I came to 1 Pet 3:15: "But sanctify the Lord God in your hearts, and always *be* ready to *give* a defense to everyone who asks you a reason for the hope that is in you, with meekness and fear." This sentence made a huge impact upon me, such that night and day I studied the Bible, seeking to comprehend the world, in order to help people believe in the only saving truth and receive the hope of eternal glory.² In order to redeem time lost in the previous fifty years, I resolved to do two days' work each day, making my evening dinner "breakfast for the next [working] day," resuming work from eight in the evening until three or four the next morning, then lying down to sleep for a while, arising again at half past six in the morning. This sort of extreme diligence shocked my entire family. My second son, Changde, when he came from Taiwan to America, discovered that I was still awake in the middle of the night, and was utterly dumbfounded. He would sit in my room until I had gone to

---

1. See chap. 1 of this book.
2. See Chang, *Jiushi zhi Dao* (*The Way of Salvation*); Chang, *Zongti Biandaoxue* (*Comprehensive Christian Apologetics*); Chang, *Asia's Religions*; Chang, *Critique of Chinese Humanism* (in this volume); Chang, *Liguo zhi Dao* (*The Foundation of a Nation*); *Shijie Renmin zhi Xiwang* (*The Hope of Mankind*); and other works.

bed, but when he had left I arose and returned to work. Afterwards, my family observed that I had actually become stronger and healthier. The stomach ulcer which I had had because of working too hard healed of itself, without any medicine. So, they stopped bothering me. Although I am now already about eighty years old, I run without becoming weary, and mount up on wings like an eagle (Isa 40:31). May God's name be praised!

The first book I wrote after my conversion to Christ was *Yuan Dao* (*The Way: An Investigation Concerning Divine Truth*). Then I wrote *Shengdao Tongquan* (*Exposition of the Truth: A Christian View of Culture*), first focusing on China's ancient concept of the Heavenly Way, in which I quoted many classic Chinese works, such as the *Book of History*; the *Book of Songs*; the *Book of Changes*; the *Analects* of Confucius; the *Dao De Jing*; *Zuozhuan*; *Records of History*; as well as the works of Confucians such as Dong Zhongshu, Zhou Dunyi, Cheng Mingdao, Chen Yichuan, Lu Xiangshan, Zhu Xi, Shao Kangjie, Wang Yangming, and others. As I said earlier, this led to great misunderstanding on the part of some conservative Christians, who thought I was promoting indigenous theology and were about to initiate a movement against me, not realizing that I was actually opposing indigenous theology. They had good motives, for sure, for they were trying to prevent the development of heresy, lest my mistakes become mainstream thinking. They were quite wrong in their understanding of what I was doing, however. Nor did they appreciate my hard work and evangelistic strategy. The purpose of my efforts was "pulling down strongholds" (2 Cor 10:4) and destroying the stereotypes among my countrymen, especially the intellectual leaders, about Confucianism, Buddhism, and Daoism, in order to get to the heart of the matter and eradicate the root of indigenous theology, thus removing obstacles to the Christian message. My strategy was to "go with the flow"[3] so that I could lead them to wholehearted agreement, turning from the hollow concept of the Heavenly Way to a humble search and pursuit of the truth, so that they could sincerely accept Christian doctrine. I wanted my fellow Chinese to be freed from the error of thinking that Christianity is a foreign religion, and help them not to believe the propaganda of Indigenous Theologians that Christianity has a Western stench. Actually, it is closer to our traditional Chinese concept of the Heavenly Way, so that for us to believe in Christianity is definitely not to "forget our roots." This strategy does not amount to explaining things in the wrong way, but is really meant to

---

3. That is, to start with what is known and accepted and then move to what is unknown and not yet believed.—Ed.

refute the far-fetched explanations of the Indigenous Theologians. Actually, I learned this way of preaching the gospel to my countrymen from the Apostle Paul, who became a Jew to the Jews in order to win the Jews, became weak in order to win the weak, and became all things to all men, in order that he might win some (see 1 Cor 9:20–22).

Thus, to the Chinese I became a Chinese, so that I might win the Chinese; to the weak—that is, Indigenous Theologians, who are weak in faith—I became weak, to the point of being misunderstood, as if I were promoting indigenous theology. In fact, however, by "going with the flow,"[4] I was seeking to turn people from what we Chinese, and especially the proponents of indigenous theology, so greatly treasure, namely our traditional concepts of the Way and of Virtue,[5] and "the legacy of the Chinese spirit," and other "weak ideas," so that they would no longer blindly close their eyes and their minds to Christianity, but might even come to believe in Christ. Actually, there is evidence that this approach has been effective. A Chinese pastor from Washington, DC has told me that my first Christian book, *Yuan Dao* (*The Way: An Investigation Concerning Divine Truth*), though it was a very immature work composed right after I trusted in the Lord, led to the conversion of a very senior scholar in Beijing. In 1968, the *Strategy of Missions in the Orient: Christian Impact on the Pagan World*, written hurriedly in one month for the Asia-Pacific Congress on Evangelism, was highly valued by church leaders. For example the School of Missions of Fuller Theological Seminary said that "every missionary should have a copy of this book, and every mission leader should study it carefully." Dr. Stanley Mooneyham of World Vision, who convened and presided over the congress, was so moved by the volume that he held a special seminar on the book to discuss the proper approach for missions to China. I have Paul to thank for the insight he gave me. He described himself as a "Hebrew of the Hebrews, . . . a Pharisee" (Phil 3:5–6), so he possessed a thorough understanding of their culture, and thus could "scratch an itching leg from the outside of the boot." He also had, however, the remarkable experience of being brought from "darkness to light, from Satan to God" on the road to Damascus, and of being "filled with the Spirit" and having the "scales" removed from his eyes in an instant (Acts 9:18; 26:9–20). Thus, he did not propound errors or compromise, or make the same mistakes made by proponents of indigenous theology. My

---

4. That is, "guiding them in the light of the general trend."—Ed.

5. Or *Dao* and *De*, the two characters in the title of the *Daode Jing* [*Tao Te Ching*] (*Classic of the Way and of Virtue*).—Ed.

preaching and writing are not the products of book knowledge only, or illusions of the mind, but issue from my previous fifty years of wandering in the darkness of paganism and the bitter experience of existence in the vast furnace of the world.

Tearing Down Strongholds: Adopting a Comprehensive Strategy

When a people forsakes its ancient religion and accepts a new faith, there will always be cultural and philosophical questions which must be thoroughly solved. For this, we must use a comprehensive strategy to tear down the strongholds of the devil in order to transform the non-Christian, man-centered systems and structures, clear away obstacles to the gospel, and allow the seed of the truth not to be eaten at once by birds and choked by thorns (Matt 13:3, 7). Only in this way can the truth "take root downward, and bear fruit upward" (Isa 37:31). China, we noted earlier, is an ancient nation with five thousand years of culture, so the problem will be even more serious, and cannot be resolved by reckless courage or intense emotions. Mere commonplaces and slogans, or "gospel platitudes" will not lead people wholeheartedly to believe the Christian message.

As Dr. J. Gresham Machen said, "The direct influence of Christianity upon the civilized world is daily decreasing . . . We cannot merely depend on religious feelings, but must also be constantly and intentionally engaging in strenuous mental effort. Recently, a popular notion has been overwhelming the whole world, one which despises the gospel as not being in keeping with the times. This idea not only prevents people from accepting the gospel, but leads them to scorn it as utterly useless."[6] Chinese proponents of indigenous theology even go so far as to say that the gospel is not as good as Confucianism, Daoism, and Buddhism, and that Christianity deeply misleads people into superstition, comparing it to unsanitary water. They criticize those Christians who cry, "Believe in Christ and you will be saved." They even claim that some Christians who shout, "Believe and be saved," although seeming to be dynamic and flamboyant, are really offering people poisonous wine to slake their thirst, thus killing them; such pastors, they say are really world-class criminals![7] They denigrate the gospel and despise it, saying it is poisonous. But some preachers

---

6. Machen, *Christian Faith in the Modern World*; and Machen, *What Is Christianity?*, chap. 12.

7. See chap. 3 of this book.

with pure faith, and most church publishing houses, seldom publish works which expound the mysteries of the faith. They write inconsistently, not understanding the culture, philosophy, and religion of China. They cannot, therefore, understand themselves or their enemies in order to win the battle for the mind. Especially the traditional literati consider Christianity to be naïve and shallow, far inferior to the profundity of Zhuangzi, the loftiness of Confucius and Mengzi, or the marvelous mystery of Buddhism. In this sort of environment, it is possible to for the church to gain new believers and even to seem to flourish for a while, but not really "take root downward, and bear fruit upward" (Isa 37:31).

It is said, "To capture the brigands, we must first seize their chief. To shoot a cavalryman, first shoot his horse." As far as strategy is concerned, to win over the intellectual leaders is more effective than winning over the masses. Zeng Guofan said, "Whether the customs and ethos of a place are good or bad depends largely upon one or two men." A person in favor with the general public will always influence tens of thousands to follow his lead. Buddhism developed in China precisely because it gained the adherence of thought leaders, even capturing the minds of the royal family. Dr. Francis Schaeffer, who in our day sought to preach the gospel to intellectuals, once offered the following warning to fellow evangelicals: "In this age of doubt and unbelief, people think that our religious platitudes are out of date and without meaning. Most evangelicals mouth empty slogans, but do not have a real message to preach . . . Some of them preposterously stick to outmoded ways, belittle reason, and imagine that by relying only on piety and zeal they can gain the victory, but do not realize that we must use creative biblical theology and actively go on the offensive to vanquish spiritual enemies and gain the victory."[8] As I said at the beginning of this book, in Hudson Taylor's day, at the Shanghai Missionary Conference, Dr. Edkins said something to this effect, "Confucianism, Buddhism, and Daoism are the strongholds which Satan has erected in China, with the intent of hindering the expansion of the Christian faith. These we must most vigorously assault. When these strongholds have been destroyed, China will become a nation ruled by the Prince of Peace, the Messiah, and this will be the greatest victory won by Christianity since the conquest of Roman political power and religion, as well as Greek philosophy."[9] Sadly, these strongholds have today not only been not destroyed, but proponents of indigenous theology want to come to their aid, and even to surrender to them and promote them. This amounts

---

8. Schaeffer, "The Evangelical Outlook."
9. *Records of the Shanghai Missionary Conference, 1877.*

to betrayal of our Lord, a source of sadness to his friends and of joy to his enemies. This is a latent danger to the Chinese church.

The Error of Indigenous Theology

The ancient Chinese concept of the Heavenly Way is much purer and loftier than today's heterogeneous and impure superstitious notions which are popular at all levels of society, ideas about gods and spirits, and worship of idols, for it is what theologians call primitive monotheism, and derives from God's general revelation. As John Calvin says, "God implanted the sense of God within men's hearts, and constantly causes it to intensify; he also protects it, and does not allow it to be extinguished. The real reason why people hunger and thirst for righteousness and ponder and proclaim the truth is that the seed of religion (*semen religionis*) resides within them. That pagan nations have religion is a sign of God's infinite mercy towards them and has sown the seed of religion in them. Sadly, because of mankind's sin and corruption, we have not treasured or preserved God's gift of mercy, but have destroyed it. We cannot, however, completely extirpate what God has implanted, though we can reduce its effectiveness in our lives, or displace it with anything else. Because we cannot live entirely without God, we forge many idols created in our own image." (Even the violently atheist Communists cannot refrain from making the Party and its head into idols, thinking to create a classless "kingdom of heaven" or "socialist paradise" on earth.) According to the convincing research of a professor at Oxford University, when Lenin's life was drawing to a close, he would often chat with a friend who was a priest, to whom, near the end, he said with bitter remorse, "I have made a great mistake! My most dreaded nightmare is that I am profoundly aware that I am perishing in an ocean of the blood of the countless innocent people whom I have slaughtered! I am deeply remorseful but cannot alter what has happened. To save Russia, however, the only thing is to ask ten holy men to pray for the nation." Stalin's daughter has testified that as her father's death approached, "one could see in his eyes an expression that was full of terror and remorse. Actually, he could not talk, but only pointed towards heaven with his hand and towards the people of high rank in the party and the nation, waving continuously and seeming to evince boundless remorse."[10] God has not only planted the seed of his word in men's hearts, but has also demonstrated

---

10. See Stalin, "Only One Year"; Graham, "A World Lost in Space"; and Chang, *Shijie Renlei zhi Xiwang* (*The Hope for Mankind*), chap. 11.

his holy wisdom and majesty through the created order, along with his eternity and deity (Rom 1:19–20). Sadly, however, though God constantly reveals himself, men constantly seek to destroy and ruin the essence of the "sense of God" and the "seed of his word" which he has implanted in them. This is truly the tragedy of human history![11]

We can see this tragedy being played out in the history of China. From the ancient classics, we see how the original concept of the "Heavenly Way"—what Calvin calls the "sense of God"—has been placed upon the foundation of such mutually contradictory ideas as the "Supreme Unity" (*Tai Yi*), the "Supreme Ultimate" (*Tai Ji*), "Supreme Limitless" (*Wu Ji*), and other mysterious fantasies by those scholars who take it as their duty to preserve and transmit the body of traditional Chinese orthodox teachings, so it is no wonder that the seed of the Word cannot "take root downward and bear fruit upward" in Chinese soil. If Christianity is going to be revived in China, therefore, we must not only actively abandon the superstitious beliefs, myths of monsters and gods, and idol worship of popular religion, but also take our ancient Chinese reverence for God off the imaginary and mysterious "sand" of such concepts and establish it upon the eternal, incorruptible "rock" [of revealed religion]. From a spiritual standpoint, we can say that Chinese people are facing a spiritual crisis, as they enact the "tragedy" of their history of which Calvin spoke, and as in the parable Jesus taught about the "fall" of the "house built on sand" when the "rains descended" and the "floods came" (Matt 7:24–27).[12] What shall we use as a "firm rock in the middle of the stream" to "do one's utmost to stem a raging tide"? Only a revival of the Christian faith can enable China's people to build upon the foundation of the "rock" (Christ). In other words, we must erase all "the futile traditions inherited from our ancestors," such concepts like *Tai Ji*, "Limitless," and other empty conceits, so that seed will not be "choked and dried." This is the necessary way and fundamental approach.

Sad to say, proponents of indigenous theology do not have such a plan, but merely repeat the mistakes of our forebears. They have imbibed the poison of liberal theology, compounding the evil, redoubling their efforts and thus making the "tragedy" even worse. They get things all backwards and fail to distinguish between essence and function, by taking philosophy as the foundation for theology. They do not regard the

---

11. Calvin, *Institutes of the Christian Religion*, bk. 1.

12. See Chang, *Minzu Xinling zhi Weiji* (*The Spiritual Crisis of the Nation*); Chang, *Liguo zhi dao* (*Foundation of a Nation*); and Chang, *Sunwen Zhuyi zhi Shenxue Jichu* (*The Theological Basis of the Thought of Dr. Sun Yat-sen*).

Scriptures as the standard of truth, being completely ignorant of the absolute transcendence of the Christian faith over time and space and of the truth that God's Word is "settled in heaven" forever (Ps 119:89). Advocates of indigenous theology, in order to make theology more indigenous and more Sinicized, reverse the proper order of things by elevating the sages of China and promoting the wisdom of men. They replace theology with philosophy, put man in the place of God, and substitute the thought of men for the revelation of God. That is why they can say that "theology differs, according to particular peoples and times." If things are as they say, there will be Chinese theology, American theology, Russian theology, English theology, French theology, German theology, Indian theology, Australian theology, African theology, and the theology of different nations in Latin America, all different, and no unanimous conclusion can be drawn as to which one is correct. More than that, they want to edit a "Chinese" Bible and create a Chinese Christianity.[13] They want another, "Chinese" Old Testament and a New "Chinese" Covenant with God.[14] They claim that "each age, each nation can have its own concept of God," and that "man is the miniature of God, and God is the perfection of man."[15] That is as much as saying that God is the creation of man and parents are their children's offspring, which is not only turning things upside down and mistaking the fruit for the root but also blasphemous and traitorous. They also fail to distinguish between essence (substance) and function (use).

Thus, I wish to state clearly that I always emphasize "being clear about the essence and knowing how to apply it to particular situations."[16] Failure to distinguish between essence and function is entirely different from "*mingti dayong*," for they are polar opposites. In 1968, I went on a lecture tour of seminaries in Taiwan, Hong Kong, the Philippines, Singapore and Indonesia; everywhere, I stressed that we must "understand the essence and apply it properly." We cannot hold on to what is outdated or stand still and refuse to make any progress. We must not cling to old ways, unwilling to accept anything new or "build a cart inside our house without ever having seen a cart," but we must adjust ourselves according to changes in place and time, get out of our ruts, and come down from our ivory tower, down to Mars Hill (Acts 17:22), and "earnestly contend for

---

13. See Xie, "Zhonggwo Wenti yu Jidujiao" ("China's Problems and Christianity"), *Mingbaoyue*, no. 107.

14. See Hu, "Old Testament and New Testament," *Ching Feng*, no. 3.

15. See Xie, *Zongjiao Jexue (Philosophy of Religion)*, 154–220.

16. *Mingti dayong*.

Critique of Indigenous Theology

the truth."[17] "Function" and "strategy" depend on the situation and must be adjusted accordingly. "Essence," however, pertains to the "truth" which is "settled in heaven" forever (Ps 119:89). One can cope with shifting events by sticking to a fundamental principle, and the essence remains the same despite all apparent changes. Christian truth is a universal standard of truth, eternal and never leading us astray. Sad to say, proponents of indigenous theology talk about "not distinguishing between essence and function (or essence and function are inseparable)." They accommodate in order to compromise, and they are even willing to "cut the foot to fit the shoe." They mix truth with heresy, leaving Christianity only an empty shell with no content. We must cut the cloth to fit our body, but we can't alter the ruler to do so. If we adjust the length of the ruler, then we don't know the true size, and we lose the function of the ruler to serve as a standard. This is the kind of principle that you can easily understand by yourself, but the proponents of indigenous theology do not understand it. "Although they knew God, they did not glorify Him as God" (Rom 1:21). They talk glibly, even condescendingly, about theology, but they have no idea what theology is, not knowing its foundation, but relying on pagan thought and secular notions (see 2 Pet 2:1). This produces an empty faith, "Christian" in name only, and is generating a crisis of faith among our people.

The "Rock" on Which Theology Is Built

The Choice Between Death and Life, Calamity and Blessing

Christianity and the religions of the world totally differ as to the truth of God's special revelation, "the mystery which from the beginning of the ages has been hidden in God" which "God, who at various times and in various ways spoke in time past to the fathers by the prophets, has in these last days spoken to us by *His* Son," (the Lord Jesus). This message "first began to be spoken by the Lord, and was confirmed to us by those who heard *Him*, God also bearing witness both with signs and wonders, with various miracles, and gifts of the Holy Spirit" (Heb 1:1–2; 2:2–4). This is not the wisdom of the world, "nor of the rulers of this age, who are coming to nothing" (1 Cor 2:6), so cannot be placed into the same category as any world religion and especially cannot be equated with any culture or

---

17. See Chang, *Dongzheng Ganhuai Lu (Reminiscences of My Journey to the East)*; *Strategy of Missions to the Orient*; *A Momentous Encounter with Paganism*; *Critique of Chinese Humanism* (in this volume); and *Zongti Biandaoxue (Comprehensive Christian Apologetics)*.

philosophy. "He who is of the earth, speaks of that which is earthly." "The rulers of this age" know "the wisdom of God's mystery," but seek to use "persuasive words of human wisdom" to proclaim the mystery of God; not believing in God's revelation, but using "the Supreme Unity" (*Tai Yi*), "Supreme Ultimate" (*Tai Ji*), and other concepts to explain the mystery of God, distorting God's truth in the process. They scorn the position of Christ, seeing him as only an ordinary man. They consider the Holy Spirit "nothing other than" the "sense of sympathy, sense of right and wrong, sense of propriety, sense of honor and shame," spoken of by Mencius or "the personification of love and goodness." They even proclaim the deification of man, asserting that "Man is the miniature of God," thus making those who are "dead in trespasses and sins," "conducting [themselves] in the lusts of [the] flesh, . . . [and thus] children of wrath" (Eph 2:1, 3) equal to God, in an extreme attempt to blaspheme God![18]

My study has led me to believe that the reason that proponents of indigenous theology put Christianity into the same category as other world religions and cultural religion; advocate the wisdom of the world; falsely believe in the wisdom of those who are "coming to nothing" (1 Cor 2:6); and even equate Christian truth with "unsanitary water" and mock Christian preachers as those who are "criminals" who are "dying from poison" is that they believe that Christianity is inferior to Confucianism, Buddhism, and Daoism, and give credence to Buddhism's Nirvana, not knowing that this is the "doctrine of the devil that leads to the suicide of the soul."[19] In this way, they elevate Buddhism as "the religion of the world that most enables us to know ourselves"—the reason they do all this, in all fairness, is not that they intend to despise the truth. The crux of the problem is that, as Paul wrote, "the natural man does not receive the things of the Spirit of God." ("Natural" is literally translated "fleshly," and refers to the person who is not born again.) Their limited spiritual understanding is not able to receive the revelation of God. That is why they cannot recognize the distinction between special revelation and general revelation, with the result that they indulge in far-fetched exegesis of Christian truth, making the mistake of thinking that it can be compatible with other religions. Because they are misled by the secular notion that Christianity and other religions are parallel but not contradictory, they confuse the Word of God with worldly religions and even seek to compromise with them, robbing Christianity of its distinctive essence and leaving only its name. They even

18. See chap. 3 in this volume.
19. See Xie, "Zhongguo Wenti yu Jidujiao" ("China's Problems and Christianity").

want God to acknowledge the Chinese classics as "China's Old Testament" and "establish a New, 'Chinese' Covenant."[20] They want to create a "Chinese" Bible. They do not know that the entire Bible is God's full revelation, so that "if anyone adds to these things, God will add to him the plagues that are written in this book" (Rev 22:18). Though we cannot totally obliterate the value of God's general revelation or its relationship with special revelation (see Rom 1:19, 21; 2:14–15; Acts 14:17; 17:27–28), yet we can say that general revelation is directed at the ordinary person, and that such a person, relying only on general revelation, absolutely cannot attain to full enlightenment or know the truth that leads to salvation.[21]

Why? First, because, though one can gain much vague knowledge of God, he cannot infallibly know the Triune God, or understand the spiritual things of God. All of intellectual history demonstrates that thinkers have not been able to escape error or free themselves from one-sided and narrow shackles of reason. Second, general revelation completely hides the marvelous saving grace of God, and cannot give knowledge of the only way of redemption. Third, general revelation cannot enable men to see the real meaning of sin, and even less take away the sin of the world; thus, it cannot serve as the foundation for salvation.[22] That is why China's ancient culture, philosophy, ethics, or religious thought cannot form a Chinese Old Testament. If we say that there are some redeeming features in the Chinese Classics, these derive from common grace, which enables us to tell right from wrong and to maintain some kind of morality and social order and get along with each other for a brief period of time. Otherwise, men will just kill each other and become monsters. On the other hand, pagans, liberal theologians, and proponents of indigenous theology, because they do not have the light of special revelation, cannot see the essential difference between general and special revelation, and this leads to real harm. It is really extremely serious. That is because, first, they do not know the true God, and thus fall into self-deification, fashioning God after their own image, and turning the true and living God into a philosophical concept. They "became futile in their thoughts, and their foolish hearts were darkened . . . [They] changed the glory of the incorruptible God into an image made like corruptible man"(Rom 1:21, 23), (such as Confucius, the Buddha, Lord Guan, King Yue, a local city god, ancestors), considering ghosts and gods as the same, even worshiping demons, thinking them to

---

20. See Hu, "Old Testament and New Testament," *Ching Feng*, no. 3.
21. See Calvin, *Institutes of the Christian Religion*, bk. 1, chap. 5, sec. 14.
22. See Berkhof, *Introductory Volume to Systematic Theology*.

be gods. Second, because they do not have an accurate knowledge of salvation, they mistakenly think that man can save himself, and even advocate the heresy of autosoterism. They reject the Savior, disbelieve the gospel, and imagine that "regeneration is nothing other than emphasizing the effort of self-improvement." They place their faith in the self-cultivation of Confucianism, believing that "by sudden enlightenment and training oneself to cultivate vital energy . . . one can become a virtuous gentleman . . . , which is the regenerate, new person that Paul emphasized."[23]

Third, lacking an accurate understanding of sin, they become self-righteous, coldly ignoring the horror of the wickedness of mankind, not knowing that "the wages of sin *is* death" (Rom 6:23). They are unable to escape the "sting of death"—sin (1 Cor 15:56)—and unaware that they are plunging themselves into eternal perdition.

Moses called out to heaven and earth as he presented the ways of life and death before the people of Israel and urged them not to err in their hearts so as to be seduced into the worship of other "gods." Rather, they were to love Yahweh alone and keep his ways and commands. I earnestly hope that proponents of indigenous theology will not wantonly destroy the "knowledge of God" that is in the hearts of Chinese people, the "seed of religion." May they not turn things upside down by trying to make philosophy the foundation of theology or replace the revelation of God with human speculation. May they not blindly follow the errors of heresy, thus defaming the word of God and repeating the "tragedy of human history." Otherwise, "when the Lord Jesus is revealed from heaven with his mighty angels, . . . [He will take] vengeance on those . . . who do not obey the gospel of our Lord Jesus Christ. These shall be punished with everlasting destruction from the presence of the Lord and from the glory of His power" (2 Thess 1:7–9). The Lord Jesus himself said, "Not everyone who says to Me, 'Lord, Lord,' shall enter the kingdom of heaven, but he who does the will of My father in heaven" (Matt 7:21). We are warned in the Book of Revelation that only those who "overcome" shall enter the new heaven and new earth. As for unbelievers, they "shall have their part in the lake which burns with fire and brimstone, which is the second death" (Rev 21:8). By the mercies of God, I plead with advocates of indigenous theology once again to heed the warnings of Scripture that "there is a way *that seems* right to a man, but its end *is* the way of death" (Prov 14:12). The true meaning of "all paths lead to the top of Mt. Fuji" is actually, "all die together." I hope

---

23. See Xie, *Zongjiao Zexue* (*Philosophy of Religion*).

Critique of Indigenous Theology

they will "rein in their horses at the brink of the precipice," and not go, every one, to his own way (Isa 53:6).

May God open the eyes of their hearts and bring them "from darkness to light, and *from* the power of Satan to God" (Acts 26:18), as happened to me when I was delivered from the darkness of paganism after fifty years. When I see others drowning, I feel as if I myself am also drowning. That is why I have spoken from my heart and composed this book with much toil and tears. Please do not imagine that this is just an ordinary book or regard it as unimportant. I hope that it will give you understanding and enable you to attain "to a living hope, . . . to an inheritance incorruptible and undefiled and that does not fade away" (1 Pet 1:3–4). Amen.

Critique of Humanism

Translator's Preface[1]

Samuel Ling

WITH A GREAT SENSE of honor and responsibility, China Horizon launched a translation project in 1997. The purpose: to introduce to the English-speaking public the apologetic writings of Dr. Lit-Sen Chang, the late Distinguished Professor of Missions at Gordon Conwell Theological Seminary, and author of over eighty Christian books and booklets.

As I read Dr. Chang's apologetics, I cannot help but be impressed by how his writings are biblical, relevant to the church's needs today, and written in beautiful Chinese style. I offer to you seven important reasons why Chang's writings deserve to be translated today:

1. Dr. Chang's apologetics are unashamedly biblical. Much contemporary Christian writing seeks to appease the non-Christian world by compromising in the areas of philosophy, culture, and religion. This is true today in the overseas Chinese church; it was true in the 1970s when Dr. Chang began his four-volume work on apologetics. He stands staunchly in the historical evangelical Protestant tradition in his faith, with no compromise. At every turn he provides a biblical alternative to secular philosophy, culture, and religion. (Indeed, volume 2 of the series, published in Chinese, is devoted to philosophy; volume 3 to religion; and volume 4 to culture.)

2. His apologetics are positive. Throughout his writings he offers a thoroughgoing critique of secular humanist philosophy, culture, and religion. However, the reader will miss out on the core of Dr. Chang's

---

1. Adapted from Ling, "Introducing the Apologetics of Lit-Sen Chang," in Chang, *What Is Apologetics?*, xxi–xxiv.

Critique of Humanism

thought if he/she walks away with only the critique. Dr. Chang powerfully proclaims the gospel—which he calls *sheng dao*, or "the Holy Word." Theologians call it "the whole counsel of God," or "the system of doctrine taught in Scripture." Apologetics has a negative task—exposing the errors of non-Christian thought. Apologetics also has a positive task—proclaiming the Word of God. This Dr. Chang does clearly and powerfully.

3. His apologetics are presuppositional. His critiques go to the core of non-Christian philosophy, culture, and religion, by exposing their underlying presuppositions. Thus Dr. Chang stands in the tradition of other masters of apologetics like Abraham Kuyper,[2] Cornelius Van Til,[3] and Francis Schaeffer.[4]

4. His apologetics are prophetic. Dr. Chang is not content only to critique non-Christian philosophy, culture, and religion, and to offer the gospel to his readers. He further points to both the need for, and the way to, rejuvenate culture in our day. He is convinced that Western culture and Chinese culture have both reached a crisis-point: will the world continue to decline, wallowing in secular humanist thinking and life? Or will the historic, biblical Christian faith "revive culture" by providing the powerful dynamic for a positive, Christian "all-embracing life system"?

5. His apologetics are global in scope. He spends much time evaluating Western philosophy, theories of religion, and general humanist culture. He also goes into thorough critique of Asian religions: Confucianism, Daoism, Zen Buddhism, Hinduism, and Islam. Before he became a Christian in the early 1950s, Dr. Chang's vision was to revive Asian religions and organize a Pan-Asian school of thought to save world civilization. After he became a Christian, he used his knowledge of Asian religions to offer an apologetic which speaks to minds both East and West. The reader interested in responding to contemporary New Age philosophy will find his evaluation of Hinduism especially helpful; in this Dr. Chang was prophetic.

---

2. Prime minister of the Netherlands, 1901 to 1905.—Ed.

3. Late professor of apologetics, Westminster Theological Seminary, Philadelphia.—Ed.

4. American pastor to young adult minds who lived for many years at L'Abri, Switzerland.—Ed.

6. His apologetics are spiritual. Dr. Chang defines apologetics as "theology at war." This is why he critiques secular humanism—East and West—and goes on to proclaim the gospel as the hope of world civilization. For too long, the church has either isolated herself from culture, offering only individualistic salvation with no regard to philosophical and religious challenges to the Christian faith; or the church compromises by embracing the thought-patterns of the world (e.g. the Social Gospel). Dr. Chang avoids both erroneous ways by stressing the spiritual warfare in which apologetics is engaged. This spirit of loving combat is evident throughout his writings. He has written many shorter works, addressed specifically to individual contemporary Chinese thinkers, urging them to consider Christ—for their own souls, and for the future of Chinese civilization.

7. His apologetics are clear. Dr. Chang's writing style is both high—coming from the background of a Confucian scholar—and clear—someone has commented that reading his works is like flowing along in a clear river; it just flows!

1

The Tradition of Chinese Humanism: Confucianism, Daoism, and Buddhism

CHINESE HUMANISM TOOK SHAPE through two representative traditions: Confucianism and Buddhism. It is true that other schools of thought have established themselves, such as Mozi's school of universal love, the Yang-Zhu school which advocated "each one for himself,"[1] Xu Xing (Hsu Xing) and Chen Xiang (Chen Hsiang) of the Agricultural School, Hui Shi (Hui Shih) and Gongsun Long of the School of Dialecticians, and Shang Yang and Han Feizi of the Legalist School.[2] Their influence, however, has been relatively insignificant. (The ideas of Daoism were distinct, but they were opposed to humanism, and therefore not a subject of our discussion here.) Confucianism taught the cultivation of the mind and self, and the manifestation of virtue and character. Buddhism pointed to the human heart, and taught the way to enlightenment and attainment of Buddhahood. Although they pursued very different paths, at its core, each was concerned with man in this life. They both believed that man can achieve the sagehood of Yao and Shun,[3] or Buddhahood.

---

1. *Mengzi (The Works of Mencius)*, "Jin Xin I," in Fung, 133.
2. Fung, *A History of Chinese Philosophy*, 312, 319.
3. Virtuous kings from the mythical prehistorical past.—Ed.

The Tradition of Chinese Humanism: Confucianism, Daoism, and Buddhism

Part 1. The Nature of Confucianism and Its World and Life View

Confucius' Pursuit: The Way

Throughout his life, Confucius earnestly sought the Way (*Dao*). He developed a deep understanding and awareness of life. "Having heard the Way in the morning, one may die content in the evening."[4] He was determined to cultivate himself and seek the *Dao*. He labored all his life to advance the cause of the *Dao* by teaching it to the people. He is the model teacher *par excellence* in Chinese history. All his pursuits and discipline, however, were limited to "the human" and "the earthly" realm (see John 3:12–21, 27, 31). "Human nature" (*xing*) and "the way of heaven" (*tian Dao*) are merely things "which none of us can comprehend."[5] All is vanity.[6] Even though Confucius was not an atheist, he taught that man should "respect the ghosts and spirits but keep them at a distance."[7] His famous question was: "We don't know yet about life, how can we know about death?"[8] This is a form of agnosticism, highly illustrative of its humanist core. In the beginning of *The Great Learning*,[9] he gave a clear and systematic exposition of the way to cultivate one's heart, life, family and nation:

> The Way of learning to be great[10] consists in manifesting the clear character, loving the people, and abiding (*zhi*) in the highest good . . .
>
> The ancients who wished to manifest their clear character to the world would first bring order to their states. Those who wished to bring order to their states would first regulate their families. Those who wished to regulate their families would first cultivate their personal lives. Those who wished to cultivate their personal lives would first rectify their minds. Those who wished to rectify their minds would first make their wills sincere. Those who wished to make their wills sincere would first extend their knowledge. The extension of knowledge consists in the investigation of things.

---

4. *Analects* 4:8, in de Bary, *Sources of Chinese Tradition*, 1:23.
5. *Analects* 5:12, in de Bary, *Sources of Chinese Tradition*, 1:30.
6. Chang, *Yuan Dao*, chap. 1.
7. *Analects* 6:20, in De Bary, *Sources of Chinese Tradition*, 1:29.
8. *Analects* 11:11, in ibid, 1:29.
9. *Da Xue*.—Ed.
10. Or *adult education*.

Critique of Humanism

> When things are investigated, knowledge is extended; when knowledge is extended, the will becomes sincere; when the will is sincere, the mind is rectified; when the mind is rectified, the personal life is cultivated; when the personal life is cultivated, the family will be regulated; when the family is regulated, the state will be in order; and when the state is in order, there will be peace throughout the world.
>
> From the Son of Heaven down to the common people, all must regard cultivation of the personal life as the root or foundation.[11]

The Bible's divine doctrine is: "The fear of the Lord is the beginning of wisdom" (Ps 111:10; Prov 1:7). But in Confucius's system of thought, the beginning of "the attainment (or extension) of knowledge" (*zhi zhi*) and the origin of any sincerity of will (*zheng*), uprightness (*cheng*), cultivation (*xiu*), rectification (*qi*), order (*zhi*) and world peace (*ping*) lies in "the investigation of all things" (*ge wu*) rather than "the fear of the Lord." This is a form of naturalistic humanism; it is also rationalism. Confucius's doctrines are not God centered, but man centered. So he said: "All must regard cultivation of the personal life as the root or foundation."[12] His ideal, his "kingdom of heaven," is to be built on earth. All one has to do, is to understand and manifest virtue (*ming de*) and cultivate one's own self (*xiu shen*). Good government and world peace will follow, and humanity will attain the *summum bonum*.[13] This type of humanism is thoroughly anthropocentric from beginning to end. Thus Chinese and Western scholars often refer to Confucianism as a "humanistic religion."[14]

The Ideal Government

Zhang Zai, a Confucianist thinker in the Song dynasty,[15] was an ardent student of ancient thought. He was absolutely convinced that sagehood was attainable. One could restore and revive the ideal government of the idyllic Three Dynasties.[16] Thus he wrote these ambitious words: "To build the heart for heaven and earth, to establish the mandate for the lives of the

---

11. *The Great Learning*, in Chan, *A Source Book*, 86–87.
12. *The Great Learning*, in Chan, *A Source Book*, 87.
13. Or *highest good*.—Ed.
14. Or *jen wen chiao*; Pinyin, *renwen jiao*.—Ed.
15. Also known as Zhang Hengqu (Chang Heng-ch'u), 1020–1077.—Ed.
16. The kingdoms of the mythical Yellow Emperor, Yao, and Shun.—Ed.

The Tradition of Chinese Humanism: Confucianism, Daoism, and Buddhism

people, to continue the best learning from the ancient sages, to open up world peace for ten thousand generations to come."

Before I turned to Christ by faith, before I was saved, I often quoted this passage in my writing. When my friends sought out my calligraphy, I would write these lines for them. I also hung them in my study to remind and constrain myself. I would travel widely, give lectures and stir up the Chinese people![17] After World War II, in response to the depraved mindset and lifestyle of the Chinese people, many scholars sought to revive "the spirit of Chinese humanism." They devised plans to establish a "humanistic religion" in order to propagate its principles to the world. This spirit can be vividly seen in the recent publication of "On Behalf of Chinese Culture: A Manifesto to the World" by Professors Chang Chunmai, Tang Junyi, and others.

Origin of Man and the Universe

When it comes to the origin of the universe and of mankind, Confucianism denies the doctrine of divine creation. Confucianists believe that the universe comes into being through the harmonious combination of the elements (*qi*) of *yin* and *yang*. In other words, the universe came about naturally. For example, *The Book of Changes*[18] states: "There is an intermingling of the genial influences of Heaven and Earth, and the transformation of all things proceeds abundantly. There is an intercommunication of seed between male and female, and all things are produced."[19] To be sure, *The Book of Odes*[20] says: "Heaven produces the teeming multitude; as there are things, there are their specific principles (*ze*),"[21] and "The operations of Heaven have neither sound nor smell."[22] *The Book of Changes* says: "Great is the *qian*, the originator! All things obtain their beginning from it. It unites and commands all things under heaven."[23] Nevertheless, the concept of Heaven (*tian*) is very vague and confusing. It can never be

---

17. See my books, Chang, *Zhongguo Minzu zhi Gaizao yu Zijiu* (*The Reformation and Self-Salvation of the Chinese People*); and Chang, *Zili Zhuyi—Minzu Fuxing Zhiji Benyuanli* (*The Doctrine of Self-Determination—Basic Principles for the Revival of the Chinese People*), both published by the Commercial Press.

18. Or *Yi Jing*.—Ed.

19. *I Ching*, chap. 8; Fung, *A History of Chinese Philosophy*, 461.

20. *Shi Jing*, or *Shih Ching*.—Ed.

21. Ode No. 279, in Chan, *A Source Book*, 5.

22. *Book of Odes*, Ode no. 235, in Chan, *A Source Book*, 113.

23. *Book of Changes*, Hexagram No. 1, in Chan, *A Source Book*, 264.

Critique of Humanism

compared with Christian doctrine that a personal God created mankind and all things in the universe.[24]

The Ultimate

Confucianists in the Song dynasty further developed the ideas of heaven (*tian*), earth (*di*), the negative (*yin*), the positive (*yang*), and force (*qi*). They postulated "the Great Ultimate" (*Tai ji*) as the origin of all things; and that "this Great Ultimate" came from "The Non-Ultimate" (W*u ji*),[25] or "The Ultimate of Non-Being."[26] No one can fathom its origin. They built their system on the principle of "The Great Ultimate." This Great Ultimate combined itself with the force of the universe (*qi*). At first there were no distinctions of order. The force became both negative (*yin*) and positive (*yang*). In each, the principle (*li*) operates. Because the negative and positive operate in both motion and quietude, heaven and earth became distinguished. Heaven is positive, and tends toward motion; the earth is negative, and tends toward quietude. Male and female thus were distinguished, as well as light and darkness, life and death, noble and commoner, wisdom and folly. Man receives the perfection of the principle (*li*) of heaven; material things receive the distinctions of the same principle.[27]

The Confucianist Doctrine of Human Nature

When it comes to the true condition of human nature, and whether human nature is good or evil, Confucius merely said, "By nature men are alike. Through practice they have become far apart."[28] He also said: "In education there are no class distinctions."[29] In his early thought, he did not advocate that man was originally good. Many people believe that Confucianism taught that human nature was originally good; this is not necessarily true. Xunzi,[30] a Confucianist, promoted the view that human nature was evil. He believed that laws and punishments, rites and government, were all for the

---

24. See Chang, *Yuan Dao* (*The Way*), chap. 1.
25. Chan, *A Source Book*, 639.
26. Ibid., 463.
27. See Jia Yuming (Chia Yu-ming), *Shen Dao Xue* (*Systematic Theology*), 2:99.
28. *Analects* 17:2, in Chan, *A Source Book*, 45.
29. *Analects* 15:38, in de Bary, 23.
30. Or *Hsun-tzu*.—Ed.

purpose of restraining passions and excesses. This proves that human nature is evil. Only Mencius[31] believed that human nature is good: "The tendency of human nature to do good is like that of water to flow downward. There is no man who does not tend to do good; there is no water that does not flow downward."[32] Due to the important place Mencius occupied in the Confucian tradition, and his unmatched debating abilities, his view has become the orthodox Confucian position, while Xunzi, on the other hand, is considered to be heterodox by Confucianists.

The Goal of Life

The great philosophy of life according to Confucianism consists in "manifesting clear character, loving the people, and abiding in the highest good."[33] And the steps from "manifesting clear character to abiding in the highest good are the investigation of things, the extension of knowledge, making the will sincere, rectification of the mind, cultivation of the personal life, regulation of the family, bringing order to the state, and realizing world peace." Confucianists believe that "the great attribute of Heaven and earth is giving and maintaining life."[34] The ultimate in life lies within the self. Life is man's joy. "The man of perfect virtue, wishing to be established himself, seeks also to establish others; wishing to enlarge himself, he seeks also to enlarge others."[35] On one extreme, man is content to be alone by himself; on the other, he can extend himself and benefit the whole world. Although Confucius speaks about "the mandate of Heaven" (tian ming), and said that "that which is bestowed by Heaven is called man's nature; the fulfillment of this nature is called the Way; the cultivation of the Way is called culture,"[36] he was silent on "nature"[37] and "the way of heaven."[38] "It is not to be heard."[39] It is fair to say that Confucius majored on the

---

31. Pinyin, Mengzi.—Ed.

32. Mengzi (The Works of Mencius), 6.A. 2, in de Bary, Sources of Chinese Tradition, 89.

33. The Great Learning, in Chan, Source Book, 86.

34. Yi Jing, "Xi Ci," II.

35. Analects 28:2, in Legge, The Chinese Classics, 1:194.

36. Or "instruction in the truth." The Doctrine of the Great Mean, I, in De Bary, The Source of Chinese Tradition 1:118.

37. Or xing.—Ed.

38. Or tian dao.—Ed.

39. Analects 12:5, in de Bary, Sources of Chinese Tradition, vol. 1.

minors, and minored on the majors. Thus, most Confucianist scholars think that "the way of heaven is far, the way of man is near."[40] "We don't know yet about life, how can we know about death?"[41] Their attitude toward life is to be content in the way of heaven, and accept one's fate. Their concerns are realistic ones. Their efforts are focused on cultivating one's own mind, heart, and virtues. Although they have the great cosmic goal "to build the heart for heaven and earth, to establish the mandate for the lives of the people, to continue the best learning from the ancient sages, to open up world peace for ten thousand generations to come," they have no knowledge of the mysteries of the kingdom of heaven. They do not know the great way to eternal life. They hold to a system of doctrines of "immortality" and "the ever-abiding great spirit,"[42] with which to comfort themselves, but because their attitude is, "We don't know yet about life, how can we know about death?"[43] they can never solve the mystery of life and death. This is a serious defect in Confucianism.

Part 2. The Nature of Buddhism and Its World and Life View

Buddhism: Religion or Atheism?

Most people consider Buddhism to be an otherworldly religion, but the fact is, according to orthodox Buddhism, it is an atheistic religion of self-salvation. Although Gautama Buddha did not make any statements concerning the existence of God, we can see his atheistic belief from his one statement: "Up to heaven, down to earth, only I am the highest."[44] He does not believe in anything which is higher than himself, worthy of his worship. According to the *Platform Scripture of the Sixth Patriarch* of the Tian Tai school of Buddhism, one of their principles was *"li qi"*—that is, all life has Buddhahood within it. All things on earth and in heaven (in the *phenomena* and in the *noumena*) are above reason, and equal with Buddha. The Buddhist monk Tai Xu even said that "the attainment of man is the same as the attainment of Buddha."[45] Understood in this way, one can

40. *Chun Qiu Zuo Zhuan*· Zhaogong eighteenth year.
41. *Analects* 11:11, in de Bary, *Sources of Chinese Tradition*, 1:29.
42. Or *a noble spirit will never perish.*—Ed.
43. *Analects* 11:11 Chan, *A Source Book.*
44. *Wu Deng Hui Yuan* (a Song dynasty history of Zen Buddhism in China), the first Scroll, written by Monk Puji.—Ed.
45. Chang, *Asia's Religions*, chap. 6, note 4—Lotus Sutra.

interpret Buddhism as merely a way of living; it is lowly, and devoid of any lofty truths. We do not mean to denigrate Buddhism in this; in their own words, they even call Buddha "a dry stick of dung."[46]

Basic Buddhist Doctrine:

The Four Noble Truths and the Eightfold Path

The "Four Noble Truths" of Buddhism are: (1) *Dukkha* (suffering)—to live is evil in itself because it involves suffering. (2) *Samudaya* (origin of suffering)—this is the thirst for being, which leads from birth to birth; lust and desire, which find gratification here and there; the thirst for pleasures; and the thirst for power. (3) *Nirodha* (extinction or destruction)—in order to be delivered from suffering, one must separate himself from desire, let it go, expel it, give it no room, and completely destroy it. (4) *Marga* (way)—the way which leads to the extinction of suffering is called the Eightfold Noble Path. Their Eightfold Noble Path consists of the following:

1. Right view: rejecting unworthy attitudes and acts.
2. Right desire: free from lust, ill will and cruelty, with wholesome zeal to achieve the highest ends.
3. Right speech: abhorring lying and harsh and vain talk, being gentle, soothing to the ear, useful, rightly timed and according to fact.
4. Right conduct: charity, abstaining from killing any living being, from stealing, and from unlawful sexual intercourse.
5. Right mode of livelihood: free from luxury, harming no one, taking up that which will be useful for fellow-men.
6. Right effort: self-control, self-discipline.
7. Right thought: dedication to Buddha's doctrines.
8. Right meditation: passing beyond sensation of pleasure and pain into a state of transcendent consciousness, attaining full enlightenment or "Buddhahood."[47]

These principles are nothing more than a philosophy of life, or principles for cultivating one's mind and heart, that echoes much that is in Confucianism's pursuit of cultivation, rectification, and knowledge.

46. See Chang, *Zen-Existentialism*, 31.
47. See Chang, *Asia's Religions*, 112.

Critique of Humanism

Confucianism vs. Buddhism

Both Confucianism and Buddhism believe that man is by nature bright and good. But man lives in darkness because he is not covered by light, and the spirits are not revealed. For Confucianists, man is covered with external things, so he deceives his own conscience; for Buddhists, man holds on to his desires with greed, so he becomes lost. The difference is that "Buddhism focuses on the cause and its effect; if one is to be enlightened concerning human nature, one must understand the cause before achieving the effect." This is why the "enlightenment of the cause" (*yin-ming*) school of Buddhist self-cultivation is so effective.

Confucianists speak of the unity of Heaven and man.[48] Man comes into harmony with the way of Heaven; man's heart corresponds to the virtue of Heaven (*tian de*). Therefore, the work of self-cultivation depends on "self-enlightenment" (*zi ming*). This is what Confucius meant by "the manifestation of clear character," or "manifestation of virtue" (*ming de*). The Buddhists put it differently—to enlighten the heart and to see man's true nature; the underlying meaning, however, is the same. Therefore Buddhists who believe in "finding the cause and seeking enlightenment" (*yin-ming*) and Confucianists who "manifest clear character and cultivate the personality" have much in common. To put it simply, *yin-ming* is an understanding of why things are the way they are. It is the same as the Confucianists' theory of "the investigation of all things and the extension of knowledge." "Investigate all things, then one will attain knowledge; with knowledge, one's will becomes sincere; when one's will is sincere, then one's heart is rectified; when one's heart is rectified, his self is cultivated." "The use of *yin-ming* is the discernment of good and evil, truth and error; this is exactly the same as the work of investigating all things and extending knowledge. It is also a necessary condition for cultivating oneself in this life." "Compassion for all life[49] is to be understood in the same way."[50]

Therefore we can see that neither Confucianists nor Buddhists think that man needs the supernatural help of God. One can save himself by understanding the nature of things and cultivating his personhood, or enlightening his heart and attaining his true nature. In other words, man's savior is himself; there is no need to seek help from another. Clearly, these are strong versions of humanism. Just as Prof. Tang Junyi said, "There is mutual

---

48. Or *tian ren he yi*.
49. Or *ji shi du zhong*.—Ed.
50. Hu, "Yin ming yu ming de xiu yang."

penetration between Buddhist and the Chinese humanist spirit." Beginning with the time of the *Tian Tai* and *Hua-yan* schools, Buddhist doctrine evolved into the thought of the *Chan* (Zen) school. Eventually, Buddhism brought about the rejuvenation of the existing humanist spirit in China. We see this in the Neo-Confucianism of the Sung[51] and Ming dynasties.[52] This should provide some support for the present writer's argument.[53]

Siddhartha Gautama was an atheist himself. He believed that "in the world, including the heavens, there is no one like unto me. I am the holy one in the world. I am the Supreme Master. I alone am the Perfect Buddha."[54] Buddhism believes that life is a product of the constant change in the three realms and the six degrees of incarnation. Everything is an illusion, the product of the constant transmutation of karma. All things are impermanent and changing; the self (or soul) does not exist. The five components of life (the five *Skandas*: form and matter, sensations, perceptions, psychological dispositions, and consciousness) all amount to vanity.[55] For example, a chair is a form made up of different physical substances. Once it is dismembered, the chair will not exist at all. It is the same with human life. This is the strongest form of materialism, which denies the existence of the soul!

Human Nature

The general Buddhist teaching on human nature is that all men have Buddhahood in them. Actually there are two theories. On the one hand, "Every sentient being has a potential Buddha in it."[56] "All life has a pure mind."[57] "The purity of the mind is like the [reflection of] the moon in the water."[58] "The mind is by nature pure."[59] On the other hand, "The heart is the karma

---

51. Or in Pinyin, *Song*.—Ed.

52. See Tang Junyi, *The Development of the Chinese Humanist Spirit* (*Zhongguo Renwen Jingshen zhi Fajan*), 33.

53. There are numerous schools of Buddhist thought, each with its own theories. We have given only a brief survey here. I have evaluated Buddhism in other books. See Chang, *Zongti Biandaoxue* (*Comprehensive Christian Apologetics*), vol. 3.

54. Mahavagga, I: 6, 8; quoted in *Asia's Religions*, chap. 7, note 20.

55. De Bary, *Sources of Chinese Tradition*, 1:267.

56. *Nirvana Scripture*.

57. *Da Ji Jing*, or *Mahavaipulya mahasamghata sutra*.

58. *Da Bao Ji Jing*, or *Maharatnakuta sutra*.

59. *Wenshu Shili Wen Jing*.

of evil."⁶⁰ "The heart is the source of the five roots, more horrible than the poisonous snake and the wild beast."⁶¹ Hinayana Scriptures also point to ignorance and delusion⁶² as the source of all evil. So we can conclude that there are two gates to the heart: one true, one false. The former is pure and empty, the other is evil.

Illusory Nature of Life

There are three basic doctrines in Buddhism: (1) all things are impermanent and in flux; (2) there is no soul (the non-atman doctrine); (3) Nirvana is the realm of extinction. They believe that all phenomena in the universe are illusory and impermanent. The life of man is one of the illusions in the universe. Man's perception of himself is merely an illusion. Though every man has the (potential) nature of Buddha in him, and thus all men have sufficient light, because of sins committed in previous existences, and because of the obstacles in this life, desires grow and obscure light. Man is thus entangled in the sorrows of life and death. The great goal in the Buddhist life, therefore, is to be enlightened, and escape from the lure of the three realms (the realms of desire, form and formlessness). There is a great enlightenment as one becomes Bodhisattva, and enters Nirvana.

Autosoterism

Since Buddhism is atheistic, it does not believe in any outside source of help. Enlightenment originates from within oneself. Strictly speaking, therefore, Buddhism is not a religion, but a school of philosophy. Their own words support this interpretation. A sage in the Tian Tai school begins his exposition of the "six stages of a Boddhisattva's development" (*liu ji*) this way: "*Li* is Buddha." The monk Tai Xu says: "The attainment of man is the attainment of Buddha."⁶³ The great enlightenment which Siddhartha Gautama attained under the Bo tree was merely that "I have seen the secret of life, the mystery of reincarnation." Under close scrutiny, it is nothing more than a philosophy of life. The Buddhist perspective on life is, the retribution of the illusory world is all sorrow! For example, there is more

---

60. *Fo Shuo Ba Da Ren Jue Jing*.
61. *Fo Yi Jiao Jing* (*Sutra on the Buddha's Bequeathed Teaching*).
62. Or *Avidya* and *moha*.—Ed.
63. From "Zhen Xianshi Song," a poem written by monk Tai Xu in 1936.

The Tradition of Chinese Humanism: Confucianism, Daoism, and Buddhism

suffering than pleasure in our bodies. We live, become old and sick, and die; at every moment, we are subject to constant change. This is sorrow. We are lost because of worries. In order to extinguish this sorrow, we must enter Nirvana, which is extinction. To enter this extinction, one must first cultivate himself in Buddhist doctrine.[64] There are thirty-seven *pin* in the way to Nirvana. They are all ways for the cultivator to discipline his mind. The eightfold noble path is particularly ethical by nature: (1) a right view, (2) right desire, (3) right speech, (4) right conduct, (5) right mode of livelihood, (6) right effort, (7) right thought, and (8) right meditation.

Buddhists believe that the universe is one great illusion. There are the five *Skhandas* (form, sensation, perception, character, and mental power)[65] and the six elements (earth, water, wind, fire, air, and perception). All phenomena in the universe are the result of interaction between mental images[66] in the world of desire[67] and physical phenomena. They believe that everyone goes through the wheel of incarnation. There are 84,000 kinds of sorrow among humans; we are all born, we all become old and sick, and we all die. All of life is inseparable from sorrow. Thus Buddhists seek, through their philosophy of sorrow and emptiness, to awaken people who are drowning in their desires. But what they seek to attain is an illusory, vague state of *bhutatathata* (genuine thus-ness; *zhen ru*)[68], not the knowledge of the true God. The end is the extinction of life in Nirvana, and not eternal life. How regretful!

Part 3. The Nature of Daoism and Its World and Life View

The Origin of the Universe: The Nameless Dao

Daoism, likewise, does not have a clear understanding of the Creator of the world. It merely states, concerning the origin of mankind and the universe: "The Nameless is the origin of Heaven and Earth; the Named is the mother of all things."[69] "All things in the world come from being. And being comes

---

64. Jiang Weiqiao (Chiang Wei-ch'iao), *Fojiao Qian Shuo* (*A Simple Introduction to Buddhism*).
65. Chang, *Asian Religions*, 109.
66. Or *jing shen xian xiang*.—Ed.
67. Or *qing qi shi jian*.—Ed.
68. Or *zhen ru*.—Ed.
69. *Tao Te Ching* (*Dao De Jing*) 1, in Chan, *A Source Book*, 139.

Critique of Humanism

from non-being."[70] "Dao produced the One. The One produced the two. The two produced the three. And the three produced the ten thousand things. The ten thousand things carry the *yin* and embrace the *yang*, and through the blending of the material force (*qi*) they achieve harmony."[71]

Human Nature

The Daoist understanding of human nature, and of good and evil, seeks to transcend the common, secular understanding. They think that the norms for good and evil do not originate in man; the highest good in the world lies in a return to simplicity. "When the people of the world all know beauty as beauty, there arises the recognition of ugliness."[72] "When the great declined, the doctrines of humanity (*ren*) and righteousness (*yi*) arose. When knowledge and wisdom appeared, there emerged great hypocrisy."[73] "Man models himself after Earth. Earth models itself after Heaven. Heaven models itself after Tao. And Tao models itself after Nature."[74] It also said: "Attain complete vacuity, maintain steadfast quietude. All things come into being, and I see thereby their return. All things flourish, but each one returns to its root. This return to its root means tranquility. It is called returning to its destiny. To return to destiny is called the eternal (*Tao*). To know the eternal is called enlightenment."[75]

The Goal of Life: Abandon and Return

The goal of life is to return to the mandate of Heaven; only this way will there be regularity. All rites, laws, government, and punishment are evil and dangerous. Therefore: "Heaven and earth are not humane (*ren*). They regard all things as straw dogs. The sage is not humane. He regards all people as straw dogs."[76] From this it derives: "Abandon sageliness and discard wisdom, then the people will benefit a hundredfold. Abandon humanity and discard righteousness; then the people will return to filial piety and

---

70. *Tao-te-ching* 40, in ibid., 160.
71. *Tao-te-ching* 42, in ibid.
72. *Tao-te-ching* 2, in ibid., 140.
73. *Tao-te-ching* 18, in ibid., 148.
74. *Tao-te-ching* 25, in ibid., 153.
75. *Tao-te-ching* 16, in ibid., 147.
76. *Tao-te-ching* 5, in ibid., 141.

deep love. Abandon skill and discard profit; then there will be no thieves or robbers."[77] Again, it is said: "Tao invariably takes no action, and yet there is nothing left undone."[78] "The pursuit of learning is to increase day after day. The pursuit of Tao is to decrease day after day. It is to decrease and further decrease until one reaches the point of taking no action. No action is undertaken, and yet nothing is left undone."[79]

These doctrines of "non-action" and "return to the mandate" (*fu ming*) certainly sound wiser and more lofty than the concerns of a secular, this-worldly humanism. However, empty talk about "non-action" will not necessarily "leave nothing undone." Only when men trust in "the God who can do all things," will they be able "to do all things." Further, man lies in bondage under sin, so he has lost the freedom "to return to the mandate." It is impossible for man to break through the barrier between him and God. Only by trusting the blood of Jesus Christ and his great redeeming work, can this "wall" be broken down, so that the two may become one, so that God may be reconciled to man. There will then be a true return to "*ming*"[80] (see Eph 2:12–19).

The Highest Good

Since Daoists find true happiness in life in purification, nonaction, a return to simplicity, and communion with nature, they believe that only when mankind returns to and conforms with nature will they achieve the highest good. What man considers to be good is actually hypocrisy. The Daoist call to "abandon humanity and discard righteousness," and to "abandon sageliness and discard wisdom," sounds superior to Confucianist philosophy, in that it opposes human pride and self-confidence. In fact there is some implicit agreement with Christianity on this point. Jesus Christ, however, warned: "For I say to you, that unless your righteousness exceeds the righteousness of the scribes and Pharisees, you will by no means enter the kingdom of heaven" (Matt 5:20). "But seek first the kingdom of God and His righteousness" (Matt 6:33). Man is to model himself after God the Father, he is to "be perfect, just as your Father in heaven is perfect" (Matt 5:48). Daoism merely teaches man to model himself after nature: "Man models himself after Earth. Earth models itself after Heaven.

77. *Tao-te-ching* 19, in ibid., 149.
78. *Tao-te-ching* 37, in ibid., 158.
79. *Tao-te-ching* 48, in ibid., 162.
80. Or *Life, mandate*.

Critique of Humanism

Heaven models itself after Tao. And Tao models itself after Nature."[81] But their understanding of nature is merely a mass of uncertainty and confusion. It cannot be known. Upon close scrutiny, one can concede that their ideal is higher; they have a confused understanding of what it is, however. Thus, there is no truly noble goal in life; life has no value. Life turns into a sensual, licentious, deadly form of romanticism and nihilism.

The Daoist View of Death

The Daoist view of death is different from the Confucianist. When the wife of Zhuangzi[82] died, Zhuangzi was "squatting on the ground and singing, beating on an earthen bowl."[83] And when Sang-hu, one of Zhuangzi's disciples died,

> Confucius heard about it and sent his pupil Tzu-kung[84] to take part in the funeral. One of the friends was composing a song and another was playing a lute, and they sang in harmony, saying, "Alas! Sang-hu. Alas! Sang-hu. You have returned to the true state but we still remain here as men!" Tzu-kung returned and told Confucius, asking him, "What sort of men are those? There is nothing proper in their conduct. . . ." "They travel in the transcendental world," replied Confucius, "and I travel in the mundane world. There is nothing common between the two worlds, and I sent you there to mourn! How stupid! They are companions of the Creator, and roam in the universe of the one and original creative force (*qi*). They consider life as a burden like a tumor, and death as the cutting off of an abscess."[85]

Daoists regard heaven and earth—that is, nature—as father and mother. Death is simply a response to the father and mother's call to return home. Life is labor, death is rest. Life is slavery, death is autonomy.[86] Zhuangzi said, "A dead infant lived the longest possible life, while

---

81. *Tao-te-ching* 25, in Chan, *A Source Book*, 153.
82. Or *Chuang-tzu*.—Ed.
83. Chan, *A Source Book*, 209.
84. In Pinyin, *Zi Gong*.—Ed.
85. *Chuang Tzu* (*Zhuangzi*), in Chan, *A Source Book*, 198.
86. *Zi zhu. Zhuang Zi—Da Zong Shi* (*The Great and Most Honored Master*).

The Tradition of Chinese Humanism: Confucianism, Daoism, and Buddhism

P'eng-Tzu[87] had an early death at eight hundred years of his age. My life is identified with the heaven and earth; I and all the creation are one."[88]

Mankind's hope and destiny is total abolition of distinctions and union with the universe: "Heaven and Earth came into being with me together, and with me, all things are one."[89] The Daoist approach to life is truly unique.[90] Their concept of the Dao, however, is ineffable and illusory. At its best, Daoism amounts to a fanciful form of pantheism. Daoists do not know the true, personal, triune God of the universe; they cannot, therefore, offer eternal life and immortality to mankind. In later generations, Daoism even degenerated into occult practices such as alchemy and the search for the elixir of immortality.

---

87. Or *Peng Zu*.—Ed.

88. *Zhuang Zi—Qi Wu Lun (The Adjustment of Controversies)*; Chang, *Asia's Religions*, chap. 4, note 12.

89. *Zhuang Zi—Qi Wu Lun (The Adjustment of Controversies)*, in Fung, *A History of Chinese Philosophy*, 1:244.

90. See *Zhuang Zi, Xiao Yao You (Enjoyment in Untroubled Ease)*. See Zhuangzi, *Zhuangzi: Basic Writings*—Ed.

2

The Renaissance of Chinese Humanism in the Twentieth Century

MODERN CHINESE INTELLECTUALS HAVE inherited the humanism of Confucianism, Daoism, and Buddhism in their thought, and at the same time have imbibed deeply of the poison of modern Western humanism. Thus there is very little in their philosophy of life worthy of emulation. The first type of modern intellectual may be represented by Professor Qian Mu,[1] the master of "humanist religion," and Professor Tang Junyi. We can call this "contemporary Chinese-type humanism." The second type of modern intellectual may be represented by Professors Wu Zhihui and Hu Shi, which can be called "contemporary Western-type humanism." We will survey each briefly.

First, Western-type humanism. One of these intellectuals was Professor Wu Zhihui, a founder of the Nationalist Party (*Guomingdang*),[2] whom Professor Hu Shi called a "great champion" in the "Philosophy of Life Debate" (1923). Wu led a movement characterized by "a scientific philosophy of life." He was an extreme materialist, who denied the existence of the soul, or the human spirit. Man is only some kind of mechanical "material reaction." In essence, man is not different from the animals. Wu therefore believed that we must "dismiss the quota of God, and exile the element of the spirit," in denial of the soul.[3] The second intellectual is Professor Hu Shi, former president of National Peking University, and now president of the Academica Sinica. He was a leader in the "New Culture Movement"

---

1. Or *Ch'ien Mu*.
2. Or *KMT*; formerly *Kuomingtang*.
3. See Chang, *Yuan Dao* (*The Way*), 177.

and enjoyed the respect of scholars both in and outside China.[4] Hu's philosophy of life is naturalistic and atheistic; in essence it is no different from Wu Zhihui's. Hu believed that "the operation of all things in the universe is natural." "A virtuous Creator in the universe" is merely an "assumption," which "cannot be established." He believed that "man is only one type of animal; he differs from other animals only in degree, not in kind." He also did not "believe in the theory of the immortality of the soul," nor "the theory of heaven and hell." "Life itself is merely a biological fact, devoid of meaning. The birth of a human being is no different from the birth of a dog or a cat!" In other words, the so-called philosophy of life of Hu Shi was not the "philosophy of (human) life," but the "philosophy of a dog and cat," an "animalistic philosophy"![5] In the modern history of China and Taiwan, there have been periods in which the entire nation rallied to oppose the inhumane philosophy of atheism and materialism. Yet, people revere this famous scholar so much, this materialist "philosopher of the animal," that a bronze statue was erected in memory of him. What a sad state of affairs among Chinese intellectuals! Chinese church, rise up to the drummer's call, and join combat in resistance!

Next, Chinese-type humanism, represented by Professors Qian Mu and Tang Junyi. They pursued interests and advocated theories which were different from Wu Zhihui and Hu Shi's. They were opposed to the philosophy of materialism, and advocated the doctrines of Heaven (*tian*) and man. They spoke of God, the soul, and even heaven and hell. They were deeply concerned about the heart of man and the progress of society; they valued the significance of religious belief. On the surface, they seemed superior to Wu and Hu. Since they promoted "humanist religion," however, their concerns were limited to human concerns. In their minds, "the way of Heaven is far, the way of man is near." Even though they have heard of God by the hearing of the ear, they have not seen Him with their own eyes (see Job 42:5). "Although they knew God, they did not glorify Him as God, nor were thankful" (see Rom 1:20-23). Therefore they regarded God as mundane, not worthy of worship. At the same time they thought

---

4. The New Culture Movement of the mid-1910s and '30s stemmed from disillusionment with traditional Chinese culture following the failure of the Chinese Republic, founded in 1912. Scholars with classical educations began a revolt against Confucianism. They called for the creation of a new Chinese culture based on global and Western standards, especially democracy and science. The movement later included promotion of vernacular literature; an end to the patriarchal family in favor of individual freedom and women's liberation; a view of China as a nation among nations, not as a uniquely Confucian culture; and democratic and egalitarian values.—Ed.

5. See Chang, *Yuan Dao* (*The Way*), 178-79.

that God was so vague and mysterious, there was no way to know him. For that reason, they took the self-existing, eternal God, the Creator of the universe, the Lord of our lives, and equated Him with "nature," "the universe," "genuine thusness,"[6] "Nirvana," "Heaven," "earth," and "the way" (Dao), and even "the self" and "my mind."

The true and living God became an abstract symbol, a mere philosophical term. Even if they truly believed in God, their God was a concept created in their own image. This is a common error among Chinese and Western philosophers, ancient and modern. Because the eyes of their spirits had not been opened, they did not receive God's revelation. "The natural man" who has not been born again "does not receive the things of the Spirit of God, for they are foolishness to him. . ." (1 Cor 2:14). Before I became a Christian, I launched a university and invited these two men to be the principal and dean of the college of liberal arts. We were travelers on the same journey. I had the deepest respect for their passion for their vocation, and have fervently prayed for them for many years, often unto tears. I do not want to treat their ideas in depth, but would point out some salient points so the reader may understand the extent to which they understood the meaning of life.

Professor Qian Mu said in "The Direction of Life":[7] "The Confucianist philosophy of life is not introverted, nor extroverted, nor neutral. They only spoke of fulfilling the true nature in man,[8] and fulfilling the nature of things." They had a high and lofty aspiration, yet this can also be considered a concern for the "here and now." It is a philosophy of life which "believed in enjoying the here and now. A blessed life is one with two feet on the ground, and walking forward." "Therefore, Confucianists do not follow the path of religion, and do not seek to build a god." (Author's note: God is the self-existing, eternal Creator; he can never be "built" by a creature! To speak of "building a god" is like building a square circle. This is an impossibility! And for a creature to be the Creator, treating God as a creature! This is truly blasphemy.) They believe that man is good by nature; they speak of "fulfilling one's own nature; in this way God will live in one's own nature." (Author's note: *The Doctrine of the Mean* says: "One who knows man must not be ignorant about heaven."[9] Also: "The mandate

---

6. Or *zhen ru*.

7. Qian, Mu (Chi'en Mu). *Rensheng Shilun* (*Ten Essays on Life*).

8. Or *Jin ji zhi xing*.

9. Chang, *Liji·Zhong Yong* (*The Classic of Rites—The State of Equilibrium and Harmony*).

The Renaissance of Chinese Humanism in the Twentieth Century

of heaven is human nature."[10] We can see, therefore, that if one does not know Heaven (God), one cannot fulfill his nature, just as a person cannot see his own appearance, whether beautiful or ugly, without a mirror. Since Qian is reputed to be a master of Confucianism, how can he not understand this principle? How can he go against his own belief? I have written other books on this subject.)

Qian, therefore, was an opponent of Christianity. He said that "man arranges for a god because of the external search of his spirit; he founds religions, and completes church organization." (Note: God is the Creator of the universe; he is not "arranged" by men. Christianity is God's self-revelation, it is not "founded" by men, nor by the "basic principles of the world" (Col 2:8); the church is the body of Christ, not a human, worldly organization.) "Yet God and religion may turn their face against humanity; they will turn around and become an obstacle to life. They may swallow up the life of men, and prohibit man from advancing forward!" (Note: God only turns his face against sinners, but does not "prohibit man from advancing forward." God is the source of all blessing for the life of mankind; he is our shepherd. "Surely goodness and mercy shall follow me all the days of my life"! (Ps 23:6) God is the Lord of life. How would he swallow up life?)

In "The Purpose and Freedom of Life,"[11] Qian further stated: "Since the purposes of life are freely chosen by man, there is no hierarchy, no right or wrong between purposes. If one likes to take a walk, he takes a walk; if he likes to go to the movies, he goes to the movies." He even said: "To commit suicide and to seek death is also the free choice of man." "Whether you go to the movies, or commit suicide, it is all up to your free choice. Others cannot interfere with you, and they should not interfere with you." (Note: Confucianism teaches that "all men have the mind of right and wrong"; how can it be said that "there should be no right and wrong"? It also teaches: "Do not see what is against decorum (*li*)"; how can we watch movies indiscriminately? Confucianism also teaches that "the virtue of heaven and earth lives on daily";[12] thus, suicide is no virtue. Qian's ideas go against his own Confucian beliefs. How can he explain his self-contradiction?)

In the same article, Qian said: "The norms with which man discerns good and evil are based on the extent of freedom which man hopes to attain. This is the starting point for these norms." "Evil is simply that which

---

10. Ibid.
11. Or *Ren sheng mudi he ziyou*.
12. *I Ching* 2 (translated by Chiuhwa Liu).

is inferior; it is that which is not so good. Evil is a matter of culture and life; if one cannot choose the best, he has to choose the second best, if the second best is not available, he will choose the not-so-good. Before the second best was available, the not-so-good was considered to be good. When man faces starvation, when he has nothing to wear, when human society returns to the base line of nature, at that time even cannibalism cannot be considered to be evil! It is still a matter of human free choice!"[13]

According to Qian, "evil is a matter of culture and life." It is not an ethical issue, not a moral question. Even "cannibalism cannot be considered to be evil"! This not only totally goes against the Confucian idea that "starvation and death is a small matter," and the ideal "to manifest clear character and to attain the highest good." It also destroys all absolute norms for right and wrong, good and evil. It kills the lofty spirit of ethics, human morality, and decorum. Qian's theory of "free choice" will become a defense of doing evil, for the end justifies the means. How can Qian explain his "humanist religion" on this basis? If his religion teaches that "suicide" is "the free choice of man" and even "cannibalism cannot be considered evil," not only will there be no "arts and letters,"[14] there will be no human beings left! Is this not a declaration of the bankruptcy of "the humanist religion"?

Second, Professor Tang Junyi, in his recent work, *An Introduction to Philosophy*,[15] said in Part Four, "The Philosophy of Life"[16]:

> The Old Testament says that, after God created every creature, it was good in his eyes. Man lived in Paradise in the beginning. Even today, missionaries prove God's existence, God's grace to mankind, and the original good of the universe by pointing to the intricacies of man's organism, and the fact that all things were created to support man. For example, man and all living things originated on earth. Suppose the earth were 100 miles closer to the sun, all mankind and all forms of life would die from the heat. If it were 100 miles further away, all forms of life would freeze to death. Man's body is so intricately put together that he cannot continue to live without one part. Doesn't this prove that God originally created the universe as good? If we exchange the name "God" for "nature" in the above argument, our conclusion would still be the same. In other words, man

---

13. See Qian, *Rensheng Shilun* (*Ten Essays on Life*).
14. Or *wen*.—Ed.
15. Or *Zhexue Gailun*.—Ed.
16. Or *Ren Dao Lun*.—Ed.

and other forms of life, which emerged in nature, can exist in harmony with the environment on earth.[17]

Mr. Tang Junyi treats God as merely "a name" that can be changed to "nature"; the two "would still be the same." Therefore, the universe has no Creator; mankind has no Lord of life. Everything is void and confusion, the product of "nature." This "little mistake" has tremendous implications. This is the source of his erroneous philosophy of life: He has turned life "upside down"![18]

First, Professor Tang reversed the order between "Heaven" and "man." He puts the ways of men above the way of Heaven. Not only did he put the two on the same level—"Heaven and man contemplate one another, complement one another, and are interdependent upon one another to move forward." He also believed that "where there is deficiency in the way of Heaven, the knowledge of the way of man will be needed to supplement the knowledge of the way of Heaven. Besides all the things which man should know about the way of Heaven, there are facts which man needs to know to establish the way of man; this is to supplement the deficiency of the way of Heaven."[19] Doesn't Tang know that, according to the teachings of Confucius, the way of Heaven is the very foundation of the way of man? "You think to know man, but you cannot be ignorant about heaven."[20] "It is only Heaven that is great, and only Yao corresponded to it."[21]

Second, Professor Tang reverses the ways of "life" and "death." He respects death, yet has no respect for the true God. He puts the Lord of life, the Risen Savior, the incarnate Son of God in the category of "the dead ones." The only difference with Christ merely lies in "his feelings which remain in the world for ten thousand generations."

> Filial sons and grandsons show their sincerity and respect in sacrificing to their ancestors; in this way the feelings of the spirits and ghosts of the ancestors are appeased. The people of a village show their sincerity and respect toward the sages among their ranks; thus, the feelings of these sages are appeased. The people in the world show their sincerity and respect by sacrificing to those who have great compassion and benevolence toward

---

17. Tang, "Ren Dao Lun" ("The Way of Man") in *Zhexue Gailun (An Introduction to Philosophy)*, 1129–30.
18. The words "upside down," *dian dao*, are Tang's own words.
19. Tang, *Zhexue Gailun (An Introduction to Philosophy)*, 1044–45.
20. *Liji·Zhong Yong (The Classic of Rites: The State of Equilibrium and Harmony)*.
21. *Mengzi (The Works of Mencius)*, "Teng Wen Gong," I.

Critique of Humanism

> mankind; they sacrifice to these immortal sages, so the feelings of these sages are appeased. In fact, people in a clan, a village, a nation or the entire world, have what it takes to fulfill the wishes of others before they die; they also have what it takes to fulfill the wishes of those who have died, so that their spirits can rest in peace in heaven. [Note: perhaps these deceased ones are not "spirits in heaven"?] These things are not the fictional imagination of writers. The truth and the facts concerning death and life all conform to the nature of men and to the existing knowledge of men. Thus, one can believe in these without doubt.[22]

Tang advocates "respect for the dead ones" and "respect for ghosts and spirits." (Note: he calls the holy, righteous, eternal living God a "ghost" or "spirit.") Man should "regard death as he regards life, regard extinction as he regards existence."[23] Thus, the object of man's worship is the deceased, not the eternal true God.

Third, Tang reverses his distinction between woe and blessing. He rebukes sinners who repent and turn to the Savior; he calls this a kind of "high-level reversal in the philosophy of life." He believes that "people believe that the highest goal for their soul's pursuit is the infinite, unfathomable truth, goodness, and holiness which totally transcend humanity. These belong to Heaven, or God, or the spirits. They do not exist in the inherent nature of man. This belief arises because of the great reversal, to project that infinite value which man has within his nature to some God or Heaven which is transcendent or wholly other." "But the great high reversal is to become conscious of the fountain of light within man himself, and to seek to transcend the darkness within. Man can open up his own light." This is the strongest type of "self-deification," promoting man and suppressing God. One can also say this is atheism in a different guise.

Fourth, Tang fails to distinguish between grace and justice, holiness and sin. He wishes to exalt compassion at the expense of justice, so that heaven and hell compromise with one another. "There is a Western poet, Blake, who wrote a poem on the marriage between heaven and hell, in which he said that man's life in this world is where heaven and hell marry one another. In reality, heaven is like a father, hell like a mother. Hell gives birth to children to live on earth; they take the surname of the father in heaven. But, if the heavenly father cannot live on earth and become compassionate, as Buddha did, how can he beget children?" Tang despises the

---

22. Tang, *Ren Sheng zhi Tiyan Xupian*, "Gui Shen zhi Zhuang yu Qin."
23. Xunzi, "Li Lun."

Christian religion and criticizes it arbitrarily. He does not seriously study the Bible, and lacks the most basic common sense. He fails to understand that only God the heavenly Father is both grace and justice personified. God so loved the world, that he became incarnate and came to earth as a man to die on the cross for the sins of men. Christ died, was buried, went to heaven, and suffered the pains of hell on behalf of sinners. On the third day he rose from the dead, so that all who believe in him will not perish, but will escape the fires of hell, and have eternal bliss and life. We were by nature children of wrath; we were dead in trespasses and sins, but by grace we have been saved through faith. We have become children of God. We have been raised together with Christ and sit together in the heavenly places in Christ Jesus (See John 3:16; 1:12; Phil 2:6–8; Eph 2:3–6).

Tang writes: "How can man attain the purification of his self? How can he turn from wickedness and become upright? How can he transform his empty life into a proper life? There is no other way than this: he needs to rid himself of all opinions and perceptions which are 'reversals,' and eliminate all roots of 'reversal' from within himself, so that the proper place of man's self, that which has infinite spirit and life within, may be restored." How may this reversal be accomplished? How can this "proper place be restored"? Tang did not propose an effective method, but said; "To get rid of all reversals is difficult, truly difficult." This just shows that his way is "empty deceit, according to the tradition of men" (Col 2:8). This is truly like a strong man who cannot lift himself. The sinner is deeply entrenched in his sin; it is impossible to uproot himself from his "reversals." Only because God himself became incarnate on earth, gave his life for us, and shed his blood to cleanse us of our guilt, can we be "justified through faith," "rid ourselves of our reversal," and "restore our true position" from being "children of wrath" to "children of God."

We will not discuss this in depth here; a separate book is called for. However, I must issue a warning to the world. As Professor Tang has said: "If one looks at man's life through his reversal, life is largely wicked and not upright, vain and not meaningful. This confirms that life is to be loathed; it is tragic and a pity." "Everywhere one goes in life, one is trapped in reversal. In fact, man lives in all kinds of reversal, every moment, everywhere. He regards the reverse as upright; this itself is reversal. The thinkers of this world are particularly prone to this!" "Those who seek to be immune from this reversal are like people who are constantly being pursued. He has just turned aside a tiger from his front door, and now a wolf has entered through the back door. The ways of the Dao are weak; the minds of men are in crisis. This crisis is so severe that, in one moment's thought the universe begins to twirl, and the high and low change places. What a predicament! The thoughts of people with a high level of knowledge and achievement have a broad and high reach; their ideas are sharp and strong. Their reversals, however, are more complex and more determined." What a moment for man to realize the destruction of his ways, and to return in repentance to God! Unfortunately, Tang only knows his ailment, but will not seek the cure. He knows that "to get rid of all reversal is difficult, truly difficult," yet he ridicules those who admit their sickness and seek the physician; he derides repentance and faith as "a high-level reversal." In his prejudice, he views his own reversal as correct vision. Thus he confuses truth with error, right with wrong, woe with blessing; he reveres ghosts and angers God. He is concerned with the ways of man, not the way of Heaven. He even thinks that heaven and hell can be mixed; that the two can be "substituted one for the other, mixed together; there is no idea which can distinguish between the two." This tremendous reversal of vision is due to sin's entrance into the human race. Just as the British philosopher George Berkeley said: "A philosopher" (Tang is a good example) "may throw stars into heaven, but gets ensnared by his own trap." Yet he rebukes others as "fallen, standing on their own heads." Bertrand Russell tried to use "the lives of numerous geniuses in the West to prove that the genius and the mad are of the same root." "This is truly the tragedy of philosophy, ancient and modern, Chinese and Western!"[24] I love Professor Tang, and would rather not enter into a debate with him. For now, I have quoted his own words to show the folly of his ideas. His arguments cannot stand, for he is "ensnared by his own trap." I exhort him to do some serious reflection and to evaluate his thinking with a calm, reasonable mind.

"There is a way that seems right to a man, but its end is the way of death" (Prov 14:12). "Enter by the narrow gate; for wide is the gate and broad is the way that leads to destruction, and there are many who go in by it. Because narrow is the gate and difficult is the way which leads to life, and there are few who find it" (Matt 7:13–14). Jesus said that his Father has "hidden these things from the wise and prudent and [has] revealed them to babes" (Matt 11:25). May the scholars of our generation humbly repent. Only in this way will they reverse their reversals and know the truth; only in this way will they indeed find life and know God the Father. This is my prayer night and day!

---

24. See Tang, *Ren Sheng zhi Tiyan Xupian* (*The Experience of Life—Continued*).

3

Twentieth-Century Chinese Humanists

CHINESE INTELLECTUALS ARE OFTEN seriously flawed in their thinking: they do not believe in God, and they blaspheme against God. Although they speak of God, they think about him according to their own speculations. They have no fear of God; they turn the most holy, most good, the all-knowing and all-powerful true God into a philosophical idea, an abstract symbol, sometimes even the equivalent of ghosts and spirits. God and man stand on the same level. Even more strangely, they contradict themselves. On the one hand, they loathe atheism and materialist philosophy, but on the other hand they deny the existence of God with all kinds of theories. Or they even attempt to "eliminate the quota for God," and "to exile the soul of the spiritual factor." (Professor Wu Zhihui is a representative of this; see below.) Or they strenuously promote a "naturalistic world and life view," and deny any "supernatural sovereign"; they "do not believe in the theory of the immortality of the soul." (Professor Hu Shi is a representative of this approach; see below.) Or they seek to "dissipate concepts of God and the soul," because "there is no value in their distinct existence." (Professor Qian Mu is a representative of this view; see below.) In other words, they oppose materialism and atheism, yet they have become captives and even end up nurturing materialistic and atheistic ideas. The evil result is something they never expected. I have tried to inspect the Chinese language textbooks of the Republic of China; I found that the essays written by the most eminent scholars often carry a strong atheistic flavor. Even those published by Chung Cheng[1] Publishers[2] are not exempt from

---

1. In Pinyin, *Zhong Zheng*.
2. Chung Cheng is another name for Chiang Kai-shek (in Pinyin, *Jiang Jieshi*).

Critique of Humanism

this. These create deep "first impressions" in the minds of Chinese youths, poisoning them for the long run. This is contrary to the educational policies of the nation, yet the government is not aware of this problem. As I think and speak about this, my heart burns with worry. I shall, therefore, give an account of the opinions of these scholars to support what I am saying here.

The Atheism of Wu Zhihui

Wu Zhihui was a founding member of the Nationalist Party (*Guomindang*), and author of "The World and Life View of a New Faith." At the time of the New Cultural Movement (1915–1927), Hu Shi hailed him as "the champion" of the Philosophy of Life Debate (1923), and a leader of the "Scientific Philosophy of Life."[3] Wu said: "Man is made up of paper on the outside; two legs were added, and somehow he received two arms. Inside, he has about 37 ounces of brain marrow, 5048 brain tissues. He is an animal which has a larger quota of nervous-system substance. Life is evolution, thus it is said that: what we call "human life" is a kind of animal which uses his hands and his brain, performing the umpteen-millionth scene in the great opera of the universe." "I believe that animals and plants consist only in the interaction of matter and energy, with radioactive reflections. There is no more than this. For example, take man. His so-called nervous system is simply a matter of matter-energy interaction. What is called the emotions, the mind, and the will, are simply a stronger dose of these interactions. We can beautify these and call it 'psychology,' or mythologize them and call them 'the soul.' At its core, what we call emotions are simply matter-energy interactions." So this senior scholar concludes with these absurd ideas: "Those awe-inspiring, fearsome terms such as 'God' would better be eliminated. Let us impeach the name of God! Let us exile the soul with its spiritual elements!" Woe! This extreme form of atheism only recognizes the material "matter-energy interaction" and denies any "spiritual element"; it seeks to "impeach God" and "exile the soul." Its goal is the destruction of the spirit. This has been the theoretical foundation and guiding principle of atheistic communism, which seeks to persecute the church and reform people's thinking. What is even more strange is that a political party (the Guomindang) and a government (Republic of China)

---

3. See Wu, *Renshengguan Lunzhan ji* (*The Philosophy-of-Life Debate: A Collection*); and Wu, *Zhihui Wen Cun* (*The Collected Works of Wu Zhihui*).

which are avowedly anti-communist would honor him as a founding father! One could only cry—yet the tears run dry!

The Atheism of Hu Shi

Next, we will consider the "naturalistic philosophy of life" of Professor Hu Shi, the former head of the Academica Sinica of the Nationalist Party. Hu said:

> According to all science, that which makes the universe and all its operations and changes intelligible, is all natural—it is thus and so, with no need for some supernatural deity, or Creator. (Author's note: This means the same thing as Professor Wu Zhihui's "impeachment of God.") According to the scientific knowledge from biology, we know about the waste and the cruelty of the competition for survival in the biological world. We further know that the presupposition for a God who is virtuous and who loves life is unjustifiable. (Author's note: This is in perfect harmony with the atheism and materialism of communism, which Hu avows to oppose.) Biology, physiology, and psychology teach us that man is only one species in the animal kingdom. Man differs from other animals only in degree, not in kind. Biology and sociology tell us that morality, ceremony, and conventions are always in change, and the reasons for change can always be determined by scientific investigation.[4]

This kind of superficial theory can be articulated by any Chinese university student. Bacon said, "Anyone who has studied a little philosophy tends to be an atheist." Although I dare not disparage Hu Shi's position with Bacon's words, the fact remains that at that time, Hu Shi was a green, idealistic young man in his twenties, yet one who has become the leader of China's New Culture Movement. His influence upon the destiny of the Chinese people has been profound! Hu also stated in his *Self-Introduction to the Selected Works of Hu Shi—An Introduction to My Thought*: "I do not believe in the theory of the immortality of the soul, I do not believe in the ideas of heaven and hell." (This is the strongest form of atheism and materialism.) "Therefore I say: I am this little self, I will become extinct. Death and extinction is a common phenomenon among all living things; there is no need for fear, no need for pity." (Attention, readers! Hu Shi says that death is a biological phenomenon for which

---

4. See Hu, *Kexue yu Renshengguan* (*Science and the Philosophy of Life*).

Critique of Humanism

we need not have pity.) He also said in his letter in "Reply to a Friend Who Inquired Whether There Is Meaning in Life": "Life itself is merely a biological fact: what meaning is there in life? To give birth to a human being is no different than the birth of a dog or a cat!"[5] Let us try to follow his line of thinking: Man is no different from dogs and cats; those who treat human beings like dogs and cats, those Communists who crush human nature and human dignity, find their theoretical foundation in Hu's thought! He does not believe in a Creator who loves life; he denies the eternal value of morality, ceremony, and conventions; he believes that one should not fear or pity death; he treats the birth of a human being, a dog, and a cat as the same. In this case, even if Hu does not regard all living things as beasts, he has certainly gone against his own liberalism, built on a tremendous respect for the dignity of mankind. We respect and love Professor Hu greatly, and so we must be fair: this was certainly not the intention of Hu when he penned these words! Yet the results of one slip, one small error, can be incalculable. Scholars, take great care when you write and speak! Hu is now dead. The Bible says, "Flesh and blood cannot inherit the kingdom of God" (1 Cor 15:50). "Where is the wise? Where is the scribe? Where is the disputer of this age?" (1 Cor 1:20). Hu has perished eternally—according to his own theory of "destruction of the spirit." Those who follow Hu's thought, take heed!

The Atheism of Qian Mu

The third is Professor Qian Mu of New Asia College, Chinese University of Hong Kong, who wrote about the "way and destiny" (*Dao* and *ming*) in his *Leisurely Thoughts by the Lake*.[6] According to him, this book was composed while he paced along the lake and the mountains, at Jiangnan University by Tai Hu Lake in Wuxi. He said that he wrote this book "not to establish a school of philosophy to teach and guide society, like the ancient Chinese Confucianists, Moists, Daoists, and Legalists; nor to establish an orthodox tradition to debunk all other schools, like the Neo-Confucianists

---

5. See Hu, *Hu Shi Wen Cun* (*The Collected Works of Hu Shi*), vol. 9. Hu Shi has expressed his own views in his essay, "She Hui Bu Xiu Lun" ("Social Immortality"). He was influenced by Fan Zhen's theory of "the destruction of God." Fan made the point that God is to form as sharpness is to a knife. No one has ever heard of sharpness which exists when a knife does not exist. So how can we say that, without physical form, God exists? This is materialist and atheist philosophy which denies the existence of the soul. Yet Hu Shi cherishes it as a great treasure and taught it to Chinese youth!

6. Or *Hu shang xian si lu*.

of the Sung and Ming periods such as the Cheng brothers,[7] Zhu Xi,[8] Lu Xiangshan,[9] and Wang Yang-ming; nor to discover objective truth and to develop a system of thought through logical deduction from a baseline, such as the Western philosophers have done." In fact, however, Qian was discussing important issues related to philosophy; he was dealing with the universe and with life, not just having "leisurely thoughts"!

In his chapter on "*Dao* and *ming*," Qian said, "God! The soul! Being! These are difficult to verify, after all." Then he said, "The Chinese people have never paid much attention to exploring the nature and origin of the universe; rather, they seek to understand the phenomena laid before them." Thirdly, he said, "The phenomena which can be seen are simply change and motion. Change is existence, but this existence cannot be explained. We cannot insist that God created the world, therefore. And this change seems to have no purpose; Chinese thought, therefore, is not interested in the end of the universe." Fourthly, he said, "Creation is to make something out of nothing. Change is to change from something into nothing. It is creation and change at the same time; things change, and things are created at the same time. We do not speak of being behind phenomena; we do not speak of the soul behind life. Therefore, God, the soul, and being are not rejected in Chinese thought. It is just that these things are immanent in all phenomena." Fifthly, he said: "The *Tao* is everywhere, and changing all the time. *Tao* is matter, *Tao* is spirit, *Tao* is heaven, *Tao* is man. *Tao* is phenomenon, *Tao* is being. The concepts of God, the soul and being disappear in this concept of Tao; there is no longer any serious reason for their existence." (Take note: He said, "God and soul ... disappear; there is no longer any reason for their existence.) Finally he said, "The motion of all things takes place only in reason (*li*) and righteousness (*yi*) and destiny (*ming*); that is, only in benevolence (*ren*) and life and the *Tao*. Conflict, war, death and calamities are natural. From all these are manifested righteousness, reason, benevolence, the *Dao*, and life. It is all humanity. But humanity is still nature. Nothing that is human can go against nature or be isolated from nature." Professor Qian is a master of humanism today; his ideas and writings are greatly respected. But if we take a closer look at his writings, we see that they amount to a conglomeration of agnosticism, positivism, phenomenalism, pantheism, naturalism, and atheism. One might say that his thought is opposite to the thought of Hu Shi, but in

---

7. Cheng Hao and Cheng Yi.
8. Or Chu Hsi.
9. Or Lu Hsiang-shan.

Critique of Humanism

terms of his "disappearance of God and the soul" and his denial of "any serious reason for their existence," his ideas are really very similar to Hu Shi's. Both are thoroughly naturalist and humanist.

The difference between Qian's thought and that of Wu Zhihui and Hu Shi lies in the outer garment of *Dao*. But when man speaks of *Dao* with no faith in God's special revelation, he only follows the falsehoods of this world, and ends in emptiness and vanity. Take Chinese philosophy, for example. Although Confucius was so alert to seeking the truth that he said, "Having heard the Way (*Tao*) in the morning, one may die content in the evening," yet he concludes that "the nature of the master and the way of Heaven" is a riddle which "cannot be heard." When Laozi[10] speaks of the *Dao*, he is in a lofty realm, not at all this-worldly like Confucius. He even rebuked Confucius, saying, "Put away your proud air and many desires, your plausibility and ungoverned will. These are of no advantage to you!"[11] Confucius returned and told his disciples that Laozi was so great, "I cannot tell how he mounts on the wind through the clouds and rises to heaven."[12] This shows how much Confucius respected Laozi.

Laozi issued a warning for today's humanists and human religions: "Abandon sageliness and discard wisdom; abandon humanity and discard righteousness." Yet, what exactly is the Dao? Laozi's answer is mystical and inscrutable: "A Tao that can be spoken about is not the constant Tao."[13] It is an empty idea! If we look at humanist philosophy in the West, we see that Heraclitus of Ephesus (ca. 535–457 BC) was merely a pantheist; he also held mysterious notions about the Logos. Anaxagoras (500?–428 BC) took the Logos to be a guiding principle which exists between God and the universe. Although Philo Judaeus (20 BC) developed a fine philosophical system with the idea of the Logos, it is really Plato's philosophy of idealism fitted onto the monotheism of the Hebrews. He is still groping in the dark, for he did not fathom the truth of "the Word become flesh."

"In the beginning was the Word, and the Word was with God, and the Word was God" (John 1:1). The Word was God's highest self-revelation. "And the Word became flesh and dwelt among us" (John 1:14); he revealed God, whom no one has seen. Through the Lord Jesus Christ, God the Son, God was made evident. This is the highest miracle of God.[14] It is some-

---

10. Formerly Lao-tzu.
11. See Chang, *Asia's Religions*, chap. 4.
12. Ibid.
13. Huang, *Tao Te Ching*, chap. 1.
14. See Chang, *Yuan Dao*, chap. 5.

thing which "many prophets and righteous men" "and kings" "desired to see ... and did not see it, and to hear ... and did not hear it" (Matt 13:17; Luke 10:24). "But God has revealed them to us through His Spirit" (see 1 Cor 2:9–10). If one reasons and deduces only with his finite mind, the best conclusion he can draw is an agnostic one: "I don't know." This is because, at its heart, humanism is empty. No wonder secular philosophers reject the holy Christian religion. This is not just an empty intellectual debate, but the conclusion from the crucible of my experience as I have contended for the faith in the past several decades.

My Prayer and Hope

Wu Zhihui, Hu Shi, and Qian Mu are all highly respected among Chinese for their character and for their writings. I also admire them very much.[15] The above are simply narratives of what each man has said or written. We have used their own words to show their own folly and contradictions. Aside from a few remarks, I have not added my own personal critique. (To critique their thought requires another book.) Quite the opposite. My reason for writing this book is precisely because I admire them personally, and would want to witness to "the mystery of the gospel" by the love of Jesus Christ, especially to the multitudes of Chinese who have blindly followed their thinking. (Unfortunately, Wu has passed away in Taiwan; his family respected his wishes, and threw his ashes into the East China Sea. So perished his theories of "impeaching God" and "exiling the soul." Hu Shi has also died of heart disease; he is gone forever, and perishes forever! As we witness their deaths, let them be a warning for the living!) Each man sensed a heavy responsibility on behalf of Chinese culture and scholarship; but as the Bible says: "The creation was subjected to futility" (Rom 8:20). Not only have these men become captives of their own thought (Col 2:8 says, "Beware lest anyone cheat you through philosophy and empty deceit, according to the tradition of men, according to the basic principles of the world, and not according to Christ"), but they have also unwittingly become defenders of "materialism" and "atheism." Oh, my fellow Chinese,

---

15. In terms of personal friendship, I have had quite a long relationship with Professors Wu and Qian. When I was appointed president of Jiangnan University in the late 1940s, I invited Professor Wu Zhihui to be chairman of the board, and Mr. Tai Zhitao as the vice-chairman. Professor Qian Mu became the dean of the college of liberal arts. At that time I had the grand vision of rejuvenating Chinese culture, and particularly emphasized this point in my inaugural address. I made this a major goal for the college of liberal arts. At that time, my own thinking was that of a very strong humanist.

please learn from these painful experiences and probe at the root of the issues: let us reflect ourselves why our nation has suffered so much, and why there have been such dramatic changes in history. We must bear our responsibility in the presence of God!

"For since the creation of the world His invisible attributes are clearly seen, being understood by the things that are made, even His eternal power and Godhead, so that they are without excuse, because, although they knew God, they did not glorify Him as God, nor were thankful, but became futile in their thoughts, and their foolish hearts were darkened. Professing to be wise, they became fools . . . who exchanged the truth of God for the lie. . . . And even as they did not like to retain God in their knowledge, God gave them over to a debased mind, to do those things which are not fitting" (from Rom 1:20–32). I pray that my fellow Chinese intellectuals may humble ourselves before the true and living God, and be enlightened by this Scripture. Let us learn from the ravages of sin on mankind, repent of our sins, and turn to God. Let us trust in the Savior Jesus Christ, and become witnesses to the truth. May we lead in the task of apologetics, and receive "an inheritance incorruptible and undefiled and that does not fade away, reserved in heaven for you" (1 Pet 1:4). This is my heart-felt prayer for Chinese intellectuals, my constant, earnest plea before God!

4

Humanism in Christian Guise: Lin Yutang

THIS CHAPTER DEALS WITH Professor Lin Yutang's misunderstanding of Christianity.

Lin returned from the United States to Taiwan and then gave open lectures in Hong Kong on his spiritual pilgrimage. Many Christians and church leaders have expressed their concern about Lin's faith because, although Lin said that he has "believed in Christ," he did not affirm many of the doctrines taught in the Bible. What a self-contradiction! He has confounded the truth with error, like the false prophets who "come . . . in sheep's clothing, but inwardly they are ravenous wolves" (Matt 7:15), to the great detriment of the Church of Jesus Christ. Due to his reputation among the Chinese, many will take offense and stumble because of him (Matt 18:7). In the West, even though there are heretical beliefs, the orthodox, evangelical camp is strong enough to offer resistance, but the Christian church is still in its budding stage in China and cannot stand such a frontal onslaught.

Even though I live far away in North America, I was consumed by zeal for God's house (see John 2:13–17), so I wrote an article to confront Lin. Because of limited space, I will not discuss issues pertaining to theological foundations; nor will I offer a systematic defense of the truth. Rather, I will follow the lines of Lin's ideas as he expressed them in Hong Kong[1] and give an objective analysis. I want to help my fellow Christians clarify our own thinking, and also urge Lin to return to the truth before it is too late, that he may truly return to the Savior and receive saving grace. I will

---

1. See Liu, "Liu Yiling Xiansheng yu Lin Shi De Chuxi Tan"; and Wu, "Issues Concerning Lin Yutang's Faith."

speak boldly, but honestly and sincerely. May Professor Lin understand and appreciate my heart.

Lin Yutang's Understanding of Christianity

Lin claims that he "has never lost his Christian faith so, strictly speaking, he cannot be regarded as a Prodigal Son." This statement of his is similar to many things which non-Christians say in order to express their goodwill toward Christianity. Yet it reveals his own lack of true understanding of the Christian truth. If Lin truly did not lose his Christian faith, then his numerous writings over the last decades could be used by the Lord as a fine testimony; his influence could possibly exceed that of C. S. Lewis![2] Moreover, Lin wrote a book called *From Pagan to Christian*; since he called himself a pagan, why does he now say that he is not a "Prodigal Son" who never lost his faith? This is self-contradictory. Or perhaps he thinks that there is no intrinsic difference between Christianity and paganism? This would show that he does not truly understand the Christian truth.

In the talk referred to above, Lin expressed his strong dislike of most pastors. He "did not admire them at all," and said that listening to them was sheer torture. On the other hand, he admired Jiang Menglin,[3] a professor who sympathized with atheism. Lin said that Jiang's autobiography was very valuable. This statement casts great doubt on Lin Yutang's own beliefs.[4]

Next, Lin Yutang indicated that although he greatly admired the teachings of Jesus, he thought that Paul had combined into a pile many sundry issues, many of which had nothing to do with Jesus' teachings. This is the old trick used by Adolf von Harnack, bifurcating the New Testament and distinguishing between the so-called "Christianity according to Jesus" and "Christianity according to Paul." It is the technique used by liberal theology to undermine biblical Christianity. These theologians wrote and spoke in the name of Jesus, so they could occupy a position in the church and subvert

---

2. C. S. Lewis was a former opponent of Christianity; later he became a Christian and wrote prolifically to witness to the truth. He is sometimes called "an apostle to the skeptics."

3. Or Chiang Meng-lin.

4. Jiang wrote an article singing Wu Zhihui's praises for the hundredth anniversary of Wu's birth. Wu was the one who wanted to "eliminate God's quota" and "exile the soul of the spiritual element" and who regarded man as a souless animal with merely a greater amount of neurological substances. Wu was a strong atheist, yet Jiang was so appreciative of him that his article was called "A Most Meaningful Life." See Jiang, "A Most Meaningful Life."

Humanism in Christian Guise: Lin Yutang

her, "and bring on themselves swift destruction" (2 Pet 2:1). With Jesus as their shield, they could perform surgery on Paul. Little did they know that they were only deceiving themselves. Just a little careful thought will show that, if Paul has compiled a "sundry lot," then the account of Paul's call to the ministry, and God's revelation to him, in the Book of Acts would be fictitious. The credibility of the Gospel of Luke, written by the author of Acts, would be questionable. If the Gospel of Luke were unreliable, then the other gospels could be questioned as well. More seriously, about one half of the New Testament books were written by the Apostle Paul. Lin's argument would make most of the New Testament "a sundry lot." Thus the authority of the Bible is lost; how can it be the infallible guide for our faith? Lin not only destroyed the foundation of his own faith, he has blasphemed against God and libeled the holy Christian religion! Let us just suppose, for argument's sake, that Lin only believed in the teachings of Jesus; how then can he not believe in the resurrection and the doctrine of hell, teachings which the Lord Jesus brought up time and again? This amounts to calling Jesus a deceiver and a liar! Thus Lin said: "Jesus told the repentant thief on the cross, 'Tonight you will be with me in Paradise.' If he was going to be in paradise, how come anyone would go to hell at the resurrection?" Not only does this show his lack of common knowledge of the Bible and of theology, but it is also illogical. Many scholars today attack the Bible in the name of "science," but they do not begin with an objective and factual study of the Bible. Instead, they use all kinds of fallacious arguments to "prove" their own theories. This is the most unscientific approach.

I have written dozens of books seeking to provide a clear exposition of the nature and mystery of the holy Christian faith, so I shall not engage in detailed theological discussion here. Furthermore, Lin has always loathed theology, so I shall only elucidate the matter with a couple of testimonies from non-theologians. For example: Friedrich W. J. Schelling said in his work, *Philosophie der Offernbarung (The Philosophy of Revelation)*, "Christianity is not an empty theory, but objective truth. Its most important reality is the work of redemption accomplished by Christ."[5] In his later years Napoleon testified of Christ: "There is a tremendous difference between Christianity and other religions; they cannot be compared on the same level. We can say to the founders of other religions: 'You are not God, nor are you representatives of God; you are only false teachers. You cannot separate yourselves from your evil desires; your fate is the same as other humans, which is destruction.'" Pagan religions are fabrications of men; those arrogant, boastful

---

5. Schelling, *Philosophie der Offernbarung (The Philosophy of Revelation)*.

founders of religions, like the rest of us, are ignorant concerning the soul of mankind, the future destiny of man, the attributes of God, and the creation of the universe. Christianity is revelation from God, not human wisdom. It is not, as Lin would say, "insight of true knowledge." Jesus Christ came to the world in order to reveal the mysteries of heaven; he came to save souls. The gospel of Jesus Christ is not merely the most holy ethic, but the greatest mystery and truth. It is the truth which eyes have not seen, and reason has not fathomed. Life is a mystery. Who am I? Where did I come from? Where am I going? The universe likewise is a mystery. How was it created? What is its future destiny? These questions are unanswerable. Christianity does not avoid these mysteries, but provides clear answers. There is an inexhaustible treasury in the Bible; in it one finds incomparable doctrines, with wondrous power to change one's heart and comfort one's spirit. The Bible is not dead; it is a living book, with living power to give life to the obedient, and death to the disobedient![6]

The Christian religion is not empty metaphysical speculation; it does not consist of philosophical arguments. Christianity is the revelation and the operation of God's love and grace. God is love, but love is not a passive attribute. It is an infinite power which is everywhere, always working itself in the hearts of men. God is the Father in heaven, but God's Fatherhood is not an empty title, but an omnipotent power which creates and re-creates, turning mankind to repent and return to him and to become his children and heirs. The Christian religion, therefore, is a historical fact. Through the power of the Holy Spirit, God has worked powerfully in human society through history, convicting hearts, reforming society, thrusting history forward, and realizing his kingdom. It is truly a dynamic faith, an ever-living, everlasting truth of salvation.[7]

The Person of Christ

Lin Yutang said that "other people paid attention to the good and the important, but only Jesus regarded the sinful and the small ones; this is something which no one in history could surpass." Therefore "Jesus is higher than Socrates, higher than Buddha." Although this shows some respect for Jesus, Lin is only regarding Christ "according to the flesh" (2 Cor

---

6. See Chang, *Religious Thought of Famous Men of the World*.

7. See Chang, *Shengdao Tong Quan* (*A General Interpretation of Christian Truth*), chaps. 1, 10.

Humanism in Christian Guise: Lin Yutang

5:16). The question of the person of Christ is a most important question, on which I have written another book to give a full exposition.[8]

Jesus Christ is truly man, but He is also truly God. Because of the deity of Christ, Christianity is qualitatively different from all other religions. If Jesus Christ is not the Word incarnate, Christianity loses its supernatural distinctiveness. Lin Yutang never had a love for theology, so I will avoid theological talk here. Let me cite the words of a British philosopher, John Stuart Mill, as testimony. Mill once said that, apart from his wife, he did not believe in any religion. However shortly before his death, he wrote three essays concerning religion. One of them was on God. He said, "Christianity is the incarnation of God in the flesh, therefore it is worthy of worship. No matter how rationalists criticize and libel it, no harm can be done to the Christian faith. The accounts in the four gospels are indisputable historical fact; all doubts and criticism arise from folly and ignorance."[9] Mill thought of Jesus Christ as a unique person in history. Jesus was not only great and noble, but also without parallel. He is unfathomable. It is not enough to call him the greatest figure in world history, because his person is incomparable. He cannot be compared with any other man in history. In the gospels, the rich young ruler saw Jesus and called him "good Teacher." Jesus responded, "Why do you call Me good? No one is good but One, that is, God" (Matt 19:16–17). We can thus see that no one can be compared with Jesus; if we call him the greatest, holiest sage, we still have not known his person, because he is the most holy, most righteous true God.

Modern scholars, in the name of "historical investigation," squeezed Jesus into their mundane, naturalistic mold. In a totally subjective way, they brought down him who was, is, and ever shall be, the eternal, ever-living God—"He who came down from heaven . . . who is in heaven" (John 3:13), the Son of the living God, Jesus Christ, Savior of mankind. In the name of the "search for the historical Jesus," they made Jesus into a mere historical figure who is different from mankind only in degree, so that Jesus may fit their superficial notions of naturalism, relativism, and historicism. But this fictitious "Jesus" whom they concocted, not in accordance with the Bible but wholly by the will of man, does not reflect the consensus of all, because each scholar has his own subjective view. Even their colleague Albert Schweitzer felt great pain. In despair he said, "We thought that we could lay hold of Jesus, so that he can live in our time; but

---

8. See Chang, *Jidu Lun* (*Christology*).

9. See Schaff, *A History of the Church*, 1:436; Chang, *Jidu Lun* (*Christology*), 280–85.

Critique of Humanism

he is very wonderful and cannot be grasped by us."[10] What a sad commentary on modern, secular liberal theologians! This proves that if we were to regard Christ only according to the flesh, we will not come to know him.[11]

The Bible and Science

Lin Yutang thought that "Jesus' teachings are very good, and will never be extinguished," but he also said that Jesus' teachings "can be understood in harmony with physics and chemistry. We are modern people, who know that many things can be understood in terms of natural science." He does not, therefore, "believe in supernatural acts," and only accepts a portion of the truths in Scripture. He only believes in teachings such as Jesus' Sermon on the Mount and regards them as "true knowledge of great insight," but he does not realize that the Christian religion is God's own revelation. "Heaven and earth will pass away, but [his] words will by no means pass away" (Matt 24:35). God's Word is established in heaven forever; it is everlasting, ever new. "He who comes from heaven is above all." "A man can receive nothing unless it has been given to him from heaven" (see Ps 119:89; John 3:27, 31). Unfortunately, Lin Yutang had been poisoned with liberal theology and trapped himself in secular naturalism; he could not overcome the shackles of humanism. Thus he did not believe in the supernatural truths of the Bible.

Modern scholars have been deeply influenced by the empiricist world-and-life view of the eighteenth-century Enlightenment. They reject all supernatural elements, and blindly follow the mechanistic "forces of nature" and "laws of nature." They seek to explain all phenomena in the universe and all matters concerning man's soul and religion mechanistically. They exalt science, so that it has climbed onto God's throne. In an effort to harmonize Christianity and the "scientific" principles of naturalism, they have discarded portions of the Bible and twisted it by their misinterpretation, so that true Christianity is transformed into something else.[12] These scholars boast of being progressive, but in fact show how ignorant and outdated they are, for, according to Francis Bacon, those who have a superficial knowledge of science and philosophy only see the secondary causes of the universe; they cannot know God and come to understand the mysteries of the Christian faith!

10. See Schweitzer, *The Quest for the Historical Jesus*.
11. See Chang, *Jidu Lun* (*Christology*), chap. 9.
12. See Chang, *Yuan Dao*, chap. 3.

Humanism in Christian Guise: Lin Yutang

The chairman of the Board of the Massachusetts Institute of Technology, Dr. Vannevar Bush, published his views in *Fortune* magazine last year (1962?).[13] He wrote, "Mankind worships science; this is actually the result of eighteenth-century superstitious faith in natural law. Actually, scientific laws can be 'true' today and 'false' yesterday; they are not unchanging truth. Science's observations are at their best a glimpse at the mechanical operations of the universe; they can never fathom the mysteries of life and of the universe. Therefore, may I plead with modern scientists, if you are to know the truth, humble yourselves and do not only rely on science; you must also have faith." The Royal Society in Great Britain was once made up of over six hundred outstanding scientists. They published a declaration, saying, "We believe that God's Word is written in Scripture, and also in nature; though the method of writing is different, the two do not conflict with one another . . . Physical science is not perfect, and is progressing all the time; at present, according to our limited understanding, we are seeing as in a glass darkly. Many modern natural scientists do not study the Bible; they only have a partial understanding by relying on their imperfect laws; they doubt and attack the Bible. These attitudes are most pitiable indeed."

The French genius and scientist Blaise Pascal realized that science and philosophy cannot unlock the key to life and to the universe, so he turned to the study of the Bible. One evening he heard God's voice speak to him in the greatest glory: "The God of Abraham, the God of Isaac, the God of Jacob, is not the God of the philosophers, nor the God of scholars."[14] He prostrated himself and trusted in the Savior. Jesus said, "I am the truth." Jesus also said: "If you abide in My word, you are My disciples indeed. And you shall know the truth, and the truth shall make you free" (John 8:31–32). May God illumine Professor Lin, so that he can be liberated from his self-centeredness, his rationalistic shackles, and his eighteenth-century naturalistic principles. May he find true freedom indeed!

Faith and Reason

Lin Yutang boasted that he was a thinker; he regarded all evangelical Christians as ignorant people. He disparaged Paul for compiling miscellanies, and said that Calvin should have been executed! Just from these

---

13. Vannevar Bush (1890–1974) was an American engineer and inventor known for his work on analog computers and for the memex, considered by many a forerunner of the World Wide Web.—Ed.

14. Pascal, *Pensees*, 285.

Critique of Humanism

statements, we can see that he has not repented of his sins, and is like those "wolves" "in sheep's clothing" (Matt 7:15) who have come to destroy the church. He does not realize that he cannot understand the truth just by using his mind; faith and reason are not in conflict. Augustine said that, in many things, knowledge comes before faith; in some things, however, faith comes before understanding. Faith is not superstition; a sound faith is reasonable, built on the evidences of assurance (Heb 11:1). A reasonable faith, however, does not rest wholly on human understanding. Herbert Spencer, an agnostic, said: "Our minds and thoughts are limited indeed. The highest truth is that power which hovers in the universe; it is unthinkable, and unfathomable by the human mind."[15]

Rene Descartes, the father of modern philosophy, made the famous statement, "I think, therefore I am" (*cogito ergo sum*). Ever since then, modern philosophy has intensified its efforts to reject faith and attack theology. The most important starting-point for all knowledge becomes doubt; all knowledge must appeal to one's reason. This not only leads mankind away from the true God, but also deifies man himself and establishes man as the ultimate. Man's mind, man's reason, becomes the only rule for truth. Little does man realize that the phenomena of the universe are not isolated, nor do they exist for themselves; rather, they transcend themselves and are vitally related to everything else in the universe. All things must exist according to the will of the Creator Lord of the universe; it is not true that "I think therefore I am." Thus, the philosopher's task is to seek the source and goal of the universe—God Himself. True philosophy, therefore, which is thinking that is truly reasonable, must have God as its starting point. Secular philosophy is "immanent" and "humanist," built on a perverted view of the universe. It denies the relationship of God to the universe and therefore is incapable of knowing the origin of the universe. It cannot attain comprehensiveness of truth. The starting-point of secular philosophers is a basically erroneous one. They do not believe in God, nor in Christ; they exalt mankind, and make man divine. They claim "infinite perfectibility" for man, and think that man can master the universe; in their view, man can rule over the world. This kind of humanist philosophy, which rebels against God and his truth, brings mankind and civilization far from God. Man becomes rootless, like "cut flowers in a vase."[16] The collapse and decline of secular philosophy today brings mankind into an unprecedented crisis. Although Lin Yutang is disappointed with human-

---

15. Spencer, *First Principles*, 45–46, 74–75, 110.
16. Trueblood, *The Predicament of Modern Man*.

ism, he does not see the root of the problem. He repeats the error of Rene Descartes, thus falling into self-contradiction. He has not gotten to the core issue. This shows that Lin has not been truly converted.

The almighty God took the initiative in his three great works: creation, redemption, and revelation. Mankind is to receive, believe, and obey. God's life is infinite, his wisdom without limit. The mind of man, no matter how lofty, can never fathom the mysteries of the Godhead (see Job 38–41). There is no ladder which man can climb to reach God in heaven. Between the two, there is only an infinite chasm. Man will always be man; he will never become God or attain divinity. Bishop William Temple[17] said: "Higher education can only bring man to a higher plane, like a ladder which man can climb so he can see a little higher. But man cannot transcend his self-centered reference-point. Man cannot become higher than what he is." Man's mind, therefore, cannot remedy the errors of man-centered philosophy. For man to know God, he cannot depend on his own wisdom or logical deductions. Man must rely on God's revelation. Man can observe and study the "instruments" (*qi*) this side of the chasm; but for man to know the Word (*Dao, logos*) which is above, he cannot depend on his sense perception. This does not mean that there is no place for the mind or that man should not develop his thinking. Rather, man must come to terms with his finitude and know his own inadequacy. Jesus said, "I thank You, Father, Lord of heaven and earth, that You have hidden these things from the wise and prudent and have revealed them to babes" (Matt 11:25). Augustine wrote, "Man cannot understand the truth, because of his arrogant nature; his pride becomes his insurmountable obstacle."

If we are to come into the presence of God, therefore, we must rid ourselves of pride. Unfortunately, modern man is exceedingly proud. He continues to come to God with his status, fame, education, and talents; he wants to share the universe with God! For example, Paul Tillich's theology has been described by some as the light, as when one lights a match. We are delighted when a light is lit in a dark room, and others groping in the dark are likewise happy, but they do not understand that they need to open their doors and windows, so that "the light of the gospel of the glory of Christ . . . should shine on them" (2 Cor 4:3–4). How pitiable! Those who reject faith in the name of reason and who boast before God with their intellectual accomplishments only show their superficiality and ignorance. Lin Yutang smacks of arrogance as he accuses Paul's doctrine

---

17. William Temple (1881–1944) served as archbishop of York (1929–42) and Archbishop of Canterbury (1942–1944).—Ed.

as being merely "miscellany" and says that Calvin should be executed. The Bible says, "Professing to be wise, they became fools" (Rom 1:22). "He who sits in the heavens shall laugh; the Lord shall hold them in derision" (Ps 2:4). Oh how sad it is!

The Holy Spirit and Revelation

Lin Yutang said, "My personal opinion is: first, do not regard the Holy Spirit as too mysterious. Man has his conscience; in the silence of the night, we can ask our hearts and will discover our conscience . . . Second, do not think that the Holy Spirit is matter. He does not have a form; he can be felt, but cannot be described with words . . . Third, do not think that the Holy Spirit is mechanical." From this we can see that Lin lacks the most basic understanding concerning the Holy Spirit. He has not been born again, and is still "dead in trespasses and sins" (Eph 2:1). Not only did he deny the personhood of the Holy Spirit; he did not know that the Holy Spirit is a person in the Trinity. He even confused man's soul with the Holy Spirit. Strictly speaking, this is blasphemy. Jesus said that the sin of blaspheming against the Holy Spirit will not be forgiven, in this life or the next (Matt 12:31–32). We will not go over Jesus' teachings concerning the Holy Spirit in detail. Jesus said that "unless one is born of water and the Spirit, he cannot enter the kingdom of God. That which is born of the flesh is flesh, and that which is born of the Spirit is spirit" (John 3:5–6). He also said, "I will pray the Father, and He will give you another Helper, that He may abide with you forever—the Spirit of truth, whom the world cannot receive, because it neither sees Him nor knows Him" (John 14:16–17a).

Lin's own published words reveal that he does not yet know the Holy Spirit; naturally he cannot receive the Holy Spirit. In other words, he is still a "natural man," after the flesh; he cannot receive the mysteries of divine wisdom, which God revealed through the Spirit (see 1 Cor 2:8–14). "If anyone does not have the Spirit of Christ, he is not His" (Rom 8:9). This is a serious life-and-death issue, "for to be carnally minded is death, but to be spiritually minded is life and peace" (Rom 8:6). "Flesh and blood cannot inherit the kingdom of God" (1 Cor 15:50). Mankind belongs to the first Adam, and is earthly, worldly, and fleshly. Christians, however, belong to the Last Adam, and are heavenly, born from above, and spiritual (see 1 Cor 15:45–50). Christians are the children of God, "born, not of blood, nor of the will of the flesh, nor of the will of man, but of God" (John 1:13).

Humanism in Christian Guise: Lin Yutang

Ducks are born from ducks; they can swim. Doves are born of doves; they cannot swim. These are simple, clear, and indisputable facts. A person who has not risen from death to life in Christ by the mercy of the Father, that is, a person who has not been born again, cannot be liberated from the corruption of sinful desires and of the world. He does not participate in the divine nature, and does not have living hope (see 2 Pet 1:4; 1 Pet 1:3) He does not live "in newness of life" (Rom 6:4). Thus, his thoughts and his words will not be Spirit-minded, for he is still at enmity with God.

Since Lin Yutang has not received the Holy Spirit, his thinking is still according to the logic of natural man and his thoughts are still those of humanism. He said: "Personally I do not believe in supernatural acts. We encounter many incidents every day. Today we think they are right, tomorrow we will think they are wrong. When we think too much, our brains cannot take it, so we put them aside. One day we understand them all of a sudden; we can call this revelation." This amounts to substituting man's thinking for God's revelation, a most dangerous mistake. The basic error in liberal theology is to put philosophy in the place of theology. (No wonder Lin said over and again that he is not a lover of theology). Secular human reason takes the place of the wisdom of the mysteries of God. "Since . . . the world through [its] wisdom did not know God" (1 Cor 1:21), it totally rejects the authority of the Bible, or even casts doubt on the existence of God. In other words, it does not believe any revelation from heaven. Worldly thinking is "through philosophy and empty deceit, according to the tradition of men, according to the basic principles of the world, and not according to Christ" (Col 2:8). Following the creed of the founder of humanism, the Greek dialectical philosopher Protagoras (480–410 BC), the world believes that "man is the measure of all things." The dialecticians do not believe in the true God or miracles. They only take man as the measure of all things; thus "man" is the greatest miracle. Having no fear of God, they are thoroughgoing humanists. The city government of Athens expelled Protagoras because of his ridiculous ideas, whereupon he set sail for Sicily and drowned in the sea. Such is the tragic fate of an unbeliever. May God have mercy, so that Lin Yutang does not follow in this path of destruction. And may people not follow Lin Yutang's "philosophy and empty deceit," nor his "basic principles of the world" to their destruction!

Critique of Humanism

Human Nature and Salvation

Lin Yutang said, "Man is by nature good in the beginning; this is correct. Man has the roots of wisdom in him, which we can call it conscience. But it has been hidden by material things. Just as *The Great Learning*[18] said, man simply needs to be renewed every day; he can move upward." This amounts to the fifth-century heresy of Pelagius's autosoterism.[19] Pelagius did not believe that sin has any subjective, inner influence on man. Man does not, therefore, need any grace or help from God; he can of his own strength and of his own initiative turn from sin and return to the way of righteousness. This Pelagian view was strongly opposed by Augustine, and was condemned as heresy at the Council of Carthage in AD 418. Unfortunately, in the nineteenth century Friedrich E. D. Schleiermacher[20] intensified this heretical view, so that "liberal" churches abandoned the preaching of the gospel, declined in their walk with God, and became powerless witnesses. It hurts me just to mention this. Schleiermacher is considered the trailblazer for liberal theology; he rejected the authority of the Bible and substituted it with man's subjective religious consciousness. He twisted the truth of the gospel and ruined God's redemptive plan. He did not believe in justification through faith, being born again, or sanctification. He did not believe in the work of the Holy Spirit. He rejected most of the doctrines in orthodox Christianity. He believed that beginning with Adam, mankind has naturally developed according to his inner strength and history's natural development. There is no room for the work of the Holy Spirit in this theology. In fact, he denies that the Holy Spirit is a person. For him, the "Holy Spirit" is actually a kind of holy life in the church. There are two laws in man: good and evil. So-called "salvation" is simply the victory of good over evil. This "doctrine of redemption" concocted by Schleiermacher is actually nothing new; it is simply an echo of the ideas of Immanuel Kant. Not only does it contradict the teaching of Scripture, it is also against the laws of history.

Arnold Toynbee, the great historian, said, "So long as original sin remains an element in human nature, Caesar will always have work to do." He further said, "I have already confessed my own adherence to the traditional Christian view that there is no reason to expect any change

---

18. Or *Da Xue*.—Ed.

19. Or *self-salvation*.—Ed.

20. Friedrich Daniel Ernst Schleiermacher (1768–1834) was a German theologian, philosopher, and biblical scholar who tried to reconcile the Romantic rejection of the Enlightenment with traditional Protestant orthodoxy.—Ed.

Humanism in Christian Guise: Lin Yutang

in unredeemed human nature while human life on Earth goes on."[21] This is the conclusion which Toynbee reached after his massive work in analyzing world history. Accordingly, David R. Davies said that Toynbee's *A Study of History* can be renamed "The Science of Original Sin"! He also said, "Six thousand years of human history has revealed to mankind a historical law. It is this: All of man's efforts have resulted in exhaustion and folly. Mankind's fate of destruction is not something from which man can save himself."[22] The Chinese sages did try to teach something good to the people; but their teachings could not result in an integration of knowledge and action in the actual life of the people. In fact, reality goes in an opposite direction. In the later period, Wang Yang Ming and others advocated "the integration of knowledge and action,"[23] but they were not able to stem the tide of the time; human hearts remain unchanged. As we look at the world today, there is so much despair and depravity of heart in the world. All the efforts of moral leaders and lofty patriots cannot heal the Chinese people of the disease of the heart.[24] Man is depraved by nature; he cannot save himself. There is no doubt about this fact, which can be demonstrated throughout history, in East and West.

Jesus Christ came into the world not only to give Christian believers a way from death to life. He also holds the key to transforming a world in crisis, for the incarnation of Jesus Christ is God's own entrance into history to re-create for Himself a new humanity—"a chosen generation, a royal priesthood, a holy nation, His own special people" (1 Pet 2:9). This is the most profound revolution in human history, rejuvenating the human race from its depravity and its fate of destruction. This transformation comes from the infinite, unfathomable, abundant grace of God and his mysterious wisdom, something which secular scholars cannot possibly understand. Sages and philosophers, East and West, have tried throughout history to understand the ways of the *Dao*[25] and to attain true knowledge,[26] so that heaven and man can work together for good[27] and arrive at the *summum bonum*.[28] They do not realize that since our ances-

---

21. Toynbee, *Civilization on Trial*, 248, 261–62.
22. See [Davies], *Down Peacock's Feathers*. Chang lists the author as Toynbee.—Ed.
23. Or *zhi xing he yi*.—Ed.
24. See Chang, *Yuan Dao*, chap. 7.
25. Or *ming ming de*.—Ed.
26. Or *zhi zhen zhi*.—Ed.
27. Or *tian ren he de*.—Ed.
28. Or *zhi yu zhi shan*.—Ed.

tors sinned and fell, mankind is at enmity with God. Man's will and God's will are at enmity, the two cannot be united. The so-called "unity between heaven and man" and a "clean conscience" are nothing but fanciful dreams smacking of human pride and revealing man's wickedness and refusal to repent. Because man's "sincere heart"[29] is not the righteousness of God; man cannot be the norm for his own moral judgments. Liberal theologians advocated the so-called New Morality in the 1960s. They claimed that man no longer needs God's laws and commandments; all he has to do is do the loving thing, that which gives him peace of mind. It is the right thing even if he commits fornication, robs, or steals. This amounts to the destruction of justice and the defense of sin itself! Turning evil into good, they "call evil good, and good evil" (Isa 5:20). They will lead mankind into a horrible dark abyss. Their own fate will be eternal destruction. Those who boast about their consciences, take heed and awake! This is your last opportunity for repentance![30] Lin Yutang is quite proud of his own conscience. This is ample proof that he has not repented. He only deceives himself (and others) with his so-called conversion.

The Pursuit of Truth: Lin Yutang's Attitude

Lin Yutang does not admit that he is a "Prodigal Son"; he says that he has "never lost the Christian faith" (see above). He does not go to church, not because he does not believe, but because ministers are not good. On the surface this argument, which is really an excuse, cannot be refuted. He says: "There are many religious doctrines which I cannot tolerate, especially the lure or threat through rewards and punishments. I really do not have any respect for it. Some preachers' sermons are so flat and outdated, it hurts me to listen to them; it is like sitting on a carpet of needles. This is an obstacle turning me away from church. Later, I heard the Rev. David Read preach in a Presbyterian church in New York City. He preached simply (truth is originally quite simple). He was dynamic, and his insights are superior. He brought out my curiosity, so I would go often to listen to him."

We need to evaluate this statement with several observations. First, a Christian who has the true life of Christ will hunger and thirst after God, "as the deer pants for the water brooks" (Ps 42:1). Like a "newborn babe," he will "desire the pure milk of [God's] word" (1 Pet 2:2). If Professor Lin

---

29. Or *zhen xin*.—Ed.

30. See Chang, *Shengdao Tong Quan* (*A General Interpretation of Christian Truth*), chap. 12.

has true faith, even if something turns him off, his spiritual hunger and thirst will push him to persist. How can he be absent from worship for several decades? How can he not love the preaching of God's Word? This is negative proof that he is not a Christian with true faith.

Second, as Paul wrote, "even if our gospel is veiled, it is veiled to those who are perishing, whose minds the god of this age has blinded, who do not believe, lest the light of the gospel of the glory of Christ, who is the image of God, should shine on them" (2 Cor 4:3–4). In the same letter, we read, "For the message of the cross is foolishness to those who are perishing, but to us who are being saved it is the power of God" (1 Cor 1:18). The same gospel seed falls by the wayside, and birds come and eat it up. Other seed falls on shallow soil and dries and withers when the sun comes up. There is no root! Other seed falls on thorns and thistles, so it is choked. Only the seed which falls on good soil brings forth fruit, thirty-fold, sixty-fold, a hundredfold (see Matt 13:3–8). On one occasion before he became a preacher, the great evangelist Charles H. Spurgeon was snow-bound, so he attended worship in a small church. A young pastor pointed his finger at the congregation and appealed to them to repent, citing Isaiah 45. Spurgeon did not feel as if he was sitting on "a carpet of needles"; he also did not look down on the youth of the preacher. Rather he repented through that sermon, was saved, and dedicated his life to preach the gospel!

Third, "God resists the proud, but gives grace to the humble" (Jas 4:6). Laozi rebuked Confucius: "Put away your proud air and many desires, your plausibility and ungoverned will!"[31] How much more should we restrain ourselves when we come to God! We need to humble ourselves and come in fear and trembling. When the prophet Isaiah saw the glory of the Lord, he confessed that he was a sinner with unclean lips: "Woe is me, for I am undone!" (see Isa 6:1–5). Job was a righteous man who fled from evil, but when he had seen the Lord, he repented in ashes and abhorred himself (Job 42:5–6). Our understanding of God's truth and awakening to faith is not merely an intellectual issue. It is very much an ethical question. What is required of us is not simply understanding in the mind, but sorrow and repentance in the heart. We must confess our sins before God (see Psalms 32, 51). Prime Minister Gladstone, the great nineteenth-century British statesman,[32] was highly respected for his knowledge and his character. The Bishop of Salisbury publicly called Gladstone a great saint. The

---

31. See Chang, *Asia's Religions*, chap. 4.

32. William Ewart Gladstone (1809–1898) was a British Liberal statesman who served as prime minister four times.—Ed.

reason? Because of Gladstone's inspiring character, Salisbury had been spared from living a wanton life in his youth. Yet when Gladstone prayed before God, he called himself "a pitiful sinner." May I ask Professor Lin Yutang, compared with Gladstone, what manner of character does he have?

Fourth, the reason why we go to church is not to listen to some great orator, or to listen to the sermon by the pastor; rather we attend church because we want to worship God "in spirit and truth" (John 4:24). Lin goes to a particular church because the pastor there is more insightful, more "dynamic"; it seems that he is worshipping man, rather than worshipping God. It is therefore understandable that he cannot receive the grace of God. There are thousands upon thousands of such people who listen to sermons in Europe and North America, "having a form of godliness but denying its power" (2 Tim 3:5). They know nothing about the saving truth of the gospel. At most, they have some kind of twisted understanding of Jesus' Sermon on the Mount. Though they go to church and praise God with their lips, they have kept the Lord Jesus outside the door. They have not opened their hearts to Him (see Rev 3:20–23). Not having experienced regeneration, they do not have a life-relationship with Christ. These so-called "Christians" are "dead, though alive." No wonder, then, that their "Christianity" is also "dead, though alive."

Fifth, I do not deny that some pastors' sermons are indeed worn out and outdated. On the other hand, if we are to regard God's rewards and punishments as "lures" and "threats," how will Professor Lin explain the words of Jesus when he rebukes the Pharisees: "Woe to you! Woe to you!"? And what about Jesus' own words about "eternal life" and "everlasting punishment?" (see Matt 23, 25). Would this not be an insult against the Savior and blasphemy against the Holy Spirit? As Professor Lin says, "Truth is originally quite simple." Eternal life and eternal punishment are spiritual truths. Take food and drink, for example. We eat and drink, and we live; we refuse food and drink, and we die. Or take the light switch; turn it on, and we see light. Turn it off, and there is no light. Eternal life or eternal punishment is a matter of the heart. My deepest desire is that Professor Lin will not follow in the footsteps of the Jewish people, who said, "This is a hard saying; who can understand it?" They grew tired of the Lord Jesus Christ. They saw, but they left (see John 6:43–68). And may Professor Lin not be turned off by the outdated ways of pastors' sermons, and thus despise the truth. This is a matter of life and death; it is not a game! Life is short, perhaps seventy years, and Lin has passed his seventieth birthday. By the grace of God, he is healthy and energetic. Do not think that

Humanism in Christian Guise: Lin Yutang

this is because you know how to take care of yourself, or that you have a real interest in life. You need to know that "in Him we live and move and have our being" (Acts 17:28). God said to the rich man, who thought he could enjoy his remaining years on earth: "O fool! I will require your soul tonight!" This is not "a threat" to Mr. Lin; this is the truth. Paul Tillich once told a colleague of mine that after he retired, he wanted to go to Asia to study Zen, so that his theology may develop in sync with Zen. Recent theologians of the "God-is-dead" movement think very highly of Tillich. One evening they were conversing with Tillich, and said that they must give credit to Tillich for their "God-is-dead" ideas. Tillich was absolutely delighted, and made an appointment with them to continue the conversation the next day. God terminated his life that night! As Professor Lin is still alive, may he treasure the present, for this is the moment in which God is waiting to save your soul. God said, "Behold, now is the accepted time; behold, now is the day of salvation" (2 Cor 6:2).

The Purpose of Life

Lin Yutang has said, "Whether I am writing or doing other things, I have a natural interest in what I do, so that the more I do, the more I get excited. I do not remember or regret things I have done in the past, even if they were mistakes or failures. The silly things in the past are not worth thinking about, not worth sighing over. Living this way, I will naturally have good health."

First, there are two kinds of sorrow. "The sorrow of the world produces death"; however, "godly sorrow produces repentance leading to salvation, not to be regretted" (2 Cor 7:10). Second, even though Paul said that he pressed forward, "forgetting those things which are behind and reaching forward to those things which are ahead" (Phil 3:13), he first had the experience of forsaking darkness and coming to the light on the road to Damascus; Paul had been transformed from death to life (see Acts 9:1–21). He now regards all things as refuse, in order that he may gain Christ; he now only wants to know Christ—and thus he has the highest goal in life (see Phil 3:7–12).

Third, true joy and peace are the fruit of the Holy Spirit, not a "natural interest" in things. True joy and peace are internal and heavenly, not affected by external factors or our circumstances. Lin refers to his good health, and credits his "interest in things." He went on to say, however, that Madam Curie, though she was fully devoted to what she was doing, "was a person with fragile health." We see Lin contradicting himself. Peace and joy may not be directly related to good health. Miss Christiana Tsai,[33] hailed as "the Queen of the Dark Chamber," was confined to her dark room for over thirty years. Though tormented with pain for decades, yet "she found peace in suffering, joy in prayer, light in darkness." Her book has been translated into over thirty languages; it is a bestseller, giving comfort to thousands of people through the testimony of her life.[34]

Fourth, Professor Lin says, "There is no greater joy in life than interest." "All progress in science has to do with curiosity; curiosity is taking an interest in things." This kind of philosophy of life is fraught with problems. The young people in the United States are curious these days; they pursue all kinds of things out of interest, and live licentious lives, just having a good time. They have become a tremendous threat to society and to their own country. Professor Lin has lived in America for many years, so he should be familiar with this fact.

Fifth, Christians do not do things just out of "natural interest." We know that "it is God who works in you both to will and to do" (Phil 2:13). Jesus said, "Without me you can do nothing" (John 15:5). The Christian's goal in life is to glorify God and to serve others. That is why we live for the Lord and offer our bodies as "a living sacrifice." We refuse to "be conformed to this world," but seek to discern what is the "good and acceptable and perfect will" of the Lord (see Rom 6:13, 12:1–2; 2 Cor 5:15; Gal 2:20; 6:14). Our hope is that God's "will be done on earth as it is in heaven" (Matt 6:10).

I write this not just to have a debate with Professor Lin, whom I love and respect greatly. What is more, the love of Christ constrains me, so that in my earnest prayer for Lin, I sense the danger his soul is facing—as others are drowning, so he is about to drown. I cannot bear the thought of him being "tossed to and fro and carried about with every wind of doctrine, by the trickery of men" (Eph 4:14). I do not want him to be deceived and perish. Thus, I take what Lin has said in Hong Kong and evaluate it according to the Bible. If Lin has been truly born again, as he said he has, he will not mind my words. My greatest comfort is to see the weakness and failure of men, and our need for God.

Lin said: "I have been observing the material progress of the twentieth century, and the conduct of nations which do not believe in God. I am convinced that humanism is not adequate. Mankind needs to be linked with a power which is greater than man himself." "Humanism believes that

33. In Pinyin, *Cai*.—Ed.
34. See Chang, *Xinxinde Shilian (Faith on Trial)*.

man's mind can remake the world; this is wrong... because man cannot be only guided by the mind." Yet as we scrutinize Lin's words, we see that he is not only "guided by the mind," but is boasting in his mind. We therefore plead with him "by the mercies of God," so that he can be liberated from the shackles of human reason and transcend the limits of humanism. May he receive salvation from God and taste the goodness of heaven.

The Christian religion is not like any other religion; it is not a matter of philosophical argument. Just as Lin said, man needs to be linked up with a power greater than himself; he needs to build a personal relationship between himself and God. However, man cannot determine the terms of this relationship himself, but must depend on God's redemptive work. In a treaty between two nations, or a contract between two parties, one cannot unilaterally lay down all the terms; the two must come to an agreement. In the matter of the plan of salvation, however, God must take the initiative. There is a "wall of separation" between mankind and God which cannot be broken down except through the finished redemptive work of the eternal Son of God, our Savior Jesus Christ. Through his cross he destroyed the "enmity," so that the two become one, and man is reconciled to God. (See Eph 2:12–16.) This great work of redemption was accomplished in history. As he died on the cross, having shed his blood for the sins of men, "the veil of the temple was torn in two from top to bottom; and the earth quaked, and the rocks were split, and the graves were opened; and many bodies of the saints who had fallen asleep were raised.... So when the centurion and those with him, who were guarding Jesus, saw the earthquake and the things that had happened, they feared greatly, saying, 'Truly this was the Son of God!'" (See Matt 27:45–54.) From now on, "a new and living way" has been opened for us to enter boldly into the Holy of Holies and come into the presence of God (Heb 10:19–23). This is indeed a great mystery; it is that scroll "sealed with seven seals," which no one can open, whether "in heaven or on the earth or under the earth." Only the Lion of Judah, the Root of David, the Lamb of God, can open this scroll, because he was slain, and redeemed men from all tribes and nations, that they may belong to God (Rev 5). Since Lin Yutang reckons that the error of humanism lies in its pretense that man's reason can reform the world, he must agree that reason cannot save the world; he should turn from his arrogance and cease to take pride in his reason!

Since Professor Lin knows that humanism is unable to save mankind, it should be clear that, in order for a humanist to break through the limitations of humanism and become a Christian, he needs more than a change

Critique of Humanism

of mind. He needs a change of heart. This kind of change is not a matter of stuffing one's mind with new ideas, or with "insightful," "dynamic" preaching from certain pastors. It is a matter of trusting in Jesus Christ and his great redemptive work, by which he saves us from being lost to living a new life. This is not a matter of external "change," but an "exchange" in our hearts, from being in Adam to being in Christ. We are liberated from the chains of our old sinful nature, so that, by the cleansing of regeneration and the renewal of the Holy Spirit, we participate in the divine nature and enter into a new relationship with God. We are restored into the glory of the freedom of the children of God and live out our new image in Christ. Our life is ushered into a new heaven and new earth; it is filled with new meaning, new goals, and a new mission.

Third, we can see from the above two considerations, that "by grace [we] have been saved through faith, and that not of [our]selves" (Eph 2:8), "that [our] faith should not be in the wisdom of men but in the power of God" (1 Cor 2:5). The first book I wrote after becoming a Christian was *Yuan Dao*. I wanted to witness to the gospel; the arguments were not well honed, the evidence was not plentiful, yet, by the power of God, certain Chinese intellectuals read the book and became saved. For example, Mr. Yuan Tongli, a leader in cultural and educational circles whom Professor Lin Yutang knows well, read my book before he passed away in Washington, D.C., and became a Christian. Praise God! We can see that we are saved not through lofty arguments, nor through the insights of pastors. Becoming a Christian is something very different from joining another religion. We must sincerely repent and commit our hearts to trust the Savior. Thus, by the blood of Jesus Christ and the mercies of God, we can be transformed from death to life, and receive a "living hope" and the inheritance reserved in heaven for us. (See Eph 2:13; 1 Pet 1:3–4.) May God have mercy on Professor Lin, that he may truly repent and enter life. May God raise up Professor Lin to be a great defender of the light of truth, a preacher of the pure gospel of Jesus Christ. This is my earnest prayer.

Bibliography

NOTE: LIT-SEN CHANG DID not provide full publication information for many of the works which he cited, including some of his own. The citations in this section of the Bibliography follow those of the author.

Works by Lit-sen Chang

Autobiography

Contending for Truth: The Story of Lit-sen and Ling Nie Chang. New York: Chinese for Christ Church, 1997.
"From Pagan to Christian." The Park Street Church *Spire* (Boston, MA) February 1961. Reprinted by Chang in "Appendix II" of *Strategy of Missions in the Orient: Christian Impact on the Pagan World*, 215–32. Hong Kong: World Outreach, 1968.
"His Amazing Grace: The Life Story of Lit-sen Chang." In *Asia's Religions: Christianity's Momentous Encounter with Paganism*, edited by Samuel Ling, 287–99. San Gabriel, CA: China Horizon, 1999.
"The Way to the True Enlightenment: From Zen to Christ, a Brief Testimony of the Author." "Appendix I." *Zen-Existentialism: The Spiritual Decline of the West*, 202–9. Phillipsburg, NJ: P & R, 1969.

Theology and Apologetics

English

"Old Serpent, New Strategy." *Christianity Today*. May 23, 1975.
Strategy of Missions in the Orient: Christian Impact on the Pagan World. Hong Kong: World Outreach, 1968.
Transcendental Meditation: A Mystic Cult of Self-Intoxication. Nutley, NJ: P & R, 1978.
The True Gospel vs. Social Activism: Beware of the New Strategy of the Old Serpent. Phillipsburg, NJ: P&R, 1976.
What Is Apologetics? Translated by Samuel Ling. Phillipsburg, NJ: P & R, 1999.
Zen-Existentialism: The Spiritual Decline of the West. Philadelphia: P & R, 1969.

Bibliography

Chinese

Dongzheng Ganhuai Lu (*Remembering My Eastern Journey*). Hong Kong: Christian Witness Press, 1972.

Jiaohui Fuxing zhi Yisyang: Shijie Renlei zhi Xiwang (*The Revival of the Church: The Hope of the World*).

Jidu Jiao de Lishi Guan (*A Christian View of History*)

Jidu Lun (*Christology*). Hong Kong: Bellman House, 1963.

Jidutu de Rensheng Guan (*The Christian View of Life*)

Jiushi zhi Dao (*The Way of Salvation*). Hong Kong: Bellman House, 1968.

Jiuyue Zonglun: Wangu Changxin zhi Dao (*Studies in the Old Testament: The Living Message of Mankind*).

Jizu Yundong Boyi (*A Rebuttal of Ancestor Worship*). Hamilton, MA: Chinese Evangelical Literature Committee, 1972.

Liguo zhi Dao (*The Foundation of a Nation*). Hong Kong: Christian Witness Press, 1971.

"Kexuejia de xinyang" ("The Faith of [Christian] Scientists"). In *Shengdao Zhengyan* (*A Defense of Christian Truth*). Hong Kong: Dao Sing Press, 1971.

Minzu Xinling zhi Weiji (*The Spiritual Crisis of a Nation*). Hong Kong: Christian Witness Press, 1972.

"Qimiao Jiuen" ("His Amazing Grace: My Life Story"). In *Zhenli de Doushi* (*Contending for the Faith*) New York: Chinese for Christ N.Y. Church, 1987.

Renmin Zhuyi Pipan (*Critique of Humanism*). Hong Kong: Alliance Press, 1963; enlarged edition, 1968.

Shengdao Tong Quan (*A General Interpretation of Christian Truth*). Hong Kong: Bellman House, 1964.

Shengdao Zhengyan (*The Defense of Christian Truth*), chapter 2: "Jidujiaode Kexueguan" ("The Christian View of Science").

Sheng Ming zhi Dao (*The Way of Life*). Hong Kong: Bellman House, 1968.

Shijie Mingren Zongjiao Guan (*Religious Thought of Famous Men of the World*). Hong Kong: Christian Witness Press, 1961.

Shijie Renlei zhi Xiwang (*The Hope for Mankind*). Hong Kong: Sheng Tao Press, 1974.

Shijie Xuandao Zhanlue Zhongxin (*Strategy of World Mission*). Hong Kong: World Outreach Publishers, 1968.

Sunwen Zhuyi zhi Shenxue Jichu (*The Theological Basis of the Teachings of Dr. Sun Yat-sen*). Hong Kong: Sheng Tao Press, 1971.

Xinxinde Shilian (*Faith on Trial*). Hong Kong: Bellman House, 1964.

Yuan Dao (*The Way: An Investigation Concerning Divine Truth*). Washington DC: International Students, 1960.

Zhongguo Minzu zhi Gaige yu Zijiu (*The Reformation and Self-Salvation of the Chinese People*). Shanghai: Commercial Press.

Zili Zhu Yi-Minzu Fuxing zhi Jiben Yuanli (*The Doctrine of Self-Determination—Basic Principles for the Revival of the Chinese People*). Changsha, China: The Commercial Press, 1938.

Zongti Biandaoxue (*Comprehensive Christian Apologetics*). 4 vols. Hong Kong: Tian Dao Book House, 1982.

Bibliography

Works Cited by Lit-sen Chang in *Critique of Indigenous Theology* and *Critique of Humanism*

Altizer, Thomas. *The Gospel of Christian Atheism*. Philadelphia: Westminster, 1966.
Altizer, Thomas, and William Hamilton. *Radical Theology and the Death of God*. Indianapolis: Bobbs-Merrill, 1966.
Anderson, Gerald H. *The Theology of Christian Mission*. New York: McGraw-Hill, 1961.
Barth, Karl. *Schleiermacher: Die Theologie und die Kirche* (*Schleiermacher: Theology and the Church*). Munich: Kaiser, 1928.
Bavinck, J. Herman. *Geneformeende Dogmatick* (*Reformed Dogmatics*), *1895–1901*. English edition: Grand Rapids: Baker Academic, 2008.
———. *The Impact of Christianity on the Non-Christian World*. Grand Rapids: Eerdmans, 1948.
———. *Our Reasonable Faith*. Grand Rapids: Baker, 1977.
Bentley-Taylor, David. *Augustine, Wayward Genius: The Life of St. Augustine of Hippo*. London: Hodder & Stoughton, 1980.
Berkhof, Louis. *Introductory Volume to Systematic Theology*. Grand Rapids: Eerdmans, 1951.
Berdyaev, Nicholai. *The Meaning of History*. 1936; republished with an introduction by Maria Nemcova Banerjee. Piscatawy, NJ: Transaction, 2006.
Blumenfield, Samuel. *Is Public Education Necessary?* New York: Devon-Adair, 1981.
Brandt, Richard B. *The Philosophy of Schleiermacher*. Westport, CT: Greenwood, 1968.
Broomhall, Marshall. *The Bible in China*. London: The China Inland Mission, 1934.
Buck, Oscar. *Christianity Tested*. New York: Macmillan, 1885.
Burkitt, F. C. *Church & Gnosis: Morse Lectures for 1931*. Cambridge: Cambridge University Press, 1932.
Bush, Vannevar. Letter to the editor. *Fortune Magazine*. May 1965.
Bowman, Alan et al. *Cambridge Ancient History*, Vol. 12, *The Imperial Crisis and Recovery*. Edited by John Bagnell Bury et al. Cambridge: Cambridge University Press, 2004.
Cailliet, Emile. *Christian Approach to Culture*. Nashville: Abingdon-Cokesbury, 1953.
———. "The Reformed Tradition in the Life and Thought of France." *Theology Today* 1 (1965) 349–60.
Calvin, John. *Institutes of the Christian Religion*. 2 vols. Grand Rapids: Eerdmans, 1957.
Chan, Wing-Tsit. *A Source Book in Chinese Philosophy*. Translated and compiled by Wing-Tsit Chan. Princeton: Princeton University Press, 1963.
Chen, Gong, "Shengren zhi yu Tiandao" ("The Heavenly Course and the Sage"), *Rensheng* (*Life*), issue 224.
Clark, Gordon H. "The Puritans and Situational Ethics." Lecture delivered in 1976. Online: http://www.trinityfoundation.org/journal.php?id=87.
———. *The Revealed Religion*. Wheaton, IL: Christianity Today, 1980.
Cochrane, Charles Norris. *Christianity and Classical Culture: A Study of Thought and Action from Augustus to Augustine*. Oxford: Clarendon, 1940.
Coleridge, Samuel Taylor. "Table Talk," March 14, 1833. *The Table Talk and Omniana of Samuel Taylor Coleridge*. London: G. Bell and Sons, 1888.
Cubberly, Edward P. *History of Education*. Boston: Houghton Mifflin, 1920.
Da Bao Ji Jing, or Mahāratnakūta sūtra.
Da Ji Jing, or Mahāvaipulya mahāsamghāta sūtra.

Bibliography

Davies, D. R. *Down Peacock's Feathers*. London: Bles, 1942. (Attributed by Chang to Arnold Toynbee).

Dawson, Christopher. *The Historic Reality of Christian Culture: A Way to the Renewal of Human Life*. Northford, CT: Harpers, 1960.

De Bary, William Theodore, Wing-Tsit Chan, and Burton Watson, editors. *Sources of Chinese Tradition*, vol. 1. 2 vols. New York: Columbia University Press, 1960.

De Waff, Maurice. *History of Medieval Philosophy*. Translated by Ernest C. Messenger. New York: Dover, 1935.

Fletcher, Joseph. *Situation Ethics: The New Morality*. Philadelphia: Westminster, 1966.

Fo Shuo Ba Da Ren Jue Jing.

Fo Yi Jiao Jing (*Sutra on the Buddha's Bequeathed Teaching*).

Fung, Yu-lan. *A History of Chinese Philosophy*. Translated by Derk Bodde. 2 vols. Princeton: Princeton University Press, 1952–53.

Gilson, Etienne. *God and Philosophy*. 2nd ed. With a new foreward by Jaroslav Pelikan. New Haven; Yale University Press, 2002.

Graham, Billy. *Day-by-Day with Billy Graham*, reading for November 9. Joan W. Brown, ed. Minneapolis: Billy Graham Evangelistic Association, 1991.

———. "A World Lost in Space." Commencement address at Wheaton College, June 1970.

Hamilton, Kenneth. *God Is Dead: The Anatomy of a Slogan*. Grand Rapids: Eerdmans, 1965.

Hamilton, William. *The New Essence of Christianity*. New York: Association Press, 1961.

Han, Yu. "Memorial on the Bone of Buddha." In *Sources of Chinese Tradition*, vol. 1, edited by William Theodore de Bary, 372–74. Records of Civilization: Sources and Studies New York: Columbia University Press, 1960.

Harnack, Adolf von. *Mission and Expansion of Christianity in the First Three Centuries*. Translated and edited by James Moffatt. 1908 edition. Gloucester, MA: Peter Smith, 1972.

———. *The Teaching of the Twelve Apostles*. Translated by Kirsopp Lake. Loeb Classical Library. Cambridge: Harvard University Press, 1912.

Henry, Carl F. H., editor. *Baker's Dictionary of Christian Ethics*.Grand Rapids: Baker, 1973.

———. "Revolution in Theology." *Christianity Today*, October 9, 1970.

Hocking, William. *Rethinking Missions: A Layman's Inquiry after One Hundred Years*. New York: Harper & Brothers, 1932.

Hodge, Charles. *Systematic Theology*. 3 vols. Grand Rapids: Eerdmans, 1968.

Hu, Huaigu. "Yin Ming yu Ming De Xiuyang," "Yin-ming and ming-de [self-cultivation]." *Ren Sheng* (*Life*), no. 245.

Hume, David. *A Treatise of Human Nature: Reprinted from the Original Edition in Three Volumes and Edited, with an Analytical Index, by L. A. Selby-Bigge, M.A.* Oxford: Clarendon, 1896.

Hu, Shi. *Hu Shi Wen Cun* (*The Collected Works* of *Hu Shih*). 1921. Beijing: Zuojia Chubanshe, 1991.

———. *Kexue yu Renshengguan* (*Science and the Philosophy of Life*). Shanghai Library, December, 1923; Huangshan Shushe, 2008.

———. "She Hui Bu Xiu Lun" ("Social Immortality"). Shanghai: Xin Qingnian (New Youth) magazine 6/2. English title: "Immortality as a Guiding Principle in Life."

Bibliography

Hu, Zhanyun. "Jiuyue yu Xinyue" ("Old Testament and New Testament"). In *Jing Feng* vol. 3.
I Ching: The Classic of Changes: A New Translation of the I Ching as Interpreted by Wang Bi (Translations from the Asian Classic). Translated by Richard John Lynn. New York: Columbia University Press, 2004.
Jackson, Herbert C. "The Forthcoming Role of the Non-Christian Religious Systems as Contributory to Christian Theology." *Occasional Bulletin of Missionary Research* 12/3 (1961) 1–15.
Jia, Yuming (Chia Yu-ming). *Shen Dao Xue (Systematic Theology)*. First published in 1921; re-published, Taipei, Campus Press, 1949; modern language edition, Taipei, Olive Press, 1996.
Jiang, Menglin. "A Most Meaningful Life." *Zhuanji Wenxue (Biographical Literature)*, March 1964. Reprinted in *Lian He Bao (United News)*, March 7, 1964.
Jiang, Tingfu. *Zhongguo Jindaishi Lunji (Modern Chinese History)*. Shanghai: Commercial Press, 1938.
Jiang, Weiqiao. *Fojiao Qian Shuo (A Simple Introduction to Buddhism)*. Shanghai: Foxue Shuju (Buddhist Press), 1932.
Kraemer, Hendrik. *The Christian Message in a Non-Christian World*. New York: Harper, 1938.
Kuyper, Abraham. *By Grace Alone* (Publication information unavailable).
———. *Encyclopaedie der Heilige Godgeleerdheid (Encyclopedia of Sacred Theology)*, 1893–1895. English edition: Grand Rapids: Baker, 1980.
———. *Lectures on Calvinism*. Grand Rapids: Eerdmans, 1943.
———. *Sacred Theology*. Reprint. Mulberry, IN: Sovereign Grace, 2001.
Lauzi (Lao-Tzu). *Dao De Jing (Tao Te Ching)*. Various editions and translations, including Huang, Chichung. *Tao Te Ching: A Literal Translation with Notes and Commentary*. Fremont, CA: Asian Humanities Press, 2003.
Li, Jingxiong. *Bense Shenxue—Jiu Geng yi Xin Keng? (Indigenous Theology: Previously Plowed Land or a Newly Cultivated Field?)*.
Liji·Zhong Yong (*The Classic of Rites—The State of Equilibrium and Harmony*). Fenghuang Chubanshe, 2011. Liji·Zhong Yong (T*he Classic of Rites—The State of Equilibrium and Harmony,* often rendered as The Doctrine of the Mean), in Li Chi or Book of Rites. Part I of II. Translated by James Legge. Oxford University Press, 1893; N.p.: Forgotten Books, 2008.
Lindsell, Harold. "Dateline Bangkok." *Christianity Today*, March 30, 1973.
Linssen, Robert. *Living Zen*. New York: Grove Press, 1988.
Liu, Yiling. "Liu Yiling Xiansheng yu Lin Shi de Chuxi Tan" ("A Heart-to-Heart Talk Between Liu Yiling and Lin Yutang"). *Dengta Magazine*, issue 121.
Machen, J. Gresham. *Christian Faith in the Modern World*. Grand Rapids: Eerdmans, 1947.
———. *What Is Christianity?* Grand Rapids: Eerdmans, 1951.
McCallum, J. R. *Abelard's Christian Theology*. Merrick, NY: Richwood, 1976.
———. *Abelard's Ethics*. Oxford: Blackwell, 1935.
McGiffert, A. M. *A History of Christian Thought*. 2 vols. New York: Scribner, 1932-33.
Mengzi (Mencius). *Mencius*. Translated by Irene Bloom, Edited and with an Introduction by Philip J. Ivanhoe. New York: Columbia University Press, 2009.
Moltmann, Jürgen. *A Theology of Hope*. Translated by James W. Leitch. New York: Harper & Row, 1967.

Bibliography

———. *Religion, Revolution and the Future*. Translated by M. Douglas Meeks. New York: Scribner, 1969.
Montgomery, John W. *The "Is God Dead?" Controversy*. Grand Rapids: Zondervan, 1966.
Moody, Raymond. *Life after Life*. San Francisco: HarperSanFrancisco, 2001.
Nirvana Scripture. Mahaparinirvana Sutra. 12 vols. Translated by Kosho Yamamoto. Edited by Tony Page. London: Nirvana Publications, 1999–2000.
Pascal, Blaise. *Pensees*. Translated by A. J. Krailsheimer. New York: Penguin, 1995.
Pollard, William G. *Chance and Providence: God's Action in a World Governed by Scientific Thought*. New York: Scribner, 1958.
Puji, *Wu Deng Hui Yuan. 1254 A.D. (History of Chinese Buddhism)*. Ann Arbor: University of Michigan Press, 1908.
Song Shi Ben Zhuan (History of the Song Dynasty).
Qian, Mu (Chi'en Mu). *Rensheng Shilun (Ten Essays on Life)*. Hong Kong: Rensheng Press, 1955. Reprinted, Guangxi Shifan Daxue Chubanshe (Guangxi Normal University Press), 2004.
Qiang, Weqiao. *Fojiao Qian Shuo (A Simple Introduction to Buddhism)*.
Qualben, Lars P. *A History of the Christian Church*, vol. 2. Eugene, OR: Wipf & Stock, 2008.
Records of the General Conference of the Protestant Missionaries of China held at Shanghai, May 10–24, 1877. Shanghai, 1878.
Ritschl, Albrecht. *The Christian Doctrine of Justification and Reconciliation*. Edited by H. R. Mackintosh. Edinburgh: T & T Clark, 1902.
———. *Geschichte des Pietismus (History of Pietism)*. Bonn: Marcus, 1880–1886.
———. *Unferricht in der Christlichen Religion*.(1881). Charleston, SC: Nabu, 2012.
Schaeffer, Francis. "The Evangelical Outlook." *Christianity Today*, February 12, 1965.
Schaff, Philip. *A History of the Christian Church*. New York: Scribner, 1900.
Schelling, Friedrich W. J. *Philosophie der Offernbarung. (The Philosophy of Revelation)*. Sammtliche Werke, edited by K. F. A. Schelling. Stuttgart: 1842–43.
Schmidt, Wilhelm. *Der Ursprung der Gottesidee (The Origin of the Idea of God)*, 12 vols. Münster: Aschendorff. 1912–55.
Schweitzer, Albert. *The Quest for the Historical Jesus*. First complete edition. Edited by John Bowden. Translated by W. Montogomery et al. Fortress Classics in Biblical Studies. Minneapolis: Fortress, 2001.
Shedd, William G. T. *Dogmatic Theology*. Grand Rapids: Zondervan, 1969.
Sima Qian, "Laozi." In *Records of the Grand Historian*. New York: Columbia University Press, 1996.
Song Shi Ben Zhuan (History of the Song Dynasty)
Spencer, Herbert. *First Principles*. New York: Appleton, 1897.
Spurgeon, Charles S. *Collected Works*. Charleston, SC: BiblioLife, 2008.
Stalin, Svetlana. "Only One Year." *Time*, April 28, 1967.
Strong, A. H. *Systematic Theology*. King of Prussia, PA: Judson, 2010.
Tai, Xu. *Zhen Xianshi Song*. 1936.
Tang, Jun yi. "Ren Dao Lun." In *Zhexue Gailun (An Introduction to Philosophy)*. Hong Kong: Mengshi Jiaoyu Jijinhui (Meng Educational Foundation), 1961.
———. *Rensheng Tiyan. (The Experiences of Life)*. Shanghai: Zhonghua Shuju. 1944.

———. *Ren Sheng zhi Tiyan Xupian* (*The Experience of Life—Continued*). Hong Kong: Rensheng Press, 1961. Reprinted, Taipei: Taiwan Xuesheng Shuju (Taiwan Student Press), 1996.

———. *Zhexue Gailun* (*An Introduction to Philosophy*). Hong Kong: Meng Shi Ji Jin Hui (Meng Educational Foundation), 1961. Reprinted, Beijing: Zhongguo Shehui Kexue Chubanshe (Chinese Academy of Social Sciences Press), 2005.

———. *Zhongguo Renwen Jingshen zhi Fajan* (*The Development of the Chinese Humanist Spirit*). Shanghai: Renmin Press, 1958. Reprinted, Guangxi Shifan Daxue Chubanshe (Guangxi Normal University Press), 2005.

Tertullian. *Apology*. In *The Ante-Nicene Fathers*, vol. 3. Edinburgh: T. & T. Clark, 1869.

———. *On Idolatry*. In *The Ante-Nicene Fathers*, vol. 3. Edinburgh: T. & T. Clark, 1869.

———. *De Praescriptione Haereticorum* (*Prescription against Heretics*). In *The Ante-Nicene Fathers*, vol. 2. Edinburgh: T. & T. Clark, 1869.

———. *De Spectaculis* (*On Spectacles*). In *The Ante-Nicene Fathers*, vol. 40. Edinburgh: T. & T. Clark, 1867.

———. *A Treatise on the Soul*. In *The Ante-Nicene Fathers*, vol. 3. Edinburgh: T. & T. Clark, 1869.

Toynbee, Arnold. *Civilization on Trial*. New York: Oxford University Press 1948.

Trueblood, D. Elton. *The Predicament of Modern Man*. 4th ed. New York: Harper & Brothers, 1944.

Van Til, Cornelius. *Is God Dead?* Nutley, NJ: P & R, 1966.

Warfield, Benjamin B. "The Idea of Systematic Theology." In *Selected Shorter Writings of Benjamin B. Warfield II*, edited by John E. Meeter, 219–79. Nutley, NJ: P & R, 1973.

———. "Introduction to Francis R. Beattie's *Apologetics*." In *Selected Shorter Writings of Benjamin B. Warfield II*, edited by John E. Meeter, 93–105. Nutley, NJ: P & R, 1973.

———. *The Plan of Salvation*. Avinger, TX: Simpson, 1989.

Wenshu Shili Wen Jing (Ancient Buddhist Scripture).

Whitehead, Alfred North. *Science and the Modern World*. 1925. New York: Free Press, 1997.

Wu, Leichuan. *Jidujiao yu Zhongguo Wenhua* (*Christianity and Chinese Culture*). Shanghai: Qingnian Xiehui Press, 1926. Reprinted, Shanghai: Guji Chubanshe, 2008.

Wu, Mingjie. "Issues Concerning Lin Yutang's Faith," *Shanghai Bible Magazine* 20/7.

Wu, Zhihui. *Renshengguan Lun zhan ji* (*The Philosophy-of-Life Debate: A Collection*). Shanghai, Taidong Tushu Ju, 1923.

———. *Zhihui Wen Cun* (*The Collected Works of Wu Zhihui*).

Xie, Fuya. *Nanhua Xiaozhu Shan Pang Wen*. Hong Kong: Nantian Shuye, 1972.

———. *Zhongguo Jidujiao Chulun* (*Introduction to Chinese Christianity*).

———. *Zhonghua Jidujiao Shenxue de Jige Yuanze* (*A Few Principles of Chinese Christian Theology*).

———. "Zhongguo Wenti yu Jidujiao" ("China's Problems and Christianity"). *Ming Bao Monthly* 107.

———. *Zongjiao Zhexue*. (*Philosophy of Religion*). Shanghai: Commercial Press, 1947. Reprinted by Shandong Renmin Chubanshe, 1998.

Xunzi, "Li Lun." 313–238 BCE.

Bibliography

Yang, Senfu. *Chinese Customs and Christian Faith*. Kaohsiung: Tianshi Publishing House, 1984.

Zhao, Zichen, "A Few Suggestions for Creating a Chinese Church." *Zhen Guang (True Light) Magazine* 26/6 (1927) 1–13.

Zhuangzi. *Zhuangzi: Basic Writings*. Translated by Burton Watson. New York: Columbia University Press, 2003.

Zuozhuan (Commentary by Zuo [Tso] on the Spring and Autumn Annals). Composed in the Fifth Century B.C. Beijing: Beijing Publishing House, 2008.

Works Cited by Editor

Bays, Daniel H. *A New History of Christianity in China*. Blackwell Guides to Gloal Christianity. Chichester, UK: Wiley-Blackwell, 2012.

Bevans, Stephan, and Wun-hsiung Wu. "Contextualization." In *A Dictionary of Asian Christianity*, edited by Scott W. Sunquist et al., 211–14. Grand Rapids: Eerdmans, 2001.

Campbell-Jack, W. C., and Gavin McGrath, editors. *New Dictionary of Christian Apologetics*. Downers Grove, IL: IVP Academic, 2006.

Chan, Daniel T. "Quest for Certainty: The Life and Thought of Lit-sen Chang." PhD diss., Boston University, 2000.

Chan, Wing-tsit. *A Source Book in Chinese Philosophy*. Princeton: Princeton University Press, 1963.

Charbonnier, Jean-Pierre. *Christians in China: A.D. 600 to 2000*. San Francisco: Ignatius, 2007.

Chow, Lien-Hwa. "Towards Evangelical Theology in Buddhist Cultures." In *The Bible & Theology in Asian Contexts*, edited by Bong Rin Ro and Ruth Eshenaur, 315–26. Taichung, Taiwan: Asia Theological Association, 1984.

Doyle, G. Wright. *Carl Henry—Theologian for All Seasons*. Eugene, OR: Pickwick Publications, 2010.

Edgar, William. "Christian Apologetics for a New Century." In *New Dictionary of Christian Apologetics*, edited by W. C. Campbell-Jack and Gavin McGrath, 3–14. Downers Grove, IL: IVP Academic, 2006.

Harvey, Thomas Alan. *Acquainted with Grief: Wang Mingdao's Stand for the Persecuted Church in China*. Grand Rapids: Brazos, 2002.

He, Jianming. "Dialogue between Christianity and Taoism: The Case of Lin Yutang." In *Christianity and Chinese Culture*, edited by Miikka Ruokanen and Paulos Huang, 124–44. Grand Rapids: Eerdmans, 2010.

Henry, Carl F. H. *God, Revelation, and Authority*. 6 vols. Waco: Word, 1976–83.

Huang, Chichung. *Tao Te Ching: A Literal Translation with Notes and Commentary*. Fremont, CA: Asian Humanities Press, 2003.

Ruokanen, Miikka, and Paulos Huang editors. *Christianity and Chinese Culture*. Grand Rapids: Eerdmans, 2010.

Lai, Pan-chiu, and Jason Lam, editors. *Sino-Christian Theology: A Theological Qua Cultural Movement in Contemporary China*. Studies in the Intercultural History of Christianity 152. New York: Lang, 2010.

Lam, Wing-hung. *Chinese Theology in Construction*. Pasadena, CA: William Carey Library, 1983.

Bibliography

———. "Patterns of Chinese Theology." In *The Bible & Theology in Asian Contexts*, edited by Bong Rin Ro and Ruth Eshenaur, 318–42. Taichung, Taiwan: Asia Theological Association, 1984.

Legge, James. *The Chinese Classics*. 5 vols. in 4. Taipei: Southern Materials Center, 1985.

Levi, compiler. *The Journal Once Lost: Extracts from the Diary of John Sung*. Translated by Thing Pheng Soon. Singapore: Genesis Books, 2008.

Lewis, Gordon R., and Bruce A. Demarest. *Integrative Theology*. Grand Rapids: Zondervan, 1996.

Lian, Xi. *Redeemed by Fire: The Rise of Popular Christianity in Modern China*. New Haven: Yale University Press, 2010.

Lyall, Leslie T. *A Biography of John Sung*. Singapore: Armour, 2004.

Moffett, Samuel Hugh. *A History of Christianity in Asia*. Vol. 1, *Beginnings to 1500*. Rev. and corrected ed. Maryknoll, NY: Orbis, 1998.

Ng, Peter Tze Ming. *Chinese Christianity: An Interplay between Global and Local Perspectives*. Religion in Chinese Societies 4. Leiden: Brill, 2012.

Ro, Bong Rin, and Ruth Eshenaur, editors. *The Bible & Theology in Asian Contexts*. Taichung, Taiwan: Asia Theological Association, 1984.

Sung (Song), John. *The Diaries of John Sung: An Autobiography*. Translated by Stephen L. Sheng. Brighton, MI: n.p., 1995.

Sung (Song), John. *The Journal Once Lost: Extracts from the Diary of John Sung*. Compiled by Levi. Translated by Thng Pheng Soon. Singapore: Armour, 2008.

Sunquist, Scott W., editor. *A Dictionary of Asian Christianity*. Grand Rapids: Eerdmans, 2001.

Weerasinga, Tissa. "A Critique of Theology from Buddhist Cultures." In *The Bible & Theology in Asian Contexts*, edited by Bong Rin Ro and Ruth Eshenaur, 290–341. Taichung, Taiwan: Asia Theological Association, 1984.

Yang, Huilin, and Daniel H. N. Yeung, editors. *Sino-Christian Studies in China*. Newcastle, UK: Cambridge Scholars Press, 2006.

Yang, Rain Liu. "Lin Yutang: Astride the Cultures of East and West." In *Salt and Light, Volume 3: More Lives of Faith That Shaped Modern China*, edited by Carol Lee Hamrin and Stacey Bieler, 158–75. Studies in Chinese Christianity. Eugene, OR: Pickwick Publications, 2011.

www.ingramcontent.com/pod-product-compliance
Lightning Source LLC
Chambersburg PA
CBHW050346230426
43663CB00010B/2013